EXPLAINING THE UNEXPLAINED
Mysteries of the paranormal

EXPLAINING THE UNEXPLAINED

Mysteries of the paranormal

Hans J. Eysenck and
Carl Sargent

Weidenfeld and Nicolson
London

First published in Great Britain by
Weidenfeld and Nicolson
91 Clapham High Street, London SW4 7TA

ISBN 0 297 78068 9

This book was devised and produced by
Multimedia Publications Inc., Amsterdam
Design and layout: Mike Spike
Picture research: Tessa Paul, Anne Horton
Graphics: Christopher Marshall, Charlotte Styles
Editor: Christopher Fagg

Printed in Great Britain by
Fakenham Press Limited
Fakenham, Norfolk

Frontispiece : Guessing a card by ESP –
extra-sensory perception.
Human powers of psychic
perception, or psi, are
among the greatest mysteries
of unexplained natural phenomena.

PHOTOGRAPHIC ACKNOWLEDGEMENTS

Anglia TV 16; Athena 83A, 83C; Cambridge Evening
News 83B, 83D; Cambridge University Psychology
Department 41; Camera Press 11 top, 52 top right, 62,
87, 93, 119, 129, 136, 137; Colorific Frontispiece, 111
top; Colour Library International 47, 114–115;
CERN/Science Photo Library 140; John H. Cutten
18, 33, 34, 39, 45, 54, 56, 71, 107, 116, 125, 148, 158,
166; Escher Foundation 142 bottom; Oskar Estabany
113; Mary Evans 10 top, 13, 18, 26, 27, 29, 59 bottom,
100, 103 left, 149, 166, 168–169; Fotomas 171; GEOS
Paris 170; Professor Bernard Grad 112;
Green-Armytage 139; Grisewood & Dempsey Ltd
138; Sonia Halliday 49; Professor John Hasted
120–121, 121, 122; Michael Holford 93 right; Alan
Hutchinson 176; Hulton Picture Library 30, 86;
Kobal Collection 11 bottom, 109; L. Kristal 50–51;
Manchester University Psychology Department
12–13; Mansell Collection 25, 85 left, 146–147;
Multimedia 65 (with thanks to Netherne Hospital),
135 (courtesy Professor John Hasted); Museum of
Modern Art, NY, Abby Aldrich Rockefeller Bequest
73; Novosti 63, 89; Popperfoto 58, 126–127, 136, 142
top; Rex Features 8, 15, 17, 23, 59 top, 67, 69, 70, 74,
86 top, 90–91, 94, 103 right, 106–107, 110, 123, 144,
146, 172; C. Sargent 77, 79; Ronald Sheridan 10
bottom; Dr Ernesto Spinelli 60 right; Frank
Spooner/GAMMA 68, 72, 78, 127; Vision
International 15, 76, 111, 131, 148, 149, 160–161,
165; Wellcome Institute 85 right; Zefa 124–125,
150–151, 162–163 top

CONTENTS

PREFACE

Over 75 per cent of the general population believe in ESP (extra-sensory perception), and a majority believe in 'dreams that come true' (precognition). In addition to belief, there is great public interest in 'the paranormal', reflected in an ever-increasing number of popular books, television programmes, and films dealing with the subject. What is also clear is that many people are not satisfied with accounts of the paranormal which simply amount to another list of miraculous and extraordinary events. 'Why do these things happen?' and '*How* do these things happen?' are questions frequently met with – and these questions are *scientific* questions. Even though the questioners may not be professional scientists, the nature of their queries shows that the scientific spirit – curiosity, the desire to explore, measure, and understand – is in us all.

Yet if we look at the scientific community we find that only some 10 per cent of them believe that ESP is an established fact. Is this because the scientific studies simply have not been done which would persuade them that the existence of ESP is at the least highly probable? Or are they just ignorant of the facts?

There is, in fact, a very large body of evidence suggesting that ESP, and other 'paranormal' human abilities like PK (mind-over-matter), exist, and one function for this book is to marshal and summarise this wealth of material. But there is something more. In surveying the evidence, what becomes clear is that there emerge *patterns* in the evidence, systematic relationships in experiments, a meaningfulness and lawfulness of the workings of ESP and PK. We are not just dealing with an anomaly which defies any attempt to understand it and control it; we are dealing with something which seems to make clear *sense* in the data we collect from experiments.

The reader should not get the idea into his head that this book is exclusively concerned with scientific experiment alone. The experiments only exist because, since antiquity, people had reported strange *experiences* which suggested the existence of ESP and PK: if there had been no experiences, there would be no experiments to discuss. Further, some of the most impressive evidence in *parapsychology* (as the scientific study of the paranormal is termed) has come from ESP experiments designed to create those psychological conditions which surveys of real-life experiences of ESP suggested were favourable for ESP. Nonetheless, a key point we stress in this book is that parapsychology has a clear scientific future – in terms of its possible practical value, in terms of the way parapsychologists construct and test scientific theories against results from scientific studies, in terms of its implications for other sciences and our picture of human abilities generally, and in other ways. If science is like a massive jig-saw puzzle, parapsychologists are collecting the pieces one by one and certain parts of the overall picture are becoming rather clear. There is no reason to think that the coming years will not show us more and more of the picture!

HJE/CLS November 1981

Science is a wonderfully powerful tool for investigating the Universe. The extraordinary scientific advances of the twentieth century have furnished us with profound insights into the fundamental processes of life and matter. In doing so, science has undoubtedly made the world a more dangerous place to live in. At the same time it has offered great freedoms – from disease, from hunger, from total dependence on a particular environment – which allow the possibility of a vastly enriched life for ordinary individuals. Because the successes and benefits of science are so great, it is easy to see it as a process of discovery leading smoothly towards a set of fixed and final answers. Nothing could be further from the truth or potentially more dangerous. Complacency like this actually hinders the search for knowledge. When Ernest Rutherford, the physicist who split the atom, was an undergraduate, his tutor advised him against studying physics. Scientists, Rutherford was told, now had such a complete picture of the nature of matter that only the final details remained to be settled. It would be interesting to speculate on the consequences for science had Rutherford accepted the advice.

A much more accurate description of scientific knowledge is to say that, at any time, science has a network of theories and models of how the Universe is organised and how it works. There are certain rules which govern the development and testing of these theories against the facts discovered by research: the theories should be explanatory, they should predict the outcome of experiments as yet not done, and they should be capable of being shown to be wrong. Similarly, there are rules which govern the conduct of scientific experiments; there are good ways to do experiments, and bad ones.

Moreover, science is a growing rather than a static method of acquiring knowledge. New facts, new ideas, new speculations, enter into the calculations, modifying our picture of the world. To take one recent example, the discovery of the bizarre nature of the rings of Saturn, made by the American space probe Voyager II in 1981, has caused a considerable revaluation of established thought in physics. The structure of the rings appears to defy principles of physical laws. Which just shows that no 'laws' proposed by scientists should be regarded as true for all time. Ideas have to change when they encounter anomalous facts.

At every stage in the history of science, there have been facts which could not be explained in terms of the accepted scientific theories of the time. This book is concerned with some of these anomalies which lie outside 'normal' scientific thinking and theorising. Such anomalies go

The rings of Saturn, photographed by Voyager II. Anomalous structures within the rings seem to challenge existing physical laws. True scientists are always ready to modify theories in the light of new evidence.

to make up the seemingly *paranormal*. Here, we encounter a real rag-bag of immensely varied material. There is no need to suppose that all these different events and anomalies might involve similar underlying causal mechanisms. What they do have in common, however, is that none of them are fully explained in terms of current scientific thought.

Faced with reports of paranormal events – whether to do with astrology, ESP, or the Loch Ness Monster – the scientific community tends to divide into two groups. On the one hand, there are those who say, 'OK. Let's go and have a look'. To us, they are the true scientists. Of course, they differ widely in their attitudes and interpretations. Some feel that the evidence for, say, astrology is strong, others feel that it is weak. All agree, however, that the duty of a scientist is the *impartial investigation of nature*.

On the other hand, there are those who simply cannot believe that there might be evidence worth looking at. There are scientists, for example, who feel that ESP is impossible, or that astrological theories can have no place in a scientific explanation of nature. When pinned down, they invariably base their argument on the assumption that ESP is impossible because it conflicts with the laws of physics, or that the planets cannot possibly have any effect on human behaviour because there is no known physical variable which could mediate such an effect. Now, to believe this is very dangerous. For, throughout the history of science, we come across innumerable cases of very distinguished scientists saying that various things (which are now completely accepted, even commonplace) were impossible, because they conflicted with the knowledge accepted *at the time*.

Four kinds of psi, the general term for allegedly paranormal human abilities.

Certain scientists, then, do not wish to see the paranormal investigated. They are sure in their own minds that such things cannot possibly happen, and therefore that any attempt to study them scientifically is a waste of time. Moreover, when research is done on the paranormal, these people try to discredit the evidence, often using arguments (personal attacks on the integrity of the researchers, for example) which are simply not acceptable scientific criticism.

We firmly reject this armchair scepticism. *In principle* it should be possible to investigate any anomaly scientifically. On the other hand we do need one part at least of the sceptic's mental attitude. We must adopt a *critical* view of the evidence offered to us. We must insist that 'paranormal' anomalies are supported by hard fact. Only then can we proceed to alter or challenge established scientific thought.

However, there is a crucial distinction between the sceptical and the critical view. For example, one of us knows a researcher who studies *poltergeists* – phenomena which *appear* to be (or are reported as being) 'forces' capable of moving objects and making noises in ways not understood. After some 25 years' research, this man has found only a tiny number of cases which gave him evidence he regarded as strong. Of the others, many could be explained as fraud, or ascribed to simple physical causes. This researcher is immensely *critical* when it comes to looking at evidence, but he is not *sceptical* about it. His considered opinion is that poltergeists do exist – but that good, hard evidence as to their existence is very hard to come by. We need to be like this: critical, but not sceptical.

ESP and PK

In deciding how to go about studying the paranormal scientifically, we might usefully take a strategic decision: we should concentrate our efforts, first, on phenomena which can be studied *easily*, and second on those which might have some common *linking principle*. Only if a common underlying factor can be discovered will we be obliged to change our thinking as scientists.

PSI PHENOMENA : FOUR VARIANTS ON A THEME ?

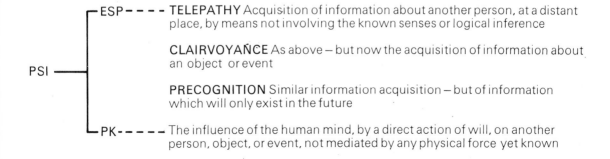

PSI —

┌ ESP - - - - **TELEPATHY** Acquisition of information about another person, at a distant place, by means not involving the known senses or logical inference

CLAIRVOYANCE As above – but now the acquisition of information about an object or event

PRECOGNITION Similar information acquisition – but of information which will only exist in the future

└ PK - - - - - The influence of the human mind, by a direct action of will, on another person, object, or event, not mediated by any physical force yet known

Two apparently paranormal human abilities stand out as being the best candidates for investigation. The first is extra-sensory perception, or ESP. This category includes the apparent ability of human beings to *detect* information about people (*telepathy*, a familiar word) or events/objects (*clairvoyance*, a less familiar one) at distant places, by unknown means. The other is mind-over-matter, psychokinesis or PK, the apparent ability of human beings to *influence* other people, or events/objects, by an effort of will alone, without involving any known physical force. ESP and PK have been with us, as reported events, since antiquity, and surveys show that many people believe that they have had experience of one or the other (particularly of telepathy).

Scientists and laymen alike realise that if ESP information does not arrive through the ordinary channels of our five senses (and the whole burden of experimentation in this field is of course the elimination of ordinary sensory information), then some extra sense must be involved – hence the term extra-sensory perception. Does the existence of such an extra sense necessarily mean that we are leaving orthodox science behind? Not at all. Consider some direction-finding experiments carried out recently. The people concerned were blindfolded, driven along circuitous routes for a long time, and then asked to point in the direction from which they had come. They succeeded much better than chance would have allowed, but their direction-finding ability seemed to vanish when the blindfolds were taken off – perhaps the chance to look around distracted them in some way. Here we seem to be dealing with some sort of extra-sensory perception – none of the known senses could have produced this particular result. However, the apparent anomaly turned out to be quite compatible with our general scientific knowledge.

It appears that many people are more or less sensitive to the magnetic field that surrounds the Earth and can therefore orient themselves in accordance with their position within that field. This unsuspected ability constitutes another sense, comparable with, but of course much weaker than, hearing or sight or touch. There is nothing paranormal about it. Indeed it can be neutralised quite simply. Scientists found that fitting an electromagnet to a person's head obliterates his direction-finding ability; the strong local field produced by the magnet obscures the much weaker field of the Earth. A similar explanation accounted for variations in direction-finding performance. Near power lines, or large electrical complexes, the weak lines of force of the Earth's magnetic field are disrupted and therefore impossible to pick up and use for the purpose of orientation.

Many more such surprises undoubtedly await us. In due course we may find that natural science explains some of the mysterious things discovered by scientists investigating ESP.

Spontaneous ESP and PK

The first thing we have to do is to take a closer look at reported cases of ESP and PK. Just what sort of events suggest that these phenomena

Student volunteers from Manchester University discover that magnetic helmets disrupt the brain's natural sense of direction – might psi, too, have a physiological basis?

may exist? Obviously, if these things were not part of our human existence, they would never have come to the attention of scientists. So we deal first with *spontaneous* cases – reports from the 'real world', if you like – rather than happenings investigated in the laboratory.

One of the strangest types of reported ESP phenomena is *precognition*. The word means, literally, 'fore-knowledge', knowledge of future events which cannot have been obtained by sensory means, or by simple logical working-out. From early times, it seems, people have believed that particular individuals have a divine ability to prophesy future events. This belief lent tremendous authority to ancient oracles such as that at Delphi in Greece. In the Old Testament, too, the prophets are seen to play a vital part in the spiritual and political history of the Jewish people.

Historical reference is one thing, but what of fact? Let's take a very dramatic example. In 1966 an appalling disaster occurred in the mining town of Aberfan, in South Wales. In the course of a few moments, 128 children and 16 adults died in a cataclysm described in one newspaper as 'the greatest single disaster that has ever hit our people in peace-time'. Here is a description of events:

'First, I saw an old school house nestling in a valley, then a Welsh miner, then an avalanche of coal hurtling down a mountainside. At the bottom of this mountain of hurtling coal was a little boy with a long fringe looking absolutely terrified to death. Then for quite a while I saw rescue operations taking place. I had an impression that the little boy was left behind and saved. He looked so grief-stricken. I could never forget him, and also with him was one of the rescuers wearing an unusual peaked cap.'

Eye-witness testimony? Of a sort. The coal tip slid down the mountainside at 9.15 a.m. on 21 October 1966. But the woman who wrote the above account 'saw' the events she reported in the form of a vision at a Spiritualist Church in Plymouth, 200 miles from Aberfan, on the evening before (i.e. the 20th). Moreover, there were six witnesses present at the time. The woman also told a neighbour about her vision at 8.30 a.m. the next day. This was not the only case of possible precognition of this dreadful disaster.

At this point we are not offering these reports as *evidence for* the existence of precognition, although they have to be taken into account on that score. We are simply indicating an example of the type of account which makes us wonder about precognition. Such events command our attention.

There are equally remarkable examples of telepathy. Consider the following report, published by the British Society for Psychical Research:

'In 1867 my only sister . . . died suddenly of cholera . . . A year or so after her death [I] became a commercial traveller, and it was in 1876 . . . that the event occurred. The hour was high noon, and the sun was shining cheerfully into my room. I suddenly became conscious that someone was sitting on my left . . . I turned and distinctly saw the form of my dead sister . . . Now comes the most remarkable *confirmation* of my statement . . . '

The sudden drama of a car crash and, far away, a vivid premonition (right) that a friend or loved one is in danger. This experience is a commonly reported form of spontaneous psi.

The man went on to explain that the apparition of his sister showed her to have a bright red scratch on the right side of her face. When he told his parents of his experience his mother was overcome. For no living person, other than herself, knew that she had accidentally scratched the face of the corpse during preparation for burial, a detail which she had never mentioned to anyone.

Is this an example of communication between the living and the dead, between a mind inside a body and a mind freed from it? Or was it telepathy between son and mother? We cannot be sure that it was either – yet reports like these are so arresting that we cannot ignore them.

A more common type of possible telepathy is that experienced by one of the authors. This is what happened. One evening he felt impelled

The horror of Aberfan. Rescuers search hopelessly through the chaos where 128 children perished. Yet the catastrophe was foreseen in a premonition the day before it happened.

Source : child victim of Aberfan
Time : 14 days before disaster
Confirmation : Both parents and local minister

Source : Woman in Sidcup
Time : 7 days before disaster
Confirmation : Two friends, one of whom confirmed in writing that this dream had been related to her four days before the disaster

Source : Woman in Aylesbury
Time : Dream, two days before disaster ; Church meeting, the night before
Confirmation (of dream and meeting events) : Friend

to pay a visit to a female friend whom he did not know very well, even though the hour was late and not one for casual social calls. When he arrived, he found her in tears, having had a blazing row with her boyfriend, who had physically attacked and hurt her. The author's unexpected arrival turned out to be greatly comforting.

Was this telepathic detection of a 'distress signal'? Perhaps. At least the idea demands thinking about. It is also interesting that this experience happened *after* the author became interested in 'psychic' phenomena, and not before.

The distinction between telepathy and clairvoyance is a hazy one. Technically, clairvoyance is the paranormal sensing of events and objects rather than thoughts. But, logically, such information can always be gleaned telepathically from those who already know it.

Finally, there is the mind-over-matter category of strange events. Very few people today have not heard of the famous (or infamous) Uri Geller, whose metal-bending feats may involve PK (and may not). Metal-bending is a fairly recent addition to recorded PK effects, which traditionally have included inexplicable movements of objects, levitation and so on. In one recorded case of mixed telepathy and PK, a woman saw an *apparition* (ghostly figure) of someone who had died at a distant place. At exactly the time the apparition appeared, a clock in the same room stopped.

These four phenomena – precognition, telepathy, clairvoyance and PK – are the core of the paranormal so far as allegedly unknown human abilities are concerned. They should not necessarily be seen as four different things, although people often think of them as such. Very often it is difficult to separate instances of ESP from instances of PK, and so the general term *psi* (short for psychical) is often used in cases where it is hard to differentiate between them. In this book we shall use the terms ESP and PK much of the time, particularly in describing experiments specifically designed to reveal one or the other, and also when use of the term 'psi' would be merely pedantic.

Now, can we look to spontaneous experiences for proof of the existence of psi? Some people, most notably Spiritualists, would argue 'Yes'. We feel, however, that even if it were possible to get firm evidence of the existence of psi from spontaneous cases – and, in our opinion, this may be possible for PK but *not* for ESP – we would still need, and want, scientific enquiry. Experience shows that researching spontaneous cases of alleged psi is a thankless task, fraught with pitfalls.

The major investigative difficulty lies in answering the question: 'Are these reports reliable accounts of true perceptions? Are the facts – as related – trustworthy?'

We can illustrate the problem with a neat example. In 1964 a British TV station, Anglia, broadcast an interview with a researcher, Tony Cornell, filmed outside an allegedly 'haunted house'. After the programme was shown, five people wrote in to say that they had 'seen' an apparition looking out over Cornell's shoulder. So the programme was broadcast again, and viewers were asked to write in if they saw anything odd during the programme. This time 27 people got in touch (which just shows that people are more likely to 'see' something if they are *led to believe* that they're going to see something). Since the evidence is immortalised on film we can actually examine it and see what is going

In this still from a TV film report, researcher Tony Cornell (left) is interviewed in front of a haunted house. Viewers reported seeing an 'apparition' in the mullioned window behind his left shoulder – a clear case of suggestibility and optical illusion!

on: behind Cornell is a grainy, mullioned window from which, with a fertile imagination, it is just possible to conjure up the figure of a 'ghost'. Needless to say, the 30 or so people all saw rather different types of 'ghost'!

From this, we learn several important things. Our senses are not reliable; people are suggestible; a reported perception *alone* is worth rather little. Indeed, this example shows us that, even when several different people have claimed to see a 'ghost', such reports may be worthless so far as evidence of anything paranormal is concerned.

Obviously, these concerns about the fallibility of our human senses apply more to some cases rather than others. Going back to the young man who saw the 'ghost' of his dead sister, the crucial evidence for psi is the *scratch*. Whether he actually 'saw' the ghost exactly as he described it is not relevant.

The next problem stems from the errors of memory which riddle human testimony. Many of us will have played the party game called 'Chinese Whispers'. In it, several people sit in a circle; the first person makes up a short story and whispers it to the second, who tries to relate it faithfully to the third, and so on round the circle. By the time the story has passed back to its original teller it has usually undergone quite startling transformations!

Second-hand or third-hand testimony, then, is just not good enough: we cannot trust it. Neither can we rely on the memory of one person, related some time after the event. Ideally, what we need from people who have cases of spontaneous psi to report is a written (or taped) account of events, made as soon as possible after the events took place. But, obviously, we cannot always have that – and, indeed, in most cases we do not get it. Few individuals are in a position to call on parapsychologists who might be interested in their experiences. Often, too, people are emotional about the events themselves and not in a sufficiently cool, detached state to realise how important such a written record can be. In some cases, also, this form of record is not a practical proposition. Nonetheless, cases without contemporaneous written records cannot be offered as strong evidence to a rational researcher.

Witnesses, obviously, strengthen the value of a spontaneous case. A good example is the independent verification of the Plymouth woman's 'vision' of the Aberfan disaster. Witnesses also help protect against the possibility of fraud, although very few people appear to hoax a researcher for the sake of it.

Then we have the problem of rational inference. Imagine a person waking up and 'seeing' an uncle, who lives in another country, standing at the foot of the bed. It subsequently transpires that the uncle has died. Would this be an example of telepathy? Possibly, if the uncle was a reasonably young man who had previously enjoyed the best of health. On the other hand, if the uncle was 85 years old and known to be bedridden with terminal cancer, then clearly we would be much less likely to consider this as a case of telepathy. The important principle to grasp is that we must know the predictability – or otherwise – of the

As Sam Goldwyn might have said, hearsay evidence for the paranormal ain't worth the paper it's written on!

event which has allegedly triggered the telepathic experience. In some cases it is extremely difficult to assess this.

Even more difficult is to examine the strength of the evidence in the light of the personality of the telepathic receiver, or *percipient*. Let us say that a mother dreams of the death of her son, who is by profession a bank clerk (hardly a hazard to life and limb), and who is healthy and young. The 'target event' is unlikely, certainly. But what if the woman is a chronic neurotic with a fixation on her son, and dreams every other night of something terrible happening to him? Now, in order to investigate that possibility, we would have to find out things about the character and integrity and personality of the individuals who report possible cases. This can be an embarrassing, and certainly subjective, business.

Testing for psi

Problems like these make the investigation of spontaneous psi a laborious and, in the end, inconclusive business. The circumstances peculiar to each individual case make it impossible to draw general conclusions from them. What can be said, however, is that there are a sufficient number of well-attested reports of psi phenomena to suggest that scientists should take a close look at them. Yet, in order to have any scientific status, our investigations must meet certain criteria. We must have some *measure* of psi abilities, we must be able to calculate the likelihood of chance and coincidence giving us false or confusing results, we must eliminate subjective factors. Most important of all, we

Joseph Banks Rhine (right), pioneer parapsychologist, conducts a test in the early days of research into ESP.

The famous ESP cards first used by Rhine and now a standard aid in ESP testing.

must conduct our experiments in such a way that others can repeat them, in order to see if they find the same results.

In looking at test methods, we can start with the most basic type: a simple, easily understood experiment. Certainly this may appear artificial, simplistic and narrow compared to the richness and strangeness of spontaneous experiences such as the vision of the Aberfan disaster, or the apparition of the girl with the scratched face. Nevertheless, with such a test we can see easily what is being done and the reasons for doing it. Later, we can look at more subtle and complex psi tests.

On the left is the five-card deck developed for ESP tests by Joseph Banks Rhine, the father of experimental parapsychology. It was his work at Duke University, North Carolina, in the 1930s, using the ESP cards, which triggered an intense controversy about ESP research and put parapsychology on the academic map. But why test with these, and how?

To answer this, we need to consider what we need from a good ESP test. In the first place, if we hope to observe the transmission of information by ESP, then the conditions in our experiment should exclude all other possibilities of acquiring the information. If we are doing an experiment on telepathy, for example, then we have to ensure that the two people being tested cannot see, hear, touch, feel, or even smell each other. *We have first to exclude conventional senses.* Next, we have to *eliminate cheating* possibilities. Again we have to *eliminate errors of memory* by recording all our results in the ESP experiment objectively and under good conditions. Most of all we need to *measure* the ESP effect – and that's where the cards come in.

Rhine's original test methods required subjects to guess the sequence of a number of packs of ESP cards. There were 25 cards in each pack – five of each kind. The packs were thoroughly shuffled to ensure that the cards were in random order. The point of a truly random order is this: at any time, a card in the sequence is equally likely to be any one of the different possibilities, and that must always be the same – with ESP cards, a 1-in-5 likelihood or *probability* – no matter which card or cards have just preceded or are about to follow it. *A random sequence is unpredictable.*

Now, we can see why this is important. We noted that, in investigating spontaneous cases of ESP, a vital problem is to establish whether or not an event (such as the death of someone with terminal cancer) could reasonably have been guessed correctly by inference, i.e. logical working out. Evidence for ESP is good when the event could not have been readily predicted. With our ESP tests, the use of random sequences of cards allows us to *eliminate* inference as an explanation of successful results since the order is unpredictable. No logic will help to beat the laws of chance.

For, using the ESP cards, we know *exactly* how unlikely any particular event is by the laws of chance. This takes us into the realm of statistics, which will both frighten some readers and arouse the suspicions of others. Suspicions? 'Lies, damned lies, and statistics' – but whoever wrote that was statistically illiterate. Fright? Yes, because many people are all too prepared to be baffled by statistics and feel certain that they cannot understand them. However, the basic logic of statistics is devastatingly simple. There are only two key principles which need to be understood, and everything else follows from them.

The first notion we have to grasp is that of a *chance average* (technically, a chance *mean*, but the more familiar term average will be used here). Let us consider an ESP card test, using a pack of 25 cards in a random order: for the moment, we shall suppose that the conditions of the experiment are such as to exclude the operation of conventional senses and cheating, and that the recording conditions are sound. We are testing two subjects – a *receiver* and a *sender* – for telepathy. To the receiver, we say: 'Now, when we start, the sender is going to be shown one card every 10 seconds. So, every 10 seconds I shall ask you what card that person is seeing. You are asked to make only one type of guess on each occasion.' The experiment starts: the sender is shown a card every 10 seconds, and an experimenter with him records what it is; the receiver makes a 'guess', which is recorded. After 4 minutes and 10 seconds the first part of the experimental test is completed.

What level of success would be obtained just by chance – with no ESP taking place? What is the *chance average*? There are 25 cards being guessed. There are five different types of card. Most people will readily understand the idea that, if you have a 1-in-5 (or $\frac{1}{5}$) chance of being correct by simply guessing (five different types of card), then a chance average score for 25 guesses would be 25 multiplied by $\frac{1}{5}$=5.00 correct guesses. This is the chance average. If we collected (say) 250 guesses, the chance average score would be 50 (20 per cent correct: 1 in 5). If we did indeed do a test involving 250 guesses, and our subject scored 50 correct, we would not think that ESP was going on, since this is a chance average score. But what if he scored 60, 70, 80 or 100? Would we be able to tell whether this was the result of ESP?

To find that out, we have to introduce the second basic concept of statistics: the notion of *scatter* (or variance, in the technical expression). The laws of chance do predict that, if we conduct a lot of tests with 25 guesses per test as above, the average will be close to 5.00. But this does not mean that chance predicts that every test will give a score of exactly 5 hits. Sometimes one would expect 4 hits (correct guesses) or 6; sometimes (but less often) 3 or 7; less frequently still, 2 or 8; even more rarely, 1 or 9; and so on.

One can test this oneself. Take two coins from your pocket, and toss them well up into the air. How do they come down? The laws of chance state that the most likely thing to happen is for the two to come down with one head and one tail showing: the average would clearly be expected to be one head (or tail) out of two, since there are two possible outcomes (head or tail). So, for two coins, the probability of any one coming down heads is 50 per cent: average, $\frac{1}{2}$ (50 per cent) times 2=one.

Sometimes, however, two heads or two tails will come down. Indeed, each of these events will happen some 25 per cent of the time.

With two coins there are four possible combinations. The bar diagram shows the possibilities: one out of four for two heads or two tails, two out of four for one head, one tail.

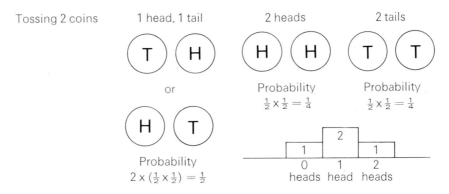

Tossing 2 coins

From this the chance average for the number of heads (or tails) is one, but we do NOT expect that the coins will always come down with one head and one tail showing. Now consider four coins:

With four coins there are 16 combinations. The bar diagram represents the various possibilities: one in 16 each for four heads and four tails, four in 16 each for one head, three tails and three heads, one tail, and so on.

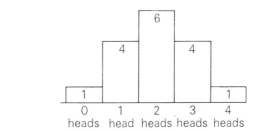

Tossing 4 coins

From this the principle of *scatter* becomes clearer. There is an average, but not all observations will be exactly at that average. Sometimes, an event will take place which is different from the average. BUT THE LIKELIHOOD OR PROBABILITY OF AN EVENT TAKING PLACE BECOMES SMALLER AS WE GO FURTHER AWAY FROM THE AVERAGE. This is clear from the four-coin example given above. Finding three heads out of four (one more than the average) is not that rare: it will happen about once every four throws. But finding four heads out of four should only happen about once every 16 throws.

It is possible to express such a range of more and less likely possibilities by means of a curve called the *normal distribution*, thus:

The average of these possibilities can be expressed as a curve – the normal distribution.

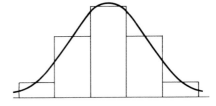

Normal distribution curve

The figure shows clearly two things: first, that the average is the most likely thing to happen as an individual observation; second, that the further away from the average one gets, the less likely something is to be observed. *Average and scatter*. These are the key concepts of statistics.

Now, there are certain arbitrary but conventional rules in science by which an experimental result can be said not to be due to chance alone. In social science, for example, the criteria are as follows. If a researcher does an experiment and observes an event which is so different from the chance average that it would only happen once in 20 similar experiments, *or even less often than that*, then he would accept that the event was not due to chance alone. Something else was responsible for it. There are no logical or empirical reasons for this being the case: it is just a convention. The smaller the probability, though, the happier one gets. One in 20 (a 5 per cent chance; the probability is .05) is acceptable, but 1 in 100 (a 1 per cent chance; the probability is .01) is more satisfying.

Let us now go back to our ESP experiment, where we collected 250 guesses from our receiver and he scored 50 hits. Or was it 60, 70, 80, 100? If it was 50, then there is no ESP. What of 60? Well, from some simple statistical calculations – based on the notions of a chance average and chance scatter – we can work out that, to get a probability of .05 or less (that 1-in-20 chance), we would need at least 61 correct guesses. So, not quite. But the probability of getting 70 hits or more by chance alone is about .001: a 1-in-1,000 shot. One way of putting this (not technically precise, but understandable) is that the 'odds against chance' for this result are 1,000 to 1. This is a large value: much bigger than the 19 to 1 which we use as our criterion for saying 'not chance'.

As one would expect, the further we get from the average, the bigger and bigger the 'odds against chance' become. For 80 or more correct guesses, over 50,000 to 1; for 100 or more, millions to one against.

The numbers are not important in this case: what is important to grasp is the idea that, in our ESP card test, there is a certain chance average and that the further one gets away from it the more unlikely it is that the score is due to chance. If that is appreciated, then the basic use of statistics in parapsychology is understood.

So, the key to the scientific, statistical ESP experiment is this: we can measure precisely what scoring rate would be expected by chance. Coincidence can be measured. If we do an ESP test and find that our receiver has scored so highly that the odds against his performance are over one million to one, we can have an *objective* confidence in that finding which we cannot have in any reported spontaneous case of possible ESP (no matter how *subjectively* interesting we find it).

This logic, of course, does not apply only to the use of cards as targets in testing. Researchers have used colours, animals, names and astrological symbols. Any materials will do, so long as the basic criteria are observed: that there is a number of different possibilities involved (so that we can do our statistical evaluations), that the targets are shielded from the subject in the test, and that they are in a random order.

Moreover, similar principles can be extended into testing for PK. As we shall see, a simple way of testing PK is to have dice thrown by machine whilst the subject is wishing for one particular face to come up.

Clearly, if only chance is occurring (and the dice are not biased) then one die in six will come up with the desired face showing.

If possibilities other than psi are reasonably excluded in an experiment, then we can see that coincidence can be eliminated as an 'explanation' of seemingly improbable events – for we know exactly how improbable they are. Further, the act of measurement allows us to *compare* different measurements. On the basis of testing we can say, for example: 'Mr X has stronger ESP ability than Mr Y; and condition A is better for eliciting PK than is condition B.' This could not be said from any survey of spontaneous cases (with some rare exceptions), because our units of measurement there are generally crude and frequently subjective.

There are still some problems left which have to be at least mentioned. Thus it might be that only successful experiments are reported in the scientific literature, while unsuccessful ones are ignored. If that were so, then the probabilities we have laboriously calculated would no longer apply. Let us assume that a psi investigator reports a statistically significant result with a probability level of 1 in 20; that would normally be acceptable. But suppose that 19 other investigators have also carried out the same experiment, but with no better than chance results. If they do not bother to publish their results, or if the usual parapsychological journals refuse to print negative results, then we would never hear about them. Yet, taken together, the 20 experiments powerfully suggest that nothing but chance was active – only 1 in 20 experiments reached the 5 per cent level of significance! Negative results are in fact reported quite frequently (one of us has published essentially negative results on precognition in rats, for instance), but nobody really knows the extent of negative findings.

The statistical methods we have summarised have been the basis for thousands of experiments on psi phenomena conducted over the last 50 years. The literature – published accounts of experiments and findings – has consequently grown to enormous proportions. What would be a rational plan for examining this vast store of published material on the paranormal? First, surely, we should examine some of the strongest evidence suggestive of its occurrence, and see if we are driven to exhaust all reasonable counter-explanations to psi. If we can do this, then we must accept that there is a high probability that psi does occur. We shall not accept its existence as proved, for proof is a concept which belongs to logic and mathematics. We shall be happy simply to say, 'The evidence is strong. It appears to us that it is probable (or highly probable) that psi exists.' On the other hand we might not find the evidence impressive at all. If we do find the evidence strong then a number of other questions arise. Do different people differ in terms of their abilities? Surely, for they do in terms of any other ability we can think of. Are there particular conditions which are very favourable to psi? Why so? Again, how does it work – can physics explain it? Or does psi contradict the 'laws' of physics? How would psi integrate with what we know in psychology? Finally, is psi relevant to the mind-body problem? Is there, as Rhine claimed, some 'non-physical' component in us which is responsible for psi – and which might survive after death?

So many questions! First, though, we have to appraise the *crème de la crème* in parapsychology – the evidence which is frequently pointed to as the strongest in the literature. We cannot survey all of it; there is simply too much. But we can examine what we consider to be a good portion of that best evidence and say why we find it strongly suggestive of the existence of psi. Three examples are given in the next chapters; two from laboratory research, and the other a nineteenth-century career in mediumship as romantic as it is staggering. We are about to enter the world of the PsiStars.

Two PsiStars

PsiStars are individuals with an exceptionally powerful ability to use psi. They provide the strongest evidence for the existence of paranormal human powers. From the literature of parapsychology we have selected two individuals in particular, the nineteenth-century medium D. D. Home, and the Czech Pavel Stepanek, whose remarkable performances in ESP experiments during the 1960s earned him a reputation as the world's most psychic man.

The amazing D. D. Home

Daniel Dunglas Home, born in Edinburgh in 1833, was reared by an aunt and at the age of nine was taken to America. A neurotic and sickly child, whose mother was thought to have 'second sight', Daniel very quickly started in the family tradition. At the age of 13, he saw an apparition of a close friend. The 'spirit' form made three circles in the air, and Daniel told his aunt and uncle that this must mean that the boy had been dead for three days. The relatives scoffed, but the news soon came that the boy had died just three days before his 'spirit' appeared to Daniel. Four years later Daniel's mother died, and he saw her ghostly

What was his secret? PsiStar Daniel Home's reputation as a medium took him from obscurity to the Imperial courts of France and Russia. He was often accused of fraud – but never detected in the act.

form also; after that, he claimed to be in constant communication with the spirits of the dead.

Mary Cook and her husband certainly had an odd child in their care, and they grew disturbed when the 'spirits' young Daniel conversed with started making their presence felt by thumping and rapping noises all over the house (this is a trademark of the poltergeist or 'noisy spirit', as we shall see later). Believing that he must have brought Satan himself into the house, the Cooks threw Daniel on to the streets.

All this took place at a time when America was in the grip of a craze for spiritualism. Beginning in 1848 in New England, where three sisters had announced that they were in communication with the spirits of the dead, a local sensation ballooned into a national obsession. Soon thousands, then millions of people all over the country were attending seances at which allegedly psychic mediums produced a bizarre selection of effects to convince those present that they were indeed in touch with another world inhabited by the spirits of dead human beings. The effects included mysterious rappings, voices, luminous apparitions, automatic writing, unearthly music – even levitations. In this milieu Home, himself a fast-developing medium, did not have to seek far for wealthy patrons. Within a very short time he was giving seances at which the spirits of the dead regularly conveyed messages to the living.

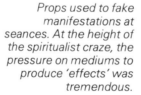

Props used to fake manifestations at seances. At the height of the spiritualist craze, the pressure on mediums to produce 'effects' was tremendous.

In this there was nothing to mark him out from the 15,000 other mediums estimated by one contemporary commentator to be operating in the United States. It quickly became clear, however, that the variety and scale of the physical effects which occurred during Home's seances set him in a class apart. Levitation of objects, even of Home himself, rappings, the grip of unseen hands clearly felt by those attending the seances – all were frequently attested by many witnesses. It is these effects which interest the researcher into the paranormal. If they really happened, they are powerful evidence for the existence of PK.

The first thing we need to do is to get the facts straight – just exactly what did Home do and under what conditions did he do them? Was he genuine – or a fraud? Looking at Home's astonishing career – spanning many years and involving seances at the royal courts of Napoleon III and Czar Alexander II of Russia – the most astonishing fact is that Home was never caught in the act of fraud nor even seriously accused of it. Most unusually for a medium, he actually *preferred* to conduct his seances in bright light, and told researchers to treat him with suspicion. He certainly never accepted any payment for his seances. These facts go to suggest that Home really was a quite exceptional figure. Let's take a closer look at the happenings which clustered around his person.

Spirit rappings were very common at Home's seances. Home would go into a light trance, at which point bangings and thumpings would be heard by the other sitters in the seance room. Could these have been produced by fraud? Two examples. The first took place at a seance held in France at the court of Napoleon III in January 1863. Home, being a royal favourite, naturally made enemies, and one of his greatest enemies at the Imperial court was the sceptical Prince Metternich. At one point in the seance, conducted in a brilliantly lit room, Home had just levitated a cloth from a table. The cloth had risen into the air as Home stood well away from it. Metternich at once leaped under the table, looking for any trick apparatus that Home might be using. He was greeted by a barrage of raps coming from *within the table itself*!

At an English seance, at which six witnesses were present, the distinguished physicist Sir William Crookes observed 'very strong vibrations of our chairs, then the table and floor, and at last the very walls and windows seemed to shake'. These events are hard to explain away. To fabricate such effects would require machinery, or confederates, or both. The whole problem of trickery will be examined shortly; but for now we can note that the scale of the effects in the Crookes seance (and others) was enormous.

Levitation was another PK effect frequently observed at Home's seances. Lord Adare, formerly a foreign correspondent for the *Daily Telegraph*, kept a model record of many of Home's seances, written down immediately after they had happened. He documented no less than 16 levitations of tables, some of them too heavy for any man to have lifted physically. Home also levitated other people and, sometimes, himself. Crookes computed that, at one time or another, over a hundred people witnessed Home levitating: on frequent occasions the witnesses were actually hanging on to his legs! Crookes himself witnessed Home levitate a chair together with a woman sitting on it.

Crookes, being a man of science, undertook experiments with Home, concentrating particularly on the levitation effect. Home enjoyed music, and one of his favourite phenomena was the levitation of an accordion which would waltz around the room playing, appropriately enough, 'Home Sweet Home'. So, Crookes bought an

Home's levitations were witnessed by many people. This contemporary illustration reflects the sensationalism with which Home was treated by the press.

accordion and placed it inside a locked cage where Home could not reach it. Despite this, the instrument levitated and flew around inside the cage, playing edifying tunes as it did so.

Home's most spectacular effects were documented towards the end of his career. Throughout his life he was often treated with hostility – Napoleon III paid conjurors and magicians to try and discredit him (which they could not do), and he was expelled from Rome because he was thought to be a wizard (questions about his treatment were raised in the British Parliament). However, we are very lucky in that we have two long contemporary accounts of Home's later activities made by Crookes and Lord Adare – men who were broadly sympathetic to him, but who were nevertheless sharp observers. Both of them recorded, together with examples of levitation, several instances of two other major possible PK effects: body elongation and fire-handling.

Body elongation was a curious phenomenon which, again, was witnessed by dozens of people. On occasions, Home would stretch his body, adding as much as six inches to his height, while people held on to him. Home generally asked spectators to watch carefully for any evidence of fraud. As he said to Crookes, 'Now, William, I want you to act as if I was a recognised conjuror, and was going to cheat you and play all the tricks I could ... Don't consider my feelings. I shall not be offended.' Yet, surrounded by people watching for tricks, holding his arms, hands, legs, feet and torso, Home was still able to extend his body. One witness reported how he felt Home's ribs passing under his hands. There are even a few reports of Home elongating the bodies of *other people*.

Lastly, *fire-handling*. Crookes saw Home at one seance take from the fire 'a red-hot piece nearly as big as an orange, and putting it on his right hand, covered it with his left hand so as to almost completely enclose it, and then blew ... until the lump of charcoal was nearly white-hot, and then drew my attention to the lambent flame which was flickering over the coal and licking round his fingers ...' Adare, too, witnessed this and both Crookes and Adare were treated (if that's the right word) to the sight of Home lying prone before an open fire and *actually placing his head among the live coals*!

This last phenomenon is so incredible that we can start a really critical scrutiny of Home here. Could this *possibly* have been some form of illusion? Crookes decided to find out. He obtained the services of a negro who claimed to be able to handle fire, and tested him. He found that the man could hold a red-hot iron for an extremely short time, but that 'the house was pervaded for hours after with the odour of roast Negro'. There was never any smell of burning when Home handled fire. Further, Crookes carefully examined Home's hands after these feats and found them to be 'soft and delicate like a woman's'.

On some occasions, Home used handkerchiefs, given to him by other people, with which to hold the coals. The handkerchiefs were not even singed. Crookes chemically analysed one such handkerchief, and found nothing out of the ordinary about it.

Locked in a cage, Home's accordion levitates, played by invisible hands. On another occasion this remarkable effect was observed closely by Sir William Crookes, a brilliant physicist and chemist, who wrote that the instrument played 'a sweet and plaintive melody'.

Were these phenomena the result of mass-hallucination? Perhaps Home was an immensely powerful hypnotist. Indeed, one 'scientific' contemporary writer in *Nature*, the distinguished journal of science, actually suggested that Home was either a mass-hypnotist or a werewolf!

The hypnosis 'explanation' runs into many problems. The major one is that only very few people are so susceptible to hypnotism that they will hallucinate if it is suggested to them. A second is that a great number of people witnessed levitations, fire-handling, and so on. A third is that the conditions under which these effects took place scarcely favoured mass-hallucination: Home liked bright lights. A fourth is that Crookes conducted experiments which showed that Home could influence the weights of objects, results which were automatically recorded on instruments. Instruments cannot hallucinate.

Errors of eye-witness testimony and memory? Certainly some witnesses were untrustworthy; certainly some people gave accounts of seances with Home some years after they took place, which contained factual errors. The question, however, is 'Can *everything* Home did be explained away like this?' The answer must be 'No', for both Adare and Crookes kept long diaries in which accounts of seance events were written down immediately afterwards. No memory lapses here.

Could Home have been just a brilliant illusionist or conjuror? Certainly, some of his effects look like tricks. Sometimes he conducted seances in the dark, sometimes he levitated glasses and made them reappear in a different place after flying into the air. We have to see, though, if illusionism is a reasonable explanation of *all* Home did, and it simply won't do.

Scrutinising the various major effects, we see that some (such as levitating tables too heavy to be lifted by one man) could only have been produced with machinery or accomplices or both. Could this have been done?

Machinery Home's seances were often conducted in public places, or even in the houses of interested people to which Home had no advance access. Moreover, Adare and others often carefully checked for apparatus of this kind.

Accomplices They would have to have been paid a lot of money and, as we've seen, Home never accepted money for seances. At one time, indeed, he was so poor that he had to give literary readings to feed himself. He would have needed many accomplices – and the financial reward for any of them who cared to tell his story to the newspapers of the time would have been enormous. On balance, the use of accomplices would have been a risky, and so not really credible, possibility. Don't forget – *Home was never seriously accused of fraud.*

In any case, there are some events – particularly the fire-handling – which seem to be virtually impossible to fake. The fires were real enough: the heat could be felt from the coals burning in Home's hands.

From the extraordinary life of this man, one episode in particular is worth discussing, because it sheds light on the psychology of some sceptics. In 1855 Home conducted a seance in the home of the poets Robert and Elizabeth Browning. As they sat around the table with other sitters, a wreath of clematis picked by the Brownings' children levitated and settled gently on to Elizabeth's head. Robert got up to watch it move through the air.

Unfortunately, Home suggested that perhaps Robert had moved so

that the wreath might fall on *his* head. Now since Robert was already jealous of his wife's poetic talents, and since after this event Elizabeth championed Home, his mind and memory became twisted. *At the time* Robert Browning wrote letters in which there was no hint that he thought Home a fraud, but in later life he convinced himself not only that Home was a fraud, but that he had actually caught him out in the act of cheating.

Robert vented his spleen in 1864 by publishing the venomous *Mr Sludge the Medium*, a long poem about a fraudulent medium. The link with Home was obvious (except to Home himself). The problem here is that the story has grown that Robert Browning exposed Home as a fraud, which is complete nonsense. His letters of the time show that this was not so, as do his statements to the pioneer psychical researcher F. W. H. Myers. Later, G. K. Chesterton wrote that *Mr Sludge* was 'a reality tangled with unrealities in a man's mind'. How stories grow in the telling – and not just on the credulous side!

Perhaps the great tragedy of Home's life was that scientists were almost all too afraid to test him, the shining exception being Crookes. Time and again Crookes invited eminent scientists to test Home, without restrictions, yet they failed to take the opportunity to do so. As a result, we are reduced to considering Home's feats as *historical* evidence alone, save for Crookes's own researches. What can we make of all this, accepting that, for the most part, we are dealing with eye-witness testimony rather than with scientific data?

Robert and Elizabeth Browning. Elizabeth's enthusiasm for spiritualism in general, and Home in particular, caused one of their few quarrels. Browning's Mr Sludge the Medium (1864) was a violent attack on Home, who was pilloried as at least nine-tenths of a charlatan.

Crookes's claim was that 'To reject the recorded evidence on this subject is to reject all human testimony whatsoever . . .' and with such a quantity of testimony, and the high quality of large parts of it, it is hard to disagree with him. At some point we *have* to trust human testimony, as we do in the courts of the land. And what is scientific fact if not the output of recording devices (of whatever kind) *seen through human eyes*?

A balanced verdict must be that, while *some* of the things reported *could* have been bad testimony, errors of memory, skilful illusions, or mass-hallucination, nevertheless a significant percentage of what was reported cannot be dismissed in these ways. Home would seem to have been the most powerful PK source ever recorded; no-one has ever equalled his feats. It may be because of this that, even after 120 years, no comprehensive sceptical examination of Home has ever been published.

Home is dead and gone. The scientist needs facts that can be re-examined and checked now. So we jump forward a hundred years, to Czechoslovakia, and to the man entered in the *Guinness Book of Records* as the world's most psychic person: Pavel Stepanek.

The psychic bank clerk

The Russians and Eastern Europeans have always had a keen interest in the links between hypnosis and ESP. With good reason, too, for hypnosis is a very effective tool for improving ESP (Chapter 5). One of the Eastern researchers working in this area was Milan Ryzl, trained in life sciences and having a keen interest in the paranormal. At the beginning of the

1960s he started experimenting with hypnosis as a tool for *training* ESP abilities. His procedure was long and complex. Subjects were trained to develop mental imagery ('seeing with the mind's eye', if you like) and to relax into deeper and deeper trance states. After this, he asked them to use ESP to complete various tasks, for example to detect objects sealed inside boxes. It was in the course of this work, which provided some promising leads, that Ryzl first met Pavel Stepanek, the man who was to spend ten years as the world's leading PsiStar.

Stepanek, a quiet and unassuming bank clerk, came along because of an interest in the psychic. Ryzl began by testing him to see if he would be a suitable subject for Ryzl's hypnosis/ESP experiments. Initially, Stepanek proved a very poor hypnotic subject, and after two visits, Ryzl was nearly ready to give up. A third session provided slightly better results, but Stepanek's performance was still unsatisfactory. Ryzl accordingly abandoned all hope of using Stepanek in his ESP-training experiments, and instead tested him for ESP using some test materials lying around from previous work.

These were white index cards about 3 in. by 5 in., painted black on one side, which were concealed inside light-proof, opaque cardboard covers. Ryzl presented each cover (containing a card) to Stepanek, and asked him to use ESP to state which side of the card – black or white – was uppermost within the cover. Even in the informal early work Ryzl made sure that the sequence of black and white was random. Stepanek responded by guessing correctly well above 50 per cent of the time. After a few weeks, both Ryzl and Stepanek were ready for formal research.

In July 1961 Ryzl and Stepanek completed a first formal experiment. At this time, Stepanek worked in a state of very light hypnosis (later, this preparation was abandoned completely). Ryzl's assistant, working alone in a closed room, took ten index cards and placed them inside opaque covers, deciding randomly whether a card should have the black or white side uppermost inside the cover. The covers and cards were given to Ryzl, who held one cover after another in front of Stepanek. Stepanek, however, could not see the covers: his face was shielded by a screen. *Stepanek neither saw nor touched the covers*, but simply guessed 'White' or 'Black'. Ryzl recorded each guess. After Stepanek had completed ten guesses, Ryzl checked them against the list of targets prepared by the assistant.

Now, with two options to choose from – black and white – chance alone will give an average success rate of 50 per cent. Since Ryzl and Stepanek completed 2,000 guesses, we would expect a chance result of about 1,000 correct guesses. In fact, Stepanek managed just over 1,140, slightly more than 57 per cent. The odds against this are well over 10 million to one.

Our statistical method tells us that the difference between 50 per cent and 57 per cent isn't chance. Still, it would be more satisfying to achieve a higher percentage, say 60 per cent or 70 per cent – and this is what Ryzl set out to do. He reasoned as follows. Suppose that, when

Stepanek is guessing, he only uses ESP now and then (since not all his guesses were correct, this must obviously be the case). If you like, what we have here is an *infrequent signal*. Something gets through every seven guesses or so. The other six are chance. If the one-in-seven is a *signal*, and the other six are just *noise*, then there is a particular technique which can be used to amplify that signal. *Stepanek can be made to guess at the same target over and over again.* The signals will then begin to add up, and they can be seen more clearly against the background of the noise.

This technique is termed a *majority-vote* experiment. Stepanek guesses at the same target many times (in fact, just ten times in the first experiment of this type) and the experimenter looks at what he says *most of the time*. If Stepanek says 'Black' seven times and 'White' only three

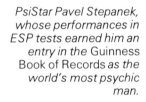

PsiStar Pavel Stepanek, whose performances in ESP tests earned him an entry in the Guinness Book of Records *as the world's most psychic man.*

times, then his guess is taken to be 'Black' – hence the *majority* vote. Accordingly, Ryzl had his assistant prepare an entire set of 100 cards, each with black or white side uppermost (random choice again), each sealed inside an opaque envelope. Just to be sure, Ryzl added some extra opaque packaging on the outside. This sequence was presented to Stepanek ten times. A majority vote was taken for the 100 sets of ten guesses, boiling them down to 100 guesses alone. In fact, there were only 93 guesses because, for seven of the targets, Stepanek said 'White' and 'Black' five times each. Obviously there is no majority vote here. Of the other 93, only 27 were wrong while 66 were right – a success rate of 71 per cent. For the record, the odds against Stepanek getting 71 per cent right by chance alone are comfortably over 20,000 to one. Clearly this is a significant finding.

Later, we shall go through all the possible counter-explanations to ESP which might be invoked to explain away the results. For the time being, let's accept that Stepanek was using ESP to guess the cards correctly. What else might we learn?

The first thing Stepanek's performance is telling us is that *ESP is lawful*, that is, it behaves consistently. It *should* be the case that a majority-vote test should bump up the scoring rate. Scientists use this type of procedure extensively to amplify weak signals, and if ESP didn't behave in this way, it would be rather surprising. Stepanek's performance is very reassuring on this count.

Stepanek's feats were so remarkable that scientists of the West soon took an interest. From the Parapsychology Laboratory of Duke University in North Carolina, Gaither Pratt visited Ryzl in Prague in 1962, hoping to test Stepanek. Pratt examined the test procedure and was present when Stepanek was tested. At this first meeting, the results were modestly above the 50/50 level, but not impressively so. When Pratt returned in 1963, however, Stepanek was right back on top form. Of 2,000 guesses 1,133 were correct, a success rate of 56.65 per cent. The odds against achieving such a result by chance are more than 10 million to one.

Between those two visits there took place the most staggering of all the experiments done with Stepanek. It occurred to Ryzl that, since going through the same sequence ten times had yielded success rates of up to 71 per cent, further repetition might produce even better results.

Ryzl arranged for Stepanek to guess a single sequence of 15 cards hundreds of times over. These were the cards on which Stepanek had been most successful. At the end of the experiment, *Stepanek had got every single one right*. The odds against chance here are 1 in 32,768.

Now for the first twist in the story. As the experiments progressed, Ryzl noticed that Stepanek began to make particular guesses quite consistently whenever a particular *envelope* was presented to him. It seemed possible that little sensory 'cues' on the envelopes – marks, scratches, and so on – were distracting him, quite without his being consciously aware of it. Might this focusing on the envelopes be inhibiting Stepanek's ability to guess the cards inside them by ESP? To exclude this possibility Ryzl and Pratt modified their procedures.

The cards were sealed inside envelopes, as before, but now the envelopes were inside opaque covers. Since Stepanek could no longer see the envelopes, it was hoped that he wouldn't be distracted by them, and would use ESP successfully on the cards.

What the researchers found was that Stepanek *continued* to make particular guesses whenever certain envelopes were present, even though he could no longer see them. The only explanation possible was that he was using ESP to detect the envelopes and, indeed, when the envelopes were moved around inside the covers, the effect stayed the same. Stepanek himself still thought that he was using ESP to guess the cards – but he was actually using ESP to guess the envelopes which contained them.

It was at this time that Pratt – who came more and more to be the dominant researcher with Stepanek – conducted one of the two experiments which he labelled as 'providing conclusive evidence that P.S. (Stepanek) was demonstrating ESP'. In it Pratt collaborated with J. G. Blom, a Dutch scientist from Amsterdam University.

Blom and Pratt prepared 40 cards (green and white now, as in most of the work with Stepanek) sealed inside 40 envelopes. They did this in

Milan Ryzl, the Czech parapsychologist who discovered Stepanek's amazing ESP powers.

such a way that neither of them alone could possibly have known which envelope contained which target colour. Pratt randomised the order of the 40 envelopes, and took eight at a time, concealing each one inside an outer cover. Stepanek made his guesses in Blom's presence when these cover/envelope/card packages were offered to him. The two experimenters carefully recorded guesses and targets for each session, and 1,000 guesses were made in all. Altogether, in four days' work, 4,000 guesses were made and recorded. Stepanek showed ESP detection of the *cards* this time, getting 2,154 right – odds of around 500,000 to one.

Over the next few years, without blinding the reader with statistics, two main advances in the work with Stepanek took place. The first was that Stepanek was able to demonstrate ESP to a large number of research scientists from all over the world. The other (and perhaps this is not exactly an advance) was that Stepanek's ESP ability detached

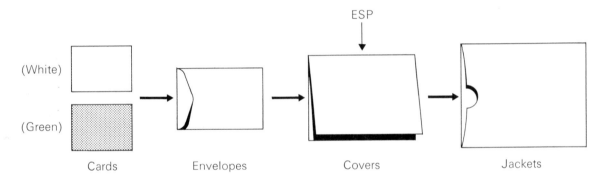

ESP

(White)

(Green)

Cards   Envelopes   Covers   Jackets

The progressive ESP mystery. Stepanek was asked to guess through the same sequence of cards many hundreds of times. Intriguingly, his ESP ability came to focus on particular cards, which he always called correctly. Attempts to 'shield' these cards first with envelopes, then covers, then jackets resulted in Stepanek's ESP fixing upon particular envelopes, covers and jackets!

itself from the cards completely, and settled first on the envelopes, then on the outer covers themselves. So the covers had to be concealed inside jackets.

Since the covers were quite bulky, the jackets had to be padded out with cotton and carefully weighed to make sure that they truly concealed the nature of the covers within them. This test procedure was used when Stepanek visited the University of Virginia to work with Pratt and Dr Ian Stevenson of that University, with Dr Jurgen Keil from Tasmania, in February 1968. Stepanek consistently called certain covers 'Green' and others 'White'; further, there were particular covers for which he guessed *one side* 'Green' and the other 'White'.

Eventually, like so many PsiStars, Stepanek went into decline and his abilities deserted him. Nevertheless, for ten years this modest and retiring man had produced the most extraordinary results in the history of ESP-testing. What are we to make of his remarkable career?

The central question is this: did Stepanek definitely show ESP? The first think we know is that chance could not possibly account for the

Hansel's Critique [Italics have been added to identify specific statements requiring comment.]	(Pratt's) Comments
In recent years, parapsychologists have discovered that ESP research is in progress behind the Iron Curtain. In Prague, Milan Ryzl, *a biochemist at the Institute of Biology of the Czechoslovak Academy of Science,* has claimed extraordinary clairvoyant powers for his subject, Pavel Stepanek.	From about 1960 Ryzl had no regular salaried position but worked unofficially in ESP research.
Stepanek's act, for it can hardly be called more than that, is as follows:	P.S. did not set the conditions for the research, so he could not have worked like a stage magician, as this sentence implies.
An observer is given a *pile of envelopes and cards.* One side of each card is *black,* and the other is white. *The observer places the cards in the envelopes with either the black or the white side uppermost. The pack of envelopes is then sorted by Stepanek,* and he is able to distinguish envelopes in which the card has its black side uppermost from those in which the card has its white side up. The envelopes are specially made and consist of *two pieces of thin cardboard stapled together. Since Stepanek handles the envelopes,* it is likely that he utilizes *cues due to bending or warping of the cards.*	Most of the research involved cards in envelopes *plus* outer covers. Most of the tests used white and *green* cards. This description reads as if someone present in the room with P.S. placed the cards in the envelopes and immediately handed them to him to call. The testing was not the casual affair that Hansel implies, but was carefully planned and carried out by experimenters who had full control over the materials and the conditions for excluding sensory cues. One strip of cardboard was folded and the edges taped for the envelopes. For the outer covers the edges were fastened by stapling them together through heavy cardboard ribs or spacing strips. This statement ignores significant series in which P.S. neither saw nor touched the objects. This statement ignores conditions used to control explicitly against bent or warped cards.
Stepanek has been tested by several independent investigators. When tested by Pratt and *J. G. Blom, one of Ryzl's colleagues,* he produced very impressive results, but *when the experiment was conducted by a psychologist,* John Beloff, of Edinburgh University, *he failed to display any clairvoyant ability.*	Blom was from Amsterdam and he had not even met Ryzl when our research, was done. Several other investigators were psychologists (Pratt, Barendregt, Freeman, Otani, Kanthamani) who obtained highly significant results.
Beloff had supplied his own cards which were made of plastic.	P.S. obtained highly significant results with Beloff present, although not with the novel materials and test procedures used in Experiment I.

results obtained. Everyone agrees on this. Instead, we need to know if any *reasonable* alternative explanation to ESP exists. The word *reasonable* must be stressed. It is, after all, theoretically *possible* that Stepanek and the 15 experimenters who obtained and reported evidence of ESP with him were all in a gigantic conspiracy to defraud the world. On the other hand, no-one would regard that as a *reasonable* alternative explanation to ESP.

In a very few of the early experiments, it seems just possible that Stepanek could have been using *heat* cues from the cards. The black and white sides of the cards may have reflected detectably different amounts of heat through the envelopes. Such a possibility could not, of course, apply to the experiments in which envelopes and covers were used, nor to those in which Stepanek did not see or touch the envelopes. This

The persistence of scepticism: C. E. M. Hansel vs. Gaither Pratt over the Stepanek affair.

needs to be mentioned because the sceptical reviewer whose opinions we shall now examine fails to mention this.

When Pratt and others published papers in *Nature* and in *New Scientist* about Stepanek, they encountered considerable scepticism. Most of it is summarised by the British sceptic C. E. M. Hansel, Professor of Psychology at Swansea. In 1966, Hansel published one book on ESP research which gave Stepanek 22 lines of text. In 1973, Pratt corrected the many errors and false inferences the Hansel text contained. Opposite, without any comment (none is needed), are the writings of Pratt and Hansel.

When Hansel returned to the fray with another book in 1980, he managed to delete many of the more egregious errors and false insinuations (for example, the one about Blom being one of Ryzl's colleagues) but other points remained the same. To take one instance, Hansel wrote in 1980 that 'In 1965, I suggested that cues due to warpage of the cards might be responsible for this result (i.e. high scoring on the cards in the earlier experiments).' Now, in fact, Pratt had controlled for this problem, carefully flexing the cards and studying the warping of unattended control samples left to return to a warped state due to the grain of the material, and so on. In 1973 he pointed this out; in 1980 Hansel simply appears to ignore it. This is depressing. Hansel also wrote once again that Ryzl was a biochemist at the Institute of Biology at the Czechoslovak Academy of Science – exactly as in 1966 and ignoring Pratt's first correction above. This is also depressing.

Other sceptics, however, had different views. The mathematician George Medhurst, a noted British sceptic, wrote to Pratt saying '. . . so far as I am concerned this looks like a clear demonstration of ESP'.

There are many possibilities for normal sensory communication being involved in Stepanek's success, but none of them – nor all of them together – will explain all, or even most, of the results. Weight differences, warping, visual clues, heat reflection: all of these were examined and controlled for, and the ESP effects still continued. The random choice of targets eliminated any predictability which might enable logical working-out to be used; nor could Stepanek get unconscious help from the experimenters, since they did not have the information about the targets that he would have needed. Unless some deliberate fraud was involved, its hard to see where else we can turn for a reasonable alternative explanation than to the ESP hypothesis. As we have noted, so many people were involved in the successful work that the possibility of fraud seems hardly reasonable. The major successes of Stepanek are such as to suggest, overwhelmingly, that ESP must have been involved in producing the results.

A last issue: what sort of man is our psychic bank clerk? Common sense suggests that anyone who spends ten years or so guessing Green versus White for cards, envelopes, covers or whatever is not an ordinary person. To many people, this must seem a dreadful prospect, boring beyond comprehension. Yet Stepanek enjoyed it, and indeed was never very successful with other types of experiments. Why was this?

A SUMMARY OF SOME OF STEPANEK'S BEST ESP PERFORMANCES

EXPERIMENT(S)	ODDS AGAINST CHANCE FOR RESULTS
1. Two majority-vote experiments, run by Ryzl, attempting to get a very high score rate on the cards by guessing over and over at the same targets. Results: 71 per cent correct in the first study, 100 per cent correct in the second.	20,000 to one 112 million million to one
2. Two key experiments viewed by Pratt (who ran them) as the best from the point of view of evidence of ESP. One (November 1963) was done with J. G. Blom of Holland as colleague, and the ESP effect was shown as a high score on the cards, 2,154 right out of 4,000 guesses. The other (February 1968) was done with Virginian Ian Stevenson and Jurgen Keil of Tasmania as colleagues, and in a series of three sub-experiments Stepanek's ESP effect revealed itself as a very high score rate on the concealed covers.	500,000 to one 10 million to one
3. Stepanek was particularly successful with visiting researchers. In the 1963 study run by Dutch experimenters, he scored 1,216 correct and only 832 incorrect for his card guesses. In other experiments with visiting Japanese, Indian, and Dutch researchers (amongst others) he was also very successful.	1,000 million million to one 1 million to one

Formal personality tests on Stepanek, and the opinions of those who worked with him and know him, point to one significant feature in his psychology. Stepanek is a rather anxious person, who adopts one type of defence in particular against that anxiety: compulsive and rather obsessional habits, the performing of rituals. As Pratt wrote, 'His life is governed more than anything else by the need to avoid social complications . . . He strives to keep matters so arranged that he can be in control at all times . . . He is afraid that personal involvements that overlap with his daily routine might make his life complicated, and he has a strong desire to *keep it as simple as possible* . . .' Pratt also stressed Stepanek's punctuality, and his deep-seated conviction that a man's word should be his bond.

Psychiatrists will readily recognise this as an obsessive-compulsive personality, reflected particularly by the need for order, control and simplicity in life. How perfect, then, the simple ESP experiment was for Stepanek. A precise, simple ritual, prearranged and adhered to at the stated time and place. There is something important to be learned here which we will need to keep in mind when examining the work on personality and ESP in a later chapter, namely that *different types of people may prefer different types of test*. It is easy to see why a type of test that would have bored most of us to tears appealed so much to Pavel Stepanek, the world's most psychic man.

The full-time score: a summary of Stepanek's best performances.

The techniques used by Ryzl, Pratt and others to test Pavel Stepanek followed directly from the original card-guessing experiments of pioneer researchers such as Rhine. It would be surprising if, in the age of the computer, new techniques had not developed which could solve the laborious business of preparing and handling materials and recording results. And, indeed, the computer, the microchip, and even the video game have come to play an increasingly important role in research on all aspects of psi.

A German-born physicist, working a decade ago for the Boeing Research Laboratories in Seattle, was the first man to use this technology to test psi in a thoroughgoing and systematic way. This man, Dr Helmut Schmidt, invented a machine that automated psi testing – generating random targets, registering subjects' guesses and recording all relevant data in a form that was both easily accessible and easy to process. With his machines, Schmidt hoped to find evidence for psi that would pre-empt all the standard criticisms of parapsychological research – usually expressed as accusations of collusion, faulty recording, inconsistencies of method, or patterning as a result of the use of non-random series of targets.

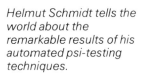

Helmut Schmidt tells the world about the remarkable results of his automated psi-testing techniques.

Schmidt's research, with the aid of his psi-testing machines, has furnished some of the most startling and provocative evidence for psi yet recorded. He has not only recorded significant ESP effects but also shown that some individuals at least are capable of using PK abilities to influence basic physical processes. But before we examine Schmidt's work as a whole, it is necessary to understand the basic principles of his machines.

At the heart of Schmidt's psi-testing machines is a naturally occurring random process – the radioactive decay of the isotope Strontium-90. As the atoms of Sr-90 decay, they emit rapidly moving electrons at random and therefore unpredictable time intervals. Sr-90 decay is thus a useful source of random targets for use in psi-testing.

Circuit diagram of Schmidt's Random Event Generator (REG).

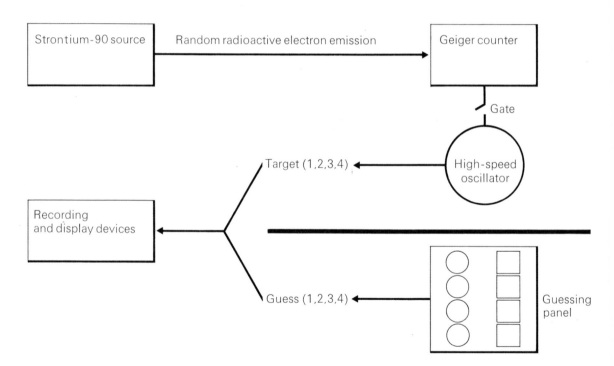

The basic elements of the Schmidt machine, then, are an isotope of Sr-90, a Geiger counter to detect electrons as they are emitted, and a high-speed electronic oscillator, constantly cycling between a number (usually four) of different electronic states. Whenever the Geiger counter detects the emission of an electron, a counter driven by the oscillator stops, registering the state – 1,2,3,4 – of the oscillator at the microsecond of emission. A simple visual display of numbered lamps allows the observer to see which state is being registered.

There are two ways of testing for psi with a Schmidt machine or random event generator (REG). One can ask a subject to guess which of the numbered lamps will light next (a precognition task, in other

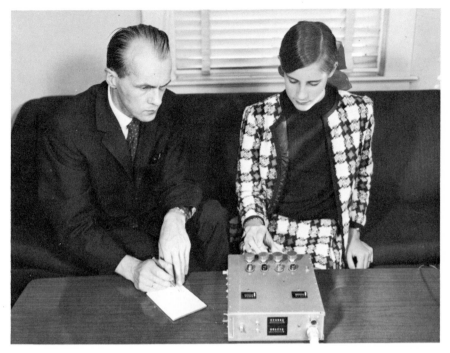

'That button gets you black coffee with no sugar': one of Schmidt's subjects gets a lesson from the inventor on how to work the machine.

words a test for ESP). Or one can ask a subject to concentrate on making one of the lamps light more than 25 per cent of the time (a test for psychokinesis, PK). The advantages of machine-testing are obvious. The events to be predicted or influenced by the subject occur in a truly random way – giving a clear measurement of the subject's success or failure in his tasks relative to chance. Further, the Schmidt machine records results automatically, eliminating the possibility of recording errors.

ESP and the Schmidt machine

Schmidt published the results of his first ESP experiments with the machine in 1969. For these, he arranged that the machine would work in the following way. The subject registered his guess by pressing one of four numbered buttons. The act of pressing the button triggered the machine to produce a target which duly resulted in one of the four lamps being illuminated. The subject's guess, together with the number of the lamp which, in the event, lit up were recorded on punched paper tape. This whole process was completed within half a second. To guard against cheating, the machine was programmed to ignore trials in which the subject pressed two or more buttons simultaneously. On the other hand, if there were more than a millionth of a second's delay between the pressing of any two or more buttons, the machine automatically registered the first signal as the subject's guess.

In his early work Schmidt tested some 100 subjects, drawn from Spiritualist communities and churches, where he thought he might have the best chance of finding people with psi abilities. Among them he found one particularly gifted individual, a doctor of physics. This physicist was able to predict the behaviour of the machine to such an extent that the odds against chance for his performance were well over 100,000 to one. Unfortunately, at this point the physicist had to move away to a new job, so Schmidt was prevented from conducting further tests with him. However, the results persuaded him that his best approach would be to concentrate on a few gifted individuals.

Through further screening, Schmidt selected three individuals for a first formal experiment. All three had a strong interest in the paranormal. One was a male medium, another a teacher of 'psychic development', while the third, a truck driver, described himself as an 'amateur psychic'. They completed some 63,066 guesses. A chance average score would be 25 per cent, or about 15,766 correct guesses. The actual number of correct guesses, or hits, was 16,458, nearly 700 hits above the chance average. This is certainly a small effect – a scoring rate of less than 27 per cent correct. However, because this slight excess of hits was recorded over such a long sequence of guesses, the odds against its coming up by chance alone are over 100 million to one!

Negative ESP

In a second experiment, Schmidt was interested in trying to establish whether his subjects could use their ESP to score *below* chance as well as above it. One of his original subjects, the medium, was unable to take

Can ESP be controlled? Schmidt's results, summarised here, suggest emphatically that the answer is yes!

SCHMIDT'S SECOND ESP EXPERIMENT : CAN PEOPLE CONTROL THEIR ESP ?

Subject	Goal	Guesses	Hits expected by chance	Hits scored	Difference	Probability by chance
O.C.	Score High	5,000	1,250	1,316	+66	1 in 50
J.B.	Score High	5,672	1,418	1,541	+123	1 in 10,000
O.C. and J.B. together		10,672	2,668	2,857	+189	1 in 100,000
J.B.	Score Low	4,328	1,082	956	−126	1 in 100,000
S.C.	Score Low	5,000	1,250	1,164	−86	1 in 500
S.C. and J.B. together		9,328	2,332	2,120	−212	1 in 500,000

Probability of the difference between +189 and −212 arising by chance is less than one in 100 million

part, so Schmidt added a new member to his team – the 16-year-old daughter of the truck driver. The sequence of testing began again as before. But in this experiment, one subject was asked to aim for an above-chance score, another to aim for a below-chance score, while one was tested under both conditions. Here again the results departed significantly from the expected average. When aiming above chance, the score level was slightly above 26 per cent; when aiming low, the score level was somewhat below 24 per cent. These differences may *seem* slight yet, reflected consistently over a long period of testing, they add up to real odds against chance of *over 1,000 million to one*.

Checks and safeguards

Before looking at some of Schmidt's other experiments we must examine the implications of the first two. The statistics tell us that the results Schmidt obtained, when combined, cannot have been the result of chance. The odds against it are a million million to one. The only possible mechanical explanation is that the results were produced by some bias in the machine itself. Well aware of this possibility, Schmidt made the following checks. Since he had the punched paper record of all the guesses that his subjects had made, in the original order, he could find out if there was anything peculiar about that particular sequence which might produce a distorted result. He fed the record into the machine and examined the total score against a fresh series of targets. It was well within chance levels. As a further check, Schmidt regularly programmed the machine to produce long sequences of targets. An original series of five million targets generated in this way, together with subsequent series, showed no evidence of patterning. Neither statistical peculiarity nor mechanical bias could explain his results.

Clairvoyance and PK

In a third experiment, Schmidt used a series of random targets generated automatically by the machine for a test of clairvoyance. The targets were stored on paper tape and sealed inside the machine, which was programmed to play them back, in the normal way, by illuminating the four numbered lamps in a random sequence. The six subjects who took part in this experiment were asked to guess the sequence in which the lamps would be lit. In attempting to do so the subjects were not trying to predict a future event, nor could they bias the machine. They were being asked to use ESP to discover, or 'read', a predetermined sequence. In all, 15,000 guesses were completed. Once again, Schmidt arranged for his subjects to try for below-average (negative ESP) scores as well as above-average scores. And once again he recorded significant results – this time at odds of over a quarter of a million to one against chance.

Had Schmidt never completed another experiment, these three would remain a major challenge to sceptics who deny that any form of ESP can exist. But further experiments produced even more extraordinary results.

REG takes a random walk: PK and the Schmidt machine

Having tested ESP, Schmidt now wanted to see if it was possible for his subjects to influence the actual operation of his machines by PK. For this work, Schmidt devised a simpler version of his machine, with two, rather than four, output states. This he termed, for obvious reasons, a binary (two-way) *random event generator* (REG). This was linked to a visual display of nine lamps arranged in a circle, of which only one lamp was illuminated at a time. As the Sr-90 isotope fired out its electrons, the REG turned them, at random, into negative and positive pulses. When a pulse of one kind was delivered to the display the light jumped one step in a clockwise direction. The other type of pulse resulted in a similar step in an anticlockwise direction. When the machine was behaving in a random manner, the lights would tend to jump clockwise and anticlockwise an even number of times (a 'random walk' around the circle of lamps). The subjects were asked to 'will' the machine to generate pulses so that the lamps would jump in a clockwise more often than an anticlockwise direction.

Interestingly, in his first experiments with the REG, Schmidt found that his subjects tended to score below chance (psi-missing, negative PK). Using a second group of 15 subjects, which included the most consistent of his psi-missers, Schmidt completed a total of 32,768 trials – in which he now hoped to find a psi-missing effect. In fact, rather than moving clockwise 50 per cent of the time (16,384 times), the lamps did so just above 49 per cent of the time (16,082 times). A small, weak psi effect, but nonetheless not a chance one: the odds against chance in this experiment are over 1,000 to one.

Two further experiments by Schmidt may be noted. The first of these was particularly ingenious. Schmidt wished to know if, in the first two experiments we have examined, the subjects were using precognition (predicting which lamp would light next) or PK (biasing the machine so that it produced the same target that they had guessed). To establish this distinction, Schmidt designed a beautifully camouflaged PK test. He modified his original, four-channel REG in such a way that, while the subject *thought* the test was one of precognition, he could in fact only succeed in it by using PK.

The modification was a logic circuit which operated so that the only way of scoring a hit was when the target produced by the machine registered on channel 4. Thus, to succeed in this test means that one has to use PK to bias the machine to generate an excess of 4's. No other action will produce an above-chance score. Subjects were not, however, told this, nor could they have guessed it.

Schmidt conducted this experiment as though it were a straight-forward ESP test. Subjects were asked to predict the sequence of illuminated lamps. What they did not know was that Schmidt had arranged for the logic circuit to be switched into and out of the test at random. In reality, therefore, Schmidt's subjects were actually taking part in two experiments – one testing ESP, the other PK testing –

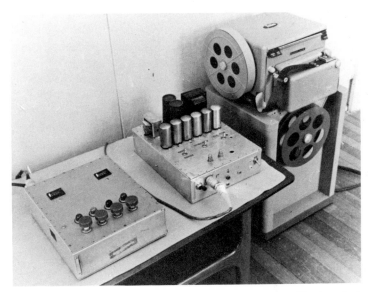

One of Schmidt's original automated psi-testing machines. Now the age of the microchip offers a bright future for accurate, easily portable psi-testing equipment.

randomly intermixed and disguised as one. Both of these 'hidden' experiments yielded significant evidence of psi (with odds against chance of over 1,000 to 1 for each phase, and of over 100,000 to 1 for the whole experiment). The scores, however, were the same for both conditions – with the logic circuit (which required pure PK to achieve a high score) and without it (PK or precognition possible). These results suggested that, in Schmidt's very first two successful experiments, the subjects could have been using PK as well as precognition – or, indeed, pure PK – to achieve their scores.

In a development of this work, Schmidt compared his subjects' PK scoring on two entirely different REGs with different mechanisms for producing the targets. One of them was a 'simple' binary REG which worked as explained above. The other was a 'complex' machine which generated a large number of individual random events, computed how many there were of each possible variety, and presented as the target the one which was most common in the whole group. The experiment was again highly successful (odds against chance of 100,000 to 1) and showed no difference in scoring between the two machines. That latter result is a very important one, and its significance will be seen in Chapter 9, when we come to examine the place of psi in physics.

Over the years Schmidt has continued to report experiments conducted with his machines. Specifically, he has been able to show that subjects can not only influence the normal operation of his machines, but that they can also influence the sequence of a pre-recorded series of events. This staggering claim is examined in more detail in Chapter 9. Briefly, however, the experiment was conducted in this manner. Schmidt arranged for a machine to generate a random series of targets, which were recorded and stored on tape. The targets were played back to the subjects in audible form as a series of clicks heard through headphones. A device ensured that the clicks should be distributed randomly between the left and the right channels of the headphones. The subjects were asked to will that more clicks should be heard through one channel than the other. In order to do this, of course, they had to use PK to influence random numbers generated *some time in the past*. The fact that Schmidt found a positive effect in this experiment is one of the most baffling results in the history of parapsychology.

At odds with sceptics

By our computations the odds against chance for all Schmidt's results put together are so huge that, if we gave them, the word 'million' would fill quite a few lines. For our purposes it is enough to know that all sceptics will admit that Schmidt's results cannot be explained by chance.

Our own review of Schmidt's evidence has left us highly impressed with the quality of his work. We find that his experiments were soundly conducted, properly recorded, and that his statistical analysis of the data was rigorously applied. Interested and knowledgeable readers may care to review the reports of his experiments for themselves, for which references are given at the end of this book. In our opinion, the only explanation, other than psi, for Schmidt's results would be wholesale fraud – but this conspiracy would also have to include other workers such as Honorton, Eve Andre, and Erlendur Haraldsson, who have independently repeated and confirmed Schmidt's experimental results. Most sceptics, indeed, have come to agree with the assessment of Ray Hyman, a distinguished critic of parapsychology. He has written:

'By almost any standard, Schmidt's work is the most challenging ever to confront critics such as myself. His approach makes many of the earlier criticisms of parapsychological research obsolete. [I am] convinced that he was sincere, honest and dedicated to being as scientific as possible ... the most sophisticated parapsychologist that I have encountered. If there are flaws in his work, they are not the more common or obvious ones.'

It would be very strange if psi abilities were limited to PsiStars like Home and Stepanek. Many ordinary people clearly have at least some ability to use psi, unless all reports of paranormal experience from ordinary people are completely fictitious. Also, as we have seen, Helmut Schmidt's impressive results have come partly from work with specially gifted individuals and partly from unselected volunteers. PsiStars are merely the tip of the iceberg.

Human beings differ enormously in intelligence, memory capacity, personality and accuracy of perception, so surely there must be a difference in their psi abilities too. Is there any link between psi ability and age, sex, race, intelligence, or personality, and if there is, why? Could the explanation lie in genetic factors, upbringing, differences in brain activity, or differences in lifestyle?

It is easy for mediums to say that the presence of disbelievers at a seance blocks out psi powers, but is there any evidence for this?

Faith and scepticism

How can we start to answer these questions? Let us begin by dividing people according to whether they are disposed to believe or disbelieve in psi. Mediums, for example, have always claimed that the presence of sceptics at seances inhibits their powers. The sceptic claims, of course, that he is a hard man to fool, and that mediums dare not play their usual tricks with him around. It would certainly be worth knowing, then, if attitudes for or against psi affect scoring in psi tests.

The Schmeidler experiments

One of the first researchers to investigate the effects of belief and disbelief on psi was Dr Gertrude Schmeidler of the City University of New York. In 1942 she started testing the psi abilities of psychologists and students from Harvard. Volunteers had to try to use ESP to guess the order of packs of ESP cards placed in a different room where no-one was looking at them. But before any testing started Schmeidler interviewed her subjects to ascertain whether they were 'sheep' or 'goats'. The sheep were the believers, those who thought ESP was at least a possibility, and the goats were those who simply refused to admit the possibility of ESP, though they were prepared to be tested, probably to help Schmeidler with her experiment.

The first three experiments gave quite clear results. In all, 58 subjects were tested and the believers came up trumps: 46 believers ploughed through a total of 389 25-card guessing runs and averaged 5.31 correct guesses per run (the chance average being 5.00). Though only fractionally above the chance average, the odds against this happening by chance were around 1,000 to one. But putting together the results of these and another four experiments in which sheep and goats were individually tested, something rather strange emerged.

One might have expected the goats to score very close to the 5.00 chance average, equivalent to nil ESP. But they scored consistently below it. Though the effect is small there is very weak ESP here, ESP of a kind one would not have expected: negative ESP or psi-missing. We met this strange effect when discussing the work of Helmut Schmidt, but usually only when subjects were deliberately trying to score below chance.

Between 1945 and 1951 Schmeidler conducted another 14 experiments in which she tested people in groups rather than individually. The results were much the same (see page 50). Taking the data from *all* her experiments together, she found that sheep consistently scored better than chance and goats consistently worse. So marked was the difference between the two groups that the odds against chance being the only explanation comfortably exceeded 10 million to one.

Schmeidler's work can be regarded as a major landmark on two counts: it showed reliable patterns of ESP from research with ordinary people, and it clearly hinted at a link between ESP and individual psychology. In total, her data base comprised some 300,000 guesses from 1,308 subjects. With numbers like these her findings cannot be dismissed. Her work has been subjected to rigorous scrutiny, but never seriously questioned. And indeed, we now have abundant confirmation of her conclusions from all over the world.

Results from post-Schmeidler experiments in India, Czechoslovakia, Argentina, and elsewhere were carefully summarised by the Californian worker John Palmer in 1971.

Durability of the sheep–goat effect

Palmer's scrutiny was rigorous but imaginative. If there really is a difference between sheep and goats, he suggested, then Schmeidler's results might be a good indication of how powerful the difference is and might be used to predict the magnitude of the difference in later experiments. Taking Schmeidler's results as an estimate of the true sheep–goat difference, Palmer predicted that about 84 per cent of all subsequent experiments should show sheep scoring better than goats, and that about 16 per cent should actually show the reverse. Looking at the 17 post-Schmeidler experiments he found that in 13 of them, equivalent to 76 per cent, sheep scored better than goats. Now the

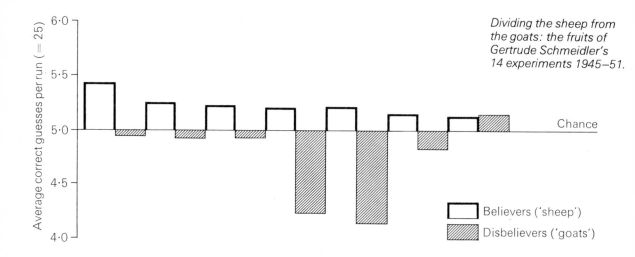

Dividing the sheep from the goats: the fruits of Gertrude Schmeidler's 14 experiments 1945–51.

difference between 84 per cent and 76 per cent is not worryingly significant. Palmer was satisfied that Schmeidler's results were essentially correct, essentially a reflection of objective reality, and vindicated by subsequent research. Though the bias is not large, believers on average score a little above chance and unbelievers a little below.

Palmer returned to the fray in 1977, looking at another set of results collected in the intervening six years, and came to the same conclusion.

So the sheep–goat effect has stood the test of time, or the last 30 years of it at any rate. Experimental results have confirmed the pro- and anti-psi attitudes expressed in interviews or formal questionnaires. But why, in particular, do goats consistently score *below* chance, rather than at chance? Does this suggest that they have some ESP ability after all, even if they are misusing it?

One possibility is that goats feel silly taking part in experiments they believe to be bunkum, and so are in a state of mental conflict which might systematically distort their use of ESP information. Assuming this to be so, it might be revealing to see if neurotics are poor at using ESP, more of which shortly. Another possibility is there are basic personality differences between sheep and goats. Research has now shown that sheep tend to be more extravert, more friendly and out-going, than goats. Because so many ESP experiences in the real world involve ESP communication about and between people, someone who is open and gregarious may be more likely to experience ESP and more likely to become a believer than a social isolate.

Personality and ESP

Although it seems, from reports of spontaneous ESP, that ESP may be triggered by strong emotions, the Schmidt, Schmeidler, and Stepanek experiments were very low-voltage affairs emotionally. Do psycho-analysts and other alleged explorers of the emotional depths of the human mind provide any clues to possible links between personality and ESP? Certainly the literature is abundant, but the facts are pretty thin.

The trouble with the psychoanalytical approach is that it is infinitely subjective, tends often to attach huge importance to entirely trivial behaviour, and lacks experimental support. Many psychoanalysts have claimed that their clients have had telepathic experiences involving deep-seated emotional drives and repressions. Unfortunately the quite unscientific nature of these 'interpretations' makes them largely valueless to the parapsychologist. We need scientific ways of looking at personality, or we will never be able to relate psi to personality scientifically.

Scientific personality researchers use three types of evidence to construct personality profiles: biographical material, objective measures of behaviour, and questionnaires which record opinions, preferences, thoughts and so on. Each source has certain advantages and problems, but put together they form an accurate and reliable picture of personality. The most exhaustive research into the measurement of personality has been that conducted by Hans J. Eysenck in Britain and Raymond B. Cattell in America. Their notions differ slightly, but they agree on one thing: the two most reliable and readily measured components of the human personality are extraversion–introversion and neuroticism–stability. And it is on these two components that parapsychologists have concentrated their research efforts. Once again, the early research was conducted in America, by Betty Humphrey at Duke University.

The famous Rohrsach Blot test was an integral part of early personality assessment. The modern personality inventories used by today's parapsychologists have helped to clarify the relationship between personality and psi ability.

The extravert–ESP effect

Humphrey used a standard personality test of the time – now thought of as rather primitive – to divide her sample of subjects into extraverts and introverts. She then ran them through ESP card-guessing, as Schmeidler did, and consistently the extraverts scored above chance and the introverts did not. Some statistical problems may have contaminated these findings. But a few years later, in 1953, Humphrey collaborated with another researcher, J. Fraser Nicol, and came up with findings entirely free of such taints. She and Nicol gave what were at the time the best personality tests available to 30 subjects, who then completed some ESP card-guessing tests. They found a clear relationship between extraversion and above-chance guess rates, just as Humphrey had done previously with inferior testing procedures. Again, their subjects were quite ordinary people, not PsiStars. Soon, confirmation of the extravert–psi effect came from other countries.

South Africa, 1959 At Rhodes University M. C. Marsh conducted a telepathy experiment in which the receivers were at Rhodes University, Grahamstown, and the sender at Cape Town, 470 miles away. Instead of using simple ESP cards, Marsh used drawings of objects as guessing targets; the receivers had to try to use ESP to guess which object the sender would draw in each test. The nature of the object was quite random. Entirely independent judges scored the guesses against the

targets, and a measure of ESP success was derived from these scorings (see Chapter 6). Marsh found that those who showed strong ESP in his experiment were much more extraverted than those who did not.

Sweden, 1965 Using the Maudsley Personality Inventory designed by Eysenck, Astrom assessed a group of 48 subjects for extraversion and introversion. In a subsequent test with ESP cards, the extraverts showed very high scoring (strong positive ESP) and the introverts scored at chance only (no ESP).

India, 1972 At Andrha University, testing high-school children with ESP cards, Kanthamani and Rao found that in three of their four experiments extraverts scored much better than introverts, a difference they could not ascribe simply to the operation of chance.

And we could continue for pages and pages with similar data ... Reviewing all the published findings in 1981, Sargent concluded that there were 18 different reports in which extraverts had scored significantly better than introverts. Chance could not possibly be the explanation. Only once did the reverse occur – introverts scoring better than the extraverts. Nevertheless, 18 to one is fairly convincing evidence of the extravert–psi effect. The exception proves the rule.

Many experiments, it must be admitted, have failed to show a major difference between extraverts and introverts, but many more have succeeded than ought to have done if chance is the only factor at work. In fact the odds against the overwhelming superiority of extraverts in ESP experiments are over 10,000 million to one. Those are long odds.

The extravert (left) scores higher in ESP tests than the introvert (above). If there is a physical basis for personality – measurable in the degree of arousal needed to stimulate cortical activity – does this mean we have a physical predisposition to more or less psi ability?

The brain arousal theory

The first suggestion as to why extraverts are better ESP subjects was put forward by Eysenck in 1967. It is fairly well established that extraverts have lower levels of cortical arousal (activity in the cortex of the brain) than introverts. This may, in part, be because extraverts are better at suppressing the activity of nerve cells in the medulla (the base of the brain) which relay incoming sensory signals to the cortex.

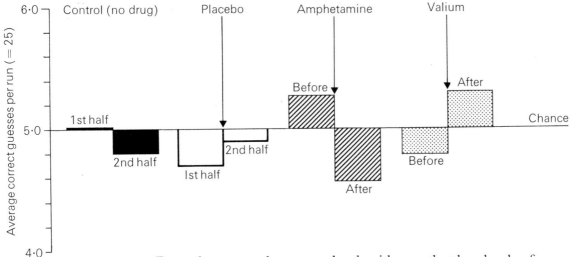

The effects of amphetamine and valium on ESP.

Can I join in? The aloof, awkward character of the introvert may itself block ESP ability.

Eysenck suggested, on anecdotal evidence, that low levels of arousal might be favourable for ESP. If this is true, one is in effect saying that the extravert–introvert psi difference reflects a difference in brain function.

To test this idea the most obvious course of action would be to measure brain activity during ESP experiments. Simple as this may sound, different researchers have come to completely different conclusions, which is disappointing, but not surprising. Many different EEG (electroencephalograph) measurement methods were used, different EEG variables were looked at, and different ESP tests tried.

The brain wave research of the early 1970s concentrated on one particular pattern of brain activity known as alpha rhythm. This is the rhythm of alert but relaxed states of consciousness. Experienced meditators, for example, can turn on alpha activity at will. Alpha activity represents an intermediate stage of arousal between beta activity (one's normal, busy, slightly anxious waking state) and delta and theta activity (characteristic of sleep). Unfortunately the evidence on ESP and alpha rhythm is weak. Extraverts and introverts do show different alpha patterns – extraverts tend to have higher alpha frequencies but of a lower amplitude than introverts – and alpha rhythms certainly do indicate relaxed, low arousal states. Overall, however, the link between alpha activity and ESP remains hazy.

However, with the foundation of a major new research centre at Duke University, with all the instrumentation and facilities for looking at ESP and brain waves properly, there may be more illuminating findings to come on this hypothesis.

Another way of tackling the brain arousal idea would be to use drugs. Amphetamine or 'speed' is a highly arousing drug. Barbiturates and valium have the opposite action – they are relaxant/de-arousing drugs. So one would expect amphetamine to reduce ESP ability and valium to stimulate it. There is some evidence that this is the case.

The notion that brain arousal is linked with ESP has some support, then. There are results from ESP experiments which fairly clearly point to a link between low arousal and psi-ability, and none which really deliver a killing blow to the theory. That said, present evidence is inadequate. Aspiring young parapsychologists will, we hope, put that right before too long.

The social influence theory

A second possible explanation of why extraverts are so much better at ESP than introverts has been offered by Ramakrishna Rao, the Indian researcher now based in America. Rao suggests that the difference is a *social* one. The atmosphere in which an experiment is conducted is all-important, Rao says. A relatively informal, friendly, well-mannered approach is vital. This is easy to achieve with extraverts because extraverts are friendly, but not with introverts because introverts tend to be aloof. This seems plausible enough. Are there any facts to support Rao's idea?

There have been experiments in which researchers asked volunteers how much they liked the person running the experiment. If the experimenter is liked, one would expect the test atmosphere to be good, and the results to be good as well. In fact, this has not been reliably the case. But the whole question of 'liking' the experimenter is a little naïve. Unless the experimenter is a complete monster, most volunteers will be polite and say 'Yes, he was quite nice really', which is far too superficial a judgement on which to base scientific conclusions. So, attractive though the idea is, we cannot prove that liking for the experimenter is conducive to ESP.

What about looking at the experimenter himself, the master of ceremonies? If subjects who are successful at ESP tasks are highly extravert, wouldn't one expect even better results if the experimenter is also an extravert, someone good at creating the informal, relaxed, friendly atmosphere Rao says is so important? There is some evidence that an extravert experimenter makes a positive difference, but too few studies have been done to be conclusive. What little evidence we have supports Rao's idea, but it is not enough.

If the extravert/introvert difference is a social one, surely familiarity with ESP-test situations would make it tend to disappear? But here one is wading into even deeper water. Let's imagine an extravert subject coming in for his first ESP test session; he bounds in, says a loud 'Hello', grins and behaves in all the ways we call extraverted. The introvert subject will tend at first to be rather subdued, a bit distant, perhaps a little nervous. By the time he comes in for a fifth or sixth test session, however, the introvert ought to have warmed up a little; he knows the drill, he knows the experimenters, he knows his fellow subjects; he begins to relax, to behave more extravertly. The extravert on the other hand, as we know from psychological research, is more prone to boredom than is the introvert. So, with the introvert feeling less anxious about the test set-up and the extravert feeling the first twinges of boredom, shouldn't the difference between them become less and less.

CONSISTENCY OF KEY ESP/PERSONALITY EXPERIMENTS

Finding	% of studies showing effect significantly (chance=5%)	Likelihood by chance alone	% of significant findings in 'right direction'	Likelihood by chance alone
1. Believers better than disbelievers	37.5	1 in 1,000 million	100	1 in 4,096
2. Extraverts better than introverts	34.6	1 in 10,000 million	95	1 in 26,214
3. Low-neurotic people better than high-neurotic (individual testing only)	33.3	1 in 100 million	100	1 in 4,096

Adding up the evidence. A review of work on personality and psi.

The evidence here is rather contradictory. Humphrey and Nicol found the opposite effect: the extraverts in their card-guessing experiments tended to do better and better as time went on. On the other hand Sargent and his colleagues, looking at picture-guessing telepathy experiments (Chapter 6), found that the extravert–introvert difference tended to fade with practice. We are left with a paradox. The 'social difference' idea gets no support from this particular line of enquiry.

One can of course manipulate the attitude of the experimenter. Charles Honorton in New York did this by instructing his experimenters to act in a 'friendly' or 'unfriendly' manner according to a prearranged plan. Sure enough, subjects tested in a 'friendly' manner did best. Here again we have a crumb of support for Rao's ideas, but a crumb only.

To summarise, then, the evidence is quite clear that extraverts are better than introverts in ESP experiments. This may be because extraverts have a lower level of brain arousal, or because they are better at generating a friendly atmosphere around them, or perhaps both. At the moment the results of experiments are not plentiful or clear-cut enough for us to be able to say which explanation, if either, is correct.

Links between neuroticism and ESP

The picture here is both more confusing and more exciting than with the studies of extraversion. The first element of confusion is that the personality factor Eysenck terms *neuroticism* is referred to by Cattell as *anxiety* – systems of description differ slightly. The second awkward element, hinted at when we were discussing the abilities of Pavel Stepanek, is that the relationship between ESP and personality tends to vary with the environment in which experiments are conducted.

In 1977 John Palmer examined every single published experiment on neuroticism and ESP and found something very interesting. In all experiments in which a significant difference emerged between low- and high-neurotic individuals, the former shared superior ESP performance. This is very neat – all the evidence points one way. Indeed the high-neurotic/low-neurotic effect is so unequivocal that we might, with justification, begin to think about possible explanations for it.

The inner-noise theory

Eysenck, Cattell, and many others would agree that one of the characteristics of highly neurotic people is a very active and reactive autonomic nervous system (ANS). The ANS is that part of our nervous system which controls automatic and involuntary activity – the production and release of hormones, the relaxation and contraction of the gut and other 'involuntary' muscles, heart rate, breathing rate, sweating, and so on, all of which can be accurately measured. Highly neurotic people tend to sweat heavily and to overreact to sudden stimuli.

Now it may be that the reason why highly neurotic people perform badly in ESP experiments is that there is a lot of 'noise' going on in their system, too much activity and overreacting for ESP 'signals' (if such they are) to penetrate. We have already seen that the poor performance of introverts in ESP experiments *may* be due to too much arousal in the brain. It may be that both introverts and neurotics simply have too much 'noise' going on inside them to pick up and use weak ESP signals. The idea is at least plausible, and will be explored in greater depth in the next chapter.

However, the really intriguing thing about neuroticism and ESP is that the inner-noise theory breaks down completely when people are tested in *groups*. No longer are the high-neurotics the inferior performers; they are, if anything, slightly superior to low-neurotics. Most of this evidence comes from comparing the results of individual and group experiments. Yet there have been some recent systematic combined experiments which not only confirm this general picture but also advance our understanding as to why this different behaviour might be occurring.

Environmental influences

In some very recent research Sargent and Trevor Harley tested a total of 186 people for ESP, 150 in two different groups and 36 individually. First they gave each subject a short personality test. Then subjects were asked to imagine a die falling down a chute and coming to rest with one face upwards. Which one? Twenty-five guesses constituted a complete test session. Guessing the 'right' face more than the chance number of times would be evidence of ESP. With 25 guesses and a 1-in-6 chance of being right without ESP the chance average of right guesses was 4.1667.

The results were very clear. When tested individually, high-

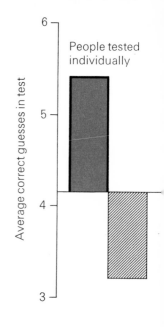

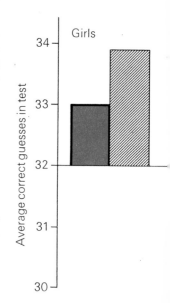

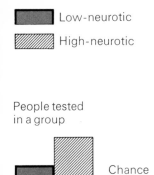

Low-neurotic

High-neurotic

People tested
in a group

Chance

*Above: Neuroticism and
ESP: the results of tests
on individuals and groups.*

*Below: In a mixed-sex
group, high-neurotics score
better in the dominant
sub-group (girls), while
in the minority group
(boys) low-neurotics
score better.*

Low-neurotic

High-neurotic

Boys

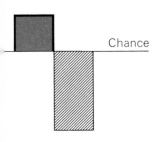

Chance

neurotics averaged just over three correct guesses, low-neurotics just over five. But when tested in groups, the difference reversed: the high-neurotics did slightly better than the low-neurotics.

This combined test certainly supports the conclusion John Palmer arrived at in 1977. ESP does seem to be affected by environment as well as personality. Palmer's explanation for this is that high-neurotics feel anxious about being tested individually, if they agree to be tested at all. Even if the researcher tells them 'We cannot *test* ESP – we don't know enough about it to be able to do that. We are *exploring* it, and are grateful to you for helping us', they still have the word TEST at the back of their mind. They cannot help feeling anxious, and so the 'noise' starts to build up. When tested they do poorly. Low-neurotics do not have this attitude or not to such a marked extent. Being tested individually does not worry them.

In a group, however, the high-neurotic can, in Palmer's words, 'lose himself in the crowd'. When he isn't singled out, he feels more at ease. Less anxiety means less noise, and he shows higher ESP ability. Palmer saw the importance of this conclusion in settings outside the ESP laboratory, in classrooms for example. The academic performance of high-neurotic children would improve, he wrote, 'where both the environment and the other group members [are] familiar and non-threatening'. Very recent research completely supports this notion.

In 1976, at about the time Palmer would have been writing his review, Sargent was becoming interested in a problem which, at first sight, appears to have little to do with neuroticism: sex differences in ESP.

The names test

To look at these differences, Sargent devised a simple test of clairvoyance. On a single duplicated sheet of paper were 64 pairs of first names, half of them boys' names, half of them girls' names. The order of the names was completely random. One name from each pair was randomly chosen by computer as the target name, and subjects were required to guess which names were the targets by ticking one of each pair of names. If one really wants to get at sex differences, why not devise an experiment in which sex differences (boys' and girls' names) are an integral part of the test material?

Of the six experiments Sargent completed between 1976 and 1980 using this test, the Names Test as it came to be called, the last one was the most interesting. After giving a lecture at an English sixth-form college the test was given to 101 people, 10 members of staff and 91 students, of whom 51 were female and 40 male. With 64 pairs of names and a 50/50 chance of being right by chance alone, the chance average score for the test is 32.

Sargent separated the 91 students from the 10 staff, and something very amusing emerged: not one of the staff scored above chance! Before the lecture and test, Sargent had been told that the staff were very sceptical. A confirmation of the sheep–goat effect perhaps?

In mixed groups, high-neurotic subjects score better in ESP tests if they are a member of the dominant sub-group, whether male or female...

Looking at the ESP scores for the students, and checking them against the personality profiles collected before the ESP test, Sargent found that for the girls the results were just as Palmer might have predicted: high-neurotic girls did better than low-neurotic girls. Indeed, the high-neurotic girls showed evidence of positive ESP. Neurotics like groups! Q.E.D. But when the ESP results for the boys were checked, it was the other way round: the low-neurotics did better than the high-neurotics. Does this knock Palmer's idea out of court?

Probably not, but what it does suggest is a refinement of Palmer's idea. Certainly neurotics will feel 'one of the crowd' in a group, but if the group has identifiably different elements in it the neurotic will only feel one of the crowd if he, or in this case she, belongs to the major or dominant subgroup. The girls were in the majority; they belonged to the dominant subgroup; for the high-neurotics among them the group testing environment was favourable. The boys were in the minority, a fact of which the obvious sex differences in the test itself would have reminded them; the high-neurotics among them would not have felt 'one of the crowd'. It is not difficult to see why the usual high/low group neurotic effect reversed for the boys.

Nevertheless, we must hold our scientific horses. No other researchers have done this kind of experiment, so we must interpret these particular findings with caution.

The lesson of group experiments is really this: social environment can influence ESP as much as personality, and social environment is far from simple. Every group has its subdivisions and differences, and our experiments must take account of them.

Summing up then, we have strong evidence that high-neurotics are poorer at ESP tests than low-neurotics when tested individually, perhaps because their autonomic nervous system generates too much

...but would the same sense of solidarity apply to high neurotics in a single-sex group? Such groups need to be tested in order to learn more about the relationship between psi and human personality.

A voodoo idol. Do psi powers flourish more easily among peoples whose beliefs are dominated by animism and magical practices?

These children claim to have seen visions of the Virgin Mary: do children have greater psi abilities than adults?

ESP-resistant 'noise'. Group tests have tended to blur this convenient picture. There are some very intriguing results around which at the very least point to new avenues of research and to some of the potential potholes.

Extraversion and neuroticism are clearly related to ESP. The evidence is so abundant that it simply cannot be dismissed by anyone who examines it in totality. Indeed the sceptical psychologist Ray Hyman wrote in the journal *Contemporary Psychology*: 'Such summaries of the hard-core laboratory data in favour of psi convince me that "something" is there.' While he is less convinced that the evidence is as strong as it may look, in his review of the book in which Palmer's summaries were published he comments: '. . . the critics, if they are to be fair, must find ways to account for the virtually hundreds of experimental studies that are summarised herein before they summarily dismiss parapsychology as a pseudoscience.'

Age and cultural differences in ESP

We have looked at intriguing evidence for the influence of personality factors on ESP performance. Are there other distinctions, too, that we can draw? What, for example, are the differences, if any, between the ESP abilities of adults and children? Given that our society makes quite different demands – chiefly in the form of rewards for ordered, logical behaviour – on adults as opposed to children, we might expect some variation. Again, twentieth-century industrial societies are organised quite differently from the hunter, hunter-gatherer and early farming communities of prehistoric times. Has this social evolution affected the ways in which people use ESP? And can we explore this question by investigating the 'primitive' societies that survive in the modern world? There is the fundamental question, too, as to whether, in terms of human evolution, ESP is evolving out or in. Since ESP is potentially useful, it could be argued that it should be evolving in. On the other hand ESP is a weak ability and somewhat unreliable. We are already highly visual creatures, and not half as gifted in sensory abilities as many other animals. Perhaps ESP is going the same way as our once highly developed sense of smell and evolving out. But if this is so one might expect to find superior ESP abilities with animals rather than people.

Adults versus children

Taking age first, the relationship is not simple. Certainly no researcher has ever reported or suggested a neat linear relationship, positive or negative, between ESP and age over the entire age range. However, many researchers have reported consistently good results with young children as ESP subjects. Children certainly appear to be better and more reliable ESP subjects than adults.

Yet when we start looking at all the published reports of child ESP in depth we find that matters are not so simple. To take one of J. B. Rhine's early ESP experiments in which children scored much higher than adults, we find that the adults were as far below chance (psi-missing again – remember the sheep–goat effect) as the children were above it. Both adults and children used ESP equally but in different ways.

Another series of experiments worth closer scrutiny are those by Margaret Anderson, a notably creative ESP researcher, in the 1950s. Only children were tested in this work, and the results were consistently excellent – clear, reliable, consistent ESP all the way along the line. However, reading exactly how Margaret Anderson did her tests reveals that some were dressed up as a science fiction game in which good (above-chance) ESP scores helped to launch a 'space rocket' and keep it on course during its 'mission'. Wonderfully imaginative. One cannot help feeling that if a similar kind of enthralment had been created for adults, they would have done just as well.

However some recent research by Dr Ernesto Spinelli of Surrey University may have propelled us beyond the stage of trying to interpret the apparent superiority of children on the basis of age alone. Spinelli, working with very large numbers of people of all ages from under three to over 70, reports that children under seven generally do very well at ESP tests (telepathy tests in this case), while older children and adults show little evidence of ESP. Now this is interesting because it is at about the age of seven, allowing of course for individual differences, that something closely resembling adult logic and reasoning develop in children. Spinelli's view is that the development of formal, logical thought and intelligence reduces – indeed, by his results virtually wipes out – ESP sensitivity. Given tricky mental tasks to carry out while trying to do ESP tests, even the ESP scores of children under seven fall away to chance. On the other hand, Spinelli found, simple mental tasks do *not* inhibit ESP.

Looking more closely at the test methods used, Spinelli's interpretations become rather doubtful. The younger children were shown how to do the ESP test by a pair of glove puppets, who acted out the test and explained the procedure, and were also given 'thinking caps' to help

Below left: Mothers often claim 'telepathic' knowledge of their children's activities and states of mind.

Below: Ernesto Spinelli (right) has developed play materials and techniques in order to involve children more deeply in ESP tests.

Investigation of psi among Australian aborigines showed that there were strong inhibitions against using psi, except among certain designated individuals, known as 'clever men'.

them. This must surely have engaged their full co-operation, and made them happy and excited in a way the adults could not have been. It seems fairly clear, looking at the methods used by Anderson, Spinelli, and others working with young children, that the outstanding results they obtained were not due to any basic difference in ESP ability between adults and children but to their great rapport with children and their talent for working with them. Adults, too, might do better in ESP tests if they were to be 'involved' in the same way as children.

The reason why children tend to be superior to adults in ESP experiments is, on the available evidence, a *social* one. Children have not learned to be sceptical. They tend to be lively and impulsive – like extraverts. The child/adult difference may be telling us a lot about the effects of *social* evolution in a society wary of the psychic, but it seems to tell us nothing about the effects of biological evolution on psi faculties. Similar problems arise when we explore cultural differences in psi abilities.

Does culture make a difference?

Impressionistic reports have seemed to suggest that some pre-industrial, tribal societies accept psi – perhaps in the form of magic – as part of everyday experience. Perhaps the most extensive work in this area was conducted in the 1950s by Ronald and Lyndon Rose among Australian aborigines, Maoris and Samoans. The Roses did both ESP and PK testing, with divergent results: the ESP tests almost invariably gave very high scores (except in Samoa), but the PK tests were uniformly completely unsuccessful. What these findings do reflect is the effect of social beliefs and attitudes on psi, the sheep–goat effect in cultural guise. The Roses' aborigines were adamant that only the 'clever men' of the tribe could possibly influence the dice used to test for PK; they were certain they could not, and so they couldn't, or rather didn't. A little PK testing was done, unsuccessfully, with the 'clever men', but very few were tested and their attitudes to the task were unclear.

Other research has been conducted with so-called 'primitive' cultures, in Liberia and Panama for example, often with quite good results. But there is really no need to spell out the details, for the Roses' findings show quite clearly that different people have different cultures which either facilitate or inhibit the development of psi abilities. Whether the abilities of Australian aborigines are basically any different from those of Central Europeans it is impossible to say.

Animal psi

Finally, there is the question of psi in non-humans. If ESP is evolving out, one might expect to find ESP more strongly in animals than in humans. It is perfectly possible to devise psi experiments for animals; much of this work has involved PK rather than ESP testing, but one can do both. For an ESP test, one can place an animal (a rat, say) in a cage divided into two halves which can be independently electrified to give the animal a weak shock. If the animal can use ESP (precognition), it might be able to avoid the half to be shocked more than 50 per cent of the time. Do animals score better than 50 per cent in such experiments? Sometimes they do and sometimes they don't. Though the picture which has emerged from numerous experiments of this kind is complex, one thing is very clear: animals do not display stronger or more reliable ESP and PK than humans. If anything their psi faculties are less reliable.

Vegetable psi

It has been reported by one researcher, who shall remain anonymous, that plants 'react' to human emotions and to the killing of other plants and small animals (like shrimps). Some authors, notably Lyall Watson, have enthusiastically taken up the cause of Plant Lib. But it has now been shown, quite conclusively, that the measuring techniques used in this work are faulty. Careful research in a number of laboratories has shown that when artefacts in the measuring equipment are eliminated by controlling such factors as draughts, temperature changes, vibration, and so on, no trace of evidence of psi in plants can be found.

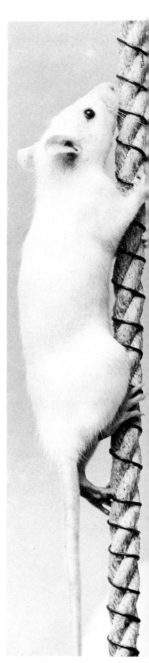

Can animals be tested for psi? Yes they can, but as yet there is no evidence to support those who swear that their pets understand everything they say!

Root-and-branch Plant Libbers have made large claims for the existence of ESP in plants. Careful testing, though, has nipped that idea in the bud.

To return to our original question, is psi evolving in or out? The only honest answer is, we don't know. Studies with children suggest that ESP may be stronger in the first few years of life than later, but this could be a function of socialisation, not of biology. Similar comments apply to work with 'primitive' cultures: the findings seem to reflect social and cultural beliefs rather than any differences in innate psi ability. And research with animals has failed to produce clear evidence that psi effects become more marked or more reliable as one moves down the evolutionary scale.

Intelligence, sanity, madness, and psi

Although Spinelli's results have been put down to social factors and to his gift for working with children, his suggestion that rational intelligence may interfere with psi, particularly with ESP, certainly seems plausible. 'Intuition', presumably part and parcel of ESP, appears to be qualitatively different from 'intelligence'. If IQ is negatively related to ESP, might not the breakdown of rational functioning in extreme cases of mental illness (the psychoses) lead to increased expression of ESP?

The relationship between IQ and ESP is easily summarised: none exists, or at least not on the present evidence. However, it is often difficult to separate intelligence from other factors. The results of an ESP experiment conducted by a young American researcher, Bob Brier, with members of Mensa, the high-IQ club, showed strong psi-missing or negative ESP (below chance). Since the Mensa members were very sceptical about ESP, Brier's result is probably further confirmation of the sheep–goat effect rather than a consequence of the high average IQ of his subjects.

Also, intelligence is not a single variable. There is evidence that it is hierarchical, comprised of different component skills which, for the sake of convenience, we lump together as 'intelligence'. In young children, for example, there is a tendency for girls to be slightly better at verbal skills and for boys to be slightly better at mathematical and spatial skills. This is only a generalisation of course. There have been attempts to pin down these sex differences by using either words or pictures in ESP tests, the theory being that differential IQ skills should show up in the expression of ESP. Sometimes girls are better than boys with verbal ESP tests, sometimes they aren't, and sometimes there is absolutely no difference. The results are consistently inconsistent.

Many schizophrenics and pre-schizophrenics believe they have telepathic powers and/or (in paranoid cases) are being persecuted telepathically. Far-fetched as it may sound, some psychiatrists have suggested that psi may be a trigger factor in the development of schizophrenia. According to this argument, the schizophrenic is 'infiltrated' by disturbing telepathic 'messages' which help to initiate the psychotic condition. So let us look at the facts. How do schizophrenics perform in ESP experiments?

There are dreadful problems involved in all research with schizophrenics. There is the whole ethical question of conducting tests with subjects who may be deeply unhappy and confused. From a purely practical point of view one has to check for problems associated with diet, drugs, mis-diagnosis, the type of schizophrenic one is working with (paranoid schizophrenics, who suffer from delusions of grandeur or persecution, are very different from other schizophrenics for

---

A TYPICAL EXAMPLE OF SCHIZOPHRENIC BELIEFS ABOUT ESP

I do want to inform you that I am myself helping psychiatric divisions to know that many of the causes are (psychic phenomena) of mind interference, thought telepathy – with knowledge of enemy action included. The Prime Minister is kept closely informed by me of all goings-on including the 'ultra-sonic soundwave activity reaching Earth' from satellites up above, trying to bring the 'voice of the dead' forward etc.
They have tried to put 'picture scenes' on my lounge and bathroom walls (possibly because I theorize that 'paranormal visions' are possible by HOLOGRAM TECHNIQUE beamed down) I have had the situation of my electric iron being 'made' to overheat and ruin a garment (the voice laughs) and of my clothes being stuck to me yet wearing 'anti-static undies' as yet another demonstration of power.

(Note : 'They', predictably enough, are the Russians, Germans, Chinese, and Japanese, which is made clear elsewhere in the letter from which this is an extract)

Right: The withdrawn, anguished world of the mentally ill is vividly conveyed by a sufferer in this painting. Victims of psychosis often report psi-like components in their delusions – but, for obvious reasons, this remains a most difficult area of research.

example), and so on. To circumvent all these problems requires great expertise and practice, plenty of time and patience, the goodwill of psychiatrists and nurses, and a lot of money. It is really not surprising that none of the work done by ESP researchers with schizophrenics meets acceptable standards. Most of the evidence we have about ESP and schizophrenia is fairly old now, but it was not conclusive either way: some experiments showed that schizophrenics had some ESP ability and some did not.

Anyone doing research in this area in the future will have to contend with all the problems mentioned above. They will also have to allow for the fact that to a schizophrenic under treatment in a mental hospital, an invitation to sit down at a table and guess through some ESP cards is not a very meaningful prospect. Immense tact, sympathy and sensitivity is called for in adapting tests to people and places.

We also have some evidence on less severe types of mental disturbance (depression, mania, hysteria, and so on) and ESP. High neuroticism is a characteristic of all persons (except for psychopaths) confined to mental hospitals, so it would be surprising if people suffering from depression, mania and other disorders were particularly good ESP subjects. Most of the evidence confirms this: mental disturbance does not equate with marked ESP ability. Research using measures of social adjustment and maturity tends to produce positive correlations between these measures and ESP ability. This is what one would expect, given the general superiority of the extravert over the introvert, and of the low-neurotic over the high-neurotic.

The myth of female superiority

Virtually every survey in existence shows a major sex difference in relation to spontaneous psi (psi experienced in everyday life). Women tend to have more ESP experiences than men or, to anticipate the argument, they *say* they do, while men are in the majority as 'senders'. This looks suspiciously like a reflection of the well-worn masculine/ feminine stereotypes – passive, intuitive females receiving messages and dynamic, dominant males sending them (the popular image of telepathy is that the 'sender' sends a 'signal' to the 'receiver'). There may be a real difference, or simply a bias in responding to surveys. Both women and men are more likely to report experiences which conform with stereotyped sex roles. Women report more ESP experiences generally, especially in the passive role of 'receiver'. Men, on the other hand, report fewer experiences, with a strong bias towards those in which they play an active role.

Most experimental investigations of sex differences in ESP have focused on children, but for every experiment in which girls have outshone boys to a degree inexplicable by chance, there is another experiment which shows the reverse.

Research with adults has not yielded evidence of any clear, simple sex difference either. In dream-telepathy experiments in New York (see Chapter 5) men scored notably better than chance as 'receivers', while women did not. In a similar type of experiment, a Ganzfeld experiment (Chapter 6), Sargent found that men slightly outdid women as receivers. In both cases the experimenters were men. Might women fare better with women experimenters? Seemingly not, for Sargent found that when sessions were run by two women the difference between the sexes increased: the men scored even better while the women scored about the same. With male or female experimenters, men scored higher than women.

Putting together surveys of both child and adult ESP experiments, it is clear that there is no simple difference between the sexes in terms of ESP ability. Possibly the differences are many and interactive. Some data suggest that males and females may use ESP in different ways, and that in group testing the ration of males to females may influence ESP patterns. The evidence, however, is too fragmented to allow one to reach a clear judgement.

It has been argued that women are more worried by laboratory tests than men and are therefore inhibited from displaying their superior

Traditionally, women have been seen as being more psychic than men. Research suggests that this is a myth fuelled by stereotyped notions of women as passive receivers of impressions.

ESP abilities. If this were the case women ought to be more at ease and less apprehensive when women are running experiments. But as we have just noted, the sex difference persists whether the experimenters are male or female, although more information on this point would be welcome. Plausible though the inhibition argument appears we cannot investigate it directly.

In conclusion, we cannot totally rule out the possibility that there may be a basic difference between the sexes in ESP ability. Nevertheless dozens of experiments have failed to discover it, in which case it is perhaps reasonable to assume that there is no difference in fact. That . does not mean to say that social mythology will not manufacture a difference or two.

The story so far ...

If *all* factors correlated clearly and significantly with ESP, then a sceptic would feel (possibly rightly) that the experiments involved must have been faulty. But this is not the case; some factors – belief, extraversion, neuroticism – do consistently relate to ESP success, while others – age, IQ, sex – do not. With this in mind, we are ready to examine some implications of the extraversion effect and the neuroticism effect. As we have suggested, the last two may have a common explanation in the concept of 'noise', high brain cortex noise in the case of the introvert, and high body noise (to put it crudely) in the case of the neurotic. In fact there is a great body of exciting research which has concentrated on boosting the impact of ESP signals by cutting down inner noise. This research is based on a hard core of ideas and theory; it uses ESP tests of great elegance and sophistication and as close to real-life situations as possible, and it has yielded very strong and consistent evidence.

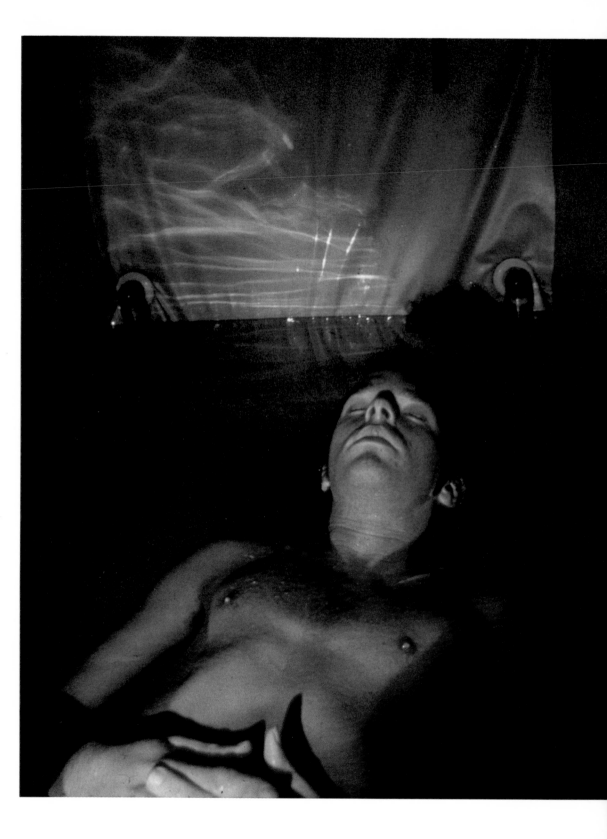

Psi researchers have found strong evidence that human psi abilities improve during periods of abnormal consciousness typical of dreams, meditation and drug-induced states. This sensory deprivation tank is one way of producing an altered state of consciousness in the laboratory.

In the last chapter we looked at evidence for and against the existence of a 'psychic personality', with a view to establishing whether or not particular types of individual are more likely to demonstrate psi abilities. We found that anxiety, a feature of the high-neurotic personality, seemed to have the effect of inhibiting psi performance – but that even high-neurotic subjects perform better in a sympathetic, non-threatening environment. Here, we want to examine some of the very exciting work that has been done to create environments – physical and mental – which might favour the occurrence of psi phenomena.

This work began in the 1960s, when the young generation of parapsychologists, many trained by Rhine, began to feel that his methods of testing for ESP were sterile and his philosophy somewhat naïve. Rhine's own pioneering work had taken place in the 1930s, when the dominant school of thought in psychology was behaviourism. In essence, behaviourists assert that psychologists can only study events and behaviour which take place, measurably, in the external world. One might show, for example, that a particular type of electrical activity in the brain is always associated with a particular mental state, but one cannot study the mental state itself, which is too subjective to be measured. Rhine wanted to beat the behaviourists at their own game by using their experimental methods to establish ESP as a reality. By the 1960s, however, a new spirit was abroad in America. The widespread use of hallucinogenic drugs – cannabis, LSD and mescalin among them

In America, the psychedelic revolution of the 1960s turned the attention of psychologists and parapsychologists to the study of altered states of consciousness.

– drew the attention of many psychologists to the inner mental life and its study. Behaviourists ignored people's introspections – but the new generation of psychologists felt that ignoring things breeds only ignorance.

Parapsychologists began to look again at reports of psi phenomena from many different sources and historical periods. Anthropological work showed that many so-called 'primitive' peoples claimed that naturally occurring hallucinogens produced psychic experiences. Ancient Sanskrit texts on the practice of yoga and meditation seemed to suggest that psi experiences – including levitation and ESP – would occur in the course of certain meditational techniques and exercises. In the more recent past, the reported demonstrations of hypnotists showed that normal human behaviour could be transformed in strange and unexplained ways. All these sources, and many more, seemed to suggest a multiplicity of new and potentially fruitful approaches to studying psi through altered mental states – in which normal consciousness was modified by drugs, through hypnosis or by meditation.

A high proportion of spontaneous psi experiences take place while the receivers are asleep or on the verge of sleep.

The dream-watchers

One particularly promising line of enquiry seemed to lie in the field of dreams. From ancient times dreams have been felt to have supernatural significance: historical accounts of prophetic dreams, such as Pharaoh's dream of famine to come, interpreted by Joseph and narrated in the Old Testament, are relatively common. Moreover, an astonishingly high proportion (some 50 per cent) of reported experiences of spontaneous ESP occur when the 'receivers' are asleep. Further research shows that people are more likely to experience ESP at night than during the daylight hours.

The first important work in dream-ESP testing was done in America by Dr Montagu Ullman, later joined by Dr Stanley Krippner. As a practising psychoanalyst, Ullman had become intrigued by precognitive dreams reported by his patients. Their experiments, con-

Stanley Krippner,
dream-watcher
extraordinary, at the
Maimonides Dream
Laboratory, New York.

ducted over several years, were funded by the Irish-born medium
Eileen Garrett through the Parapsychology Foundation, which she set
up in order to promote scientific research into parapsychology.
Between 1962 and his retirement in 1978, Ullman's dream research was
based in the Dream Laboratory of the Maimonides Medical Center in
Brooklyn, New York.

Ullman's work relied upon the discovery, by the psychologist
Nathaniel Kleitman, that it was possible to detect periods of dreaming
in sleepers. Kleitman found that, during sleep, human beings show
periodic bursts of strong, rapid fluctuations of the eye muscles. If a
person is wakened from this period of Rapid Eye Movement (REM)
sleep, he is much more likely to report a dream than if awakened at
other times. REM detectors, linked with an electroencephalograph
(EEG), which records electrical activity in the brain, can reliably be
used to pinpoint episodes of dream sleep as they occur.

The best way to show how Ullman's dream-ESP experiments
worked is to examine a study he undertook in 1964. His subject was a
psychologist, Dr William Erwin. Twelve test nights were planned but,
due to illness on the part of Erwin, only seven were completed.

The experiment took the form of a telepathy test. While Erwin,
wired up to an REM/EEG apparatus, was asleep in one room, a
'sender' in another room tried to transmit to Erwin, by telepathy, a
target picture. The picture was chosen at random from a large number
of different art prints – the choice being determined by a table of
random numbers. The sender looked at that one picture, and that one
alone, throughout the night and made an effort to 'send' the information to Erwin. During the night the experimenter who was with Erwin
would signal to the sender when Erwin was dreaming, so that the
sender could make a special effort to get the content of the picture across
to him. At the end of each burst of REM sleep, Erwin was woken and
asked to report his dreams, which were recorded.

In the morning, the sender left without seeing Erwin and the
experimenter asked Erwin to report any extra associations and dream
reports he might care to.

After seven nights the experimenters had seven target pictures and
seven nights' worth of reported dreams from Erwin. The pictures and
the dream reports were then despatched to three independent judges.
They were asked to carry out a simple task: to look at each of the dream
reports, and then to arrange the seven pictures in order, from one to
seven. The first place was to be given to the picture which seemed most
like the dream, and seventh place to the picture least like the dream.

There is a key point here: *this judging is subjective*. Not all judges will
see things the same way. Despite this problem, one can still use the
method to measure ESP. It is clear that if a judge compares dreams
with pictures and consistently puts the right picture first against the
right dream, then there must be a strong suggestion that ESP is at
work. Chance alone would give a mixture of results; some pictures
would come out top against the right dream, most would come out

somewhere in the middle, and some pictures would be put down at the bottom of the list. Take the Erwin study: given the seven dreams and the seven pictures, we would expect by chance alone that only one of the seven pictures would be placed first against the correct dream. This is because there were seven trials with a 1-in-7 chance of being completely correct each time. We would also expect that the average *rank* (number between 1 and 7) given to the right picture would be the middle number 4. How did the judges score when their different judgements were averaged out?

On only one occasion did they average a rank of 4.0, the chance level. For the other six the average rank was lower, showing that the right pictures were being scored high against the right dreams. Ullman reported that the experiment gave the first clear indications of strong and reliable dream ESP.

Much better was to come from Erwin in a second study of eight test sessions. Feldstein, a very successful 'sender', suggested an innovation: perhaps the targets would get over better if the sender was really *involved* with them. Ullman and Krippner agreed and designed 'multisensory' materials to supplement the pictures alone. Feldstein must have been embarrassed by his suggestion: on the second night of the study the picture to be 'sent' was a Japanese painting of a man with an umbrella trying to escape from the rain. Feldstein had to wander around in the Maimonides shower room with a toy umbrella...

From the second Erwin experiment the results were remarkable. Of the eight nights of experiments, six gave direct hits: on six occasions the judges ranked the correct picture first against the dream report. The two others were second and third. Now chance alone would have given only one direct hit (a $12\frac{1}{2}$ per cent success rate), but Erwin got six – a success rate of 75 per cent. The odds against this kind of success occurring by chance alone are well over 1,000 to one.

The Maimonides team went from success to success with this kind of experiment. Just one more example of their work will be mentioned, because of the remarkable nature of the experiment and the great success with it. It emerged as a result of intriguing examples of spontaneous precognition which manifested themselves during the normal course of laboratory experiments. For example, in 1969, a telepathic dream session was run with Alan Vaughan (who co-authored the book *Dream Telepathy* with Ullman and Krippner) as the dreamer. In the post-dream interview Vaughan commented, 'Chuck Honorton was there in the dream and he was marking a transcript and he was using the letter F ... He said, 'Oh, F is for failure' ... then I looked at the

The technology required for recording brain activity in sleep, and length of time needed for experiments means that dream-ESP work is very expensive.

AN EXPERIMENTAL TEST SESSION : PRECOGNITIVE DREAMING BY MALCOLM BESSENT ?

NIGHT 1
BESSENT'S DREAM REPORTS

Impression of green and purple . . . small areas of blue and white.

There was a large concrete building. A lot of concrete, for some reason. But it was architecturally designed and shaped . . . and there was a patient from upstairs escaping . . . It might have been a woman . . . she had a white coat on, like a doctor's coat.

Kind of a feeling . . . of hostility toward me by people in a group I was in daily contact with . . . My impression was that they were doctors and medical people . . .

The concrete wall was all in natural color . . . It's like a carved wall . . . I felt that . . . a patient had escaped . . . and got as far as . . . the archway.

I was dreaming . . . about breakfast . . . the cups were all white . . . drinking . . . eating . . . the cups and things were rattling . . .

NIGHT 2
TARGET WORD (Random choice):
Corridor

TARGET PICTURE (first picture in pool with word 'corridor' in title) : *Hospital Corridor at St Rémy* (1889) by Van Gogh

POST-WAKING EXPERIENCE

Rosza's 'Spellbound' played on phonograph. Recorder laughing hysterically . . . Bessent welcomed as Mr Van Gogh . . .
Paintings by mental patients shown on slide projector. Bessent given a pill and a glass of water. Bessent 'disinfected' with acetone daubed on a cotton swab.
Bessent led through a darkened corridor of the lab to reach the office.

Hospital Corridor at Saint Rémy (1889) by Vincent van Gogh, Gouache and watercolour, 61×47.3 cm. Collection, The Museum of Modern Art, New York. Abby Aldrich Rockefeller Bequest.

Amazingly, Bessent was consistently able to dream precognitively of events which were themselves selected at random.

television set there and this television set actually seemed to be part of the experiment as well . . . as I looked at it, the whole thing began to move and come to life, and there was a man holding a knife . . . and behind him was a monkey lying on the floor . . . I wonder if there might be sometime an experimental thing like this . . .'

That was on 9 April 1969; on 17 July Vaughan wrote to Ullman suggesting that this dream might be a precognition of a session yet to come.

On 12 January 1970, the Canadian TV personality Norman Perry arrived at Maimonides to act as a subject in the research. Vaughan was there as a 'back-up' just in case Perry couldn't get to sleep in the unfamiliar laboratory conditions, which included having electrodes attached to his scalp. The sender randomly chose a picture showing a

BESSENT'S PSYCHIC PREDICTIONS (DECEMBER, 1969) ;
PRECOGNITION AT WORK ?

Bessent	Eventual events
'A Greek oil tanker, black in colour, will be involved in a disaster having international significance within 4-6 months' time. (Onassis connected – perhaps the danger is symbolic, but I feel that the ship may represent him personally)'	Two months later the Onassis-owned tanker the *Arrow* was wrecked off the coast of Nova Scotia. The resulting pollution did become an 'international incident'.
'General de Gaulle will die within one year'	Eleven months later *de Gaulle* died – but he was an old man !
'Prime Minister Wilson in change of government next summer (1970)'	The Heath Government took office in the summer of 1970 in Britain and confounded political pundits and opinion polls, which had put Labour well ahead. But Bessent's prediction is not exact. He did not state that *Wilson* would be defeated although, to be fair, this is the usual sense of 'change of government'.
'Nixon will not serve another term as President'	Wrong. Nixon was overwhelmingly re-elected in 1972. And yet right : for Nixon did not complete his term of office, being forced out of it over the Watergate scandal.
'Senator Muskie will be the next President'	WRONG !

monkey holding an orange. To add impact to this the sender took an orange and *ripped it apart*.

Perry dreamed, not of a monkey, but of a large white nondescript animal. However, he placed the monkey picture first of the six possible alternatives, because the monkey in the picture was white.

Meanwhile, Vaughan dreamed too, of someone *ripping up a* loaf of bread. When he looked at the picture, he put the monkey at the bottom of the pile, a miss. *Honorton was the experimenter*. F for failure.

Vaughan watched Perry make his choice as he was being *filmed for television* ('this television set seemed to be part of the experiment as well ...'), and watched Perry place the monkey picture first, *flat on the floor* ('... a monkey lying on the floor ...'). The second choice by Perry, which he placed next to the monkey, was a picture of *a man holding an axe* ('... and there was a man holding a knife ...').

Now this *could* all be coincidence, but the number of correspondences is rather exceptional! Little wonder that the precognition phenomenon was of great interest to the people at Maimonides.

In 1969, and again in 1970, the young English psychic Malcolm Bessent arrived to be tested for precognition. Could he, having a history of predicting future events, perform to order in laboratory dream-ESP experiments? Two experiments settled any doutbs about Bessent's abilities.

In each of the experiments, there were to be eight experimental nights. On each night, Bessent would sleep with the EEG/REM

Some of British psychic Malcolm Bessent's dream predictions during his sojourn at the Maimonides Dream Laboratory.

monitors attached as usual and, on being awakened from REM sleep, would be asked to report his dreams, and so on in the orthodox manner. But at this stage there was to be no sender and no target.

After each night's dreaming was completed, an experimenter who knew nothing of Bessent's dreams used a complex random scheme to select a target *word* from the book *The Content Analysis of Dreams*. This was then matched with an art picture, and from that picture the experimenter devised a dramatised experience for Bessent. On one occasion, for example, the word 'Corridor' was chosen, and the art print was Van Gogh's *Hospital Corridor at St Rémy*. A bizarre charade was inflicted on Bessent. Immediately after dreaming and reporting, he was hauled off along a dark corridor, given a fake 'pill' to take for his 'condition', addressed as 'Mr Van Gogh', and shown paintings by mental hospital patients.

Bessent's dreams the night *before* all this happened seem to reflect uncannily just what was going to happen to him subsequently.

In order to measure these correspondences statistically, Bessent's dream report was sent to three independent judges together with the target word and seven other 'dummy' words. On the 'St Rémy' night, the other seven words were 'parka hood', 'desk', 'kitchen', 'teaspoon', 'body back', 'leaves' and 'elbow'. The judges – who, as usual, were not told which word was the real target – nonetheless rated 'Corridor' as the best fit to the content of the dream from the eight possible choices.

Sixteen nights, sixteen dreams. On each occasion a 1-in-8 chance of the judges correctly putting the right word, the target, as best fit to the dream. Chance alone would give an average of two correct dreams (16 times $\frac{1}{8}$). Bessent got ten correct, exactly five times as many as the chance average, and the odds against this being due to chance are very high indeed. It would appear that Bessent used precognition to dream of what would happen to him on the morning after each dream.

The full sequence of studies from Maimonides clearly showed far more successes than chance would allow. Other experimenters have, as usual, had mixed fortunes. Some have been able to get positive ESP effects; others have not. One major problem has been that few experimenters have had access to the facilities of Maimonides. Most have had to work under inferior conditions. Sometimes, lacking the EEG equipment to wake people up during dream sleep, they have only been able to ask for recall of dreams in the morning. However, some success has been forthcoming with this procedure. Robert Van de Castle, a sleep researcher who, with Erwin and Bessent, had been an outstandingly successful ESP-dreamer at Maimonides, used the method with members of a youth camp and found successful ESP performance in the results.

Reviews of all the experiments published show that about 50 per cent of them are successful in showing positive and significant ESP in dreams. Again the sceptic may say, 'This is an illusion; the success rate seems this high because we don't hear about the ones that fail. Psi researchers don't report chance results!' The rebuttal to this charge is simple. The success rate is ten times the chance level and, to cancel out all the reported successes, there would have to be a mountain of unpublished chance results. Since these experiments take a very long time to run, and few people have the facilities and motivation to do them, this is hardly likely. And, once again, there is the crucial point that all the successful dream ESP studies show results well *above* chance, not below. Just as in the case of the 'sheep–goat effect' (believers scoring higher than disbelievers in ESP tests) there are no reversals of the effect. The fact that all the significant results go one way seems, on the face of it, to suggest that dreams are definitely favourable to ESP. In fact, this inference is unwarranted. The dream-ESP work showed very clearly that dreams are *associated* with powerful ESP effects, but it provided no clues as to how that association occurs. Also the practical drawbacks of this type of experiment are considerable: the equipment necessary to record periods of dreaming is extremely expensive; the work is very labour-intensive – a whole night is needed for just one session; and the experimenters concerned must be very dedicated, or chronic insomniacs, to work such unsocial hours. Although the dream-ESP work was very successful in its time, particularly in reinforcing the new attention being paid to inner mental states, a more refined theoretical and experimental approach was required. In the event, this was to come from one of the Maimonides researchers, Charles (Chuck) Honorton.

Honorton's approach was informed by his own surveys of historical accounts of psi experiences, ranging from the *Yoga Sutras* of Patanjali, written in India 3,500 years ago, to the detailed surveys, published in the nineteenth century, of the British Society for Psychical Research. He also examined the memoirs and writings of nineteenth- and twentieth-century mediums and psychics. In Patanjali's text, the oldest known work on yoga meditation, ESP and PK effects are spoken of as taking place at the deepest levels of meditation, *samadhi*. *Samadhi* is the final stage of a process of disengaging Mind from the distractions of the senses, and concentrating it until it achieves absolute stillness. The work of the British Society for Psychical Research showed that a high proportion of those experiencing spontaneous psi were in a highly relaxed state, on the verge of sleep, for example, or lost in reverie. In the writings of psychics, too, Honorton found a common refrain: the best conditions for psychic experience were those in which the medium was relaxed and making a firm but gentle effort to empty the mind. From these accounts, Honorton identified two common elements – a quietening of the normal sense, and a mental inwardness – as being favourable to ESP effects. But why and how did ESP work under these conditions?

Honorton was particularly interested in the possibility that psi – in this case ESP – might be something like a weak sense, analogous to the conventional human senses. If this is true, then we might expect it to be normally drowned out by the strong signals, or 'noise', delivered by our conventional senses. In states of altered consciousness – including dreaming, reverie and perhaps hypnosis and meditation – the opera-

A dreamy, reflective state of mind – perfect conditions for psi.

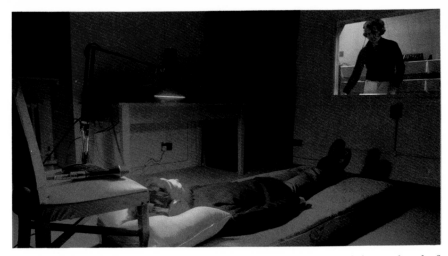

The Ganzfeld technique, (see page 79) pictured here in Sargent's Cambridge laboratory, is a cheap and effective alternative to dream-ESP work. Experiments with the Ganzfeld have yielded very strong ESP scoring.

tion of normal human senses, of course, goes on at a much lower level of activity. This might be the reason why, for example, dreaming seemed to be favourable to ESP.

We first met this notion of 'noise-reduction' in the last chapter. There we suggested that the reason that extraverts perform better than introverts in ESP tests might be because the latter feel more threatened by their environments – in other words, suffer from a higher level of distracting 'noise'. And to support this theory, we found evidence that introverts do perform better when more at ease with, less distracted by, their environment.

ESP in the twilight zone

By the early 1970s Honorton had thought out his noise-reduction ideas clearly. He suggested that the crucial reasons for the success of the dream work were twofold. First, during the dream state the 'noise' from the external world was reduced, allowing the weak ESP sense to operate more freely. Second, the attention of the mind was directed inwards. He set about designing a theoretical model which would combine his ideas, and which he could test through experiments.

Honorton's first experimental steps were into the field of sensory deprivation. It is well known that subjects insulated from their environment for a period of time begin to show symptoms of disorientation which include vivid hallucinations. Honorton reasoned that if indeed the reduction of external sensory 'noise', combined with concentration on inner mental processes, was the key to the strong, successful ESP demonstrated in Ullman's dream-work, then sensory deprivation experiments might produce the same effect.

He chose 30 volunteers. Each one, wearing a blindfold and ear-mufflers, was confined to a cradle suspended so that it could be freely moved in any direction. During the experimental sessions, the cradle was constantly in motion, being either rotated or swung backwards and forwards. The subjects had to report the ideas, thoughts and mental images they experienced. Honorton wanted to test two possible predictions: on the one hand he expected positive ESP to be produced; on the other, he predicted that the best ESP scores would come from

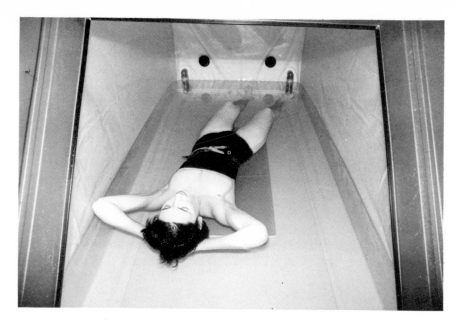

A sensory deprivation tank. Suspended in water at blood heat, insulated from the outside world, subjects become disorientated and can experience vivid hallucinations.

those volunteers most strongly affected by the experience of sensory deprivation.

The ESP test he used was similar to that used in the dream-work: a sender in a distant place looked at a randomly selected target picture. After the trip in the cradle (which lasted 30 minutes) the subject was given his report to re-examine, plus four pictures, one of which was the target, and asked to select the picture which most closely matched what he had experienced.

The results of Honorton's experiment were above chance, but not strong enough to be definite evidence of ESP. However, the subjects who scored above chance reported bigger 'shifts in state' than those who did not; the better performances came from those most strongly affected by their experiences in the cradle. Indeed, those reporting the biggest shifts showed positive ESP to a degree which could not be explained by chance alone. So Honorton's second prediction was confirmed.

So far Honorton had shown that ESP was strongly associated with disorientated mental states artificially induced by insulating people from their environment. But it soon became clear that the effects of sensory deprivation on his subjects were too extreme for sensory deprivation to be used as a standard experimental technique. The experience is certainly not a pleasant one. Even the prospect of it frightens many people.

In an attempt to produce a milder, less threatening form of deprivation, Honorton developed what he called the Ganzfeld (German *Ganzfeld* = 'whole field'). This way of creating the noise-reduction/inward-attention mix is subtly different and much more pleasant than total sensory deprivation. Instead of eliminating all sensory inputs the Ganzfeld approach maintains inputs at a constant level. We know that if the same sensory signals are fed into the brain again and again, the brain eventually stops attending to them. To put it crudely, brains are programmed to respond to change and, if nothing changes, the attention moves elsewhere – to internal mental events. Keeping sensory signals constant produces what is termed *habituation* of attention; the attention diminishes and gradually shifts elsewhere.

After much experimentation, Honorton settled on the Ganzfeld (GZ) method, which combined the best practical results with the most acceptable conditions. The subject is encouraged to relax in a restful, controlled and non-threatening environment. He or she lies on a mattress, or on a reclining chair. White noise (sound spread equally across all audible frequencies) or rhythmic sea-shore sounds are fed through headphones. The eyes are covered with halved table tennis balls, sealed round the edges with cotton wool, over which a dim light-source (usually red) is directed. The material of which the balls are made has just the right degree of translucence to spread the light evenly.

What happens to the person? There is a fairly clear sequence of effects, although not all the effects will occur to all people. As time passes, and the attention of the brain to external events grows progressively weaker, the effects become more marked.

The GZ experience is delightful if one relaxes into it; the world is a warm red glow, the noise the gentle fall of rain, or the sea, or distant thunder; one is warm, relaxed, comfortable.

The experimental procedure is similar to that of the dream-ESP work. A sender at a distant location looks at a target picture, trying to send the content to the person in GZ. That person – the receiver – gives a running commentary on what is happening to him. An experimenter tapes it and writes it down. After a predetermined time – usually 35

A volunteer subject is prepared for a Ganzfeld session.

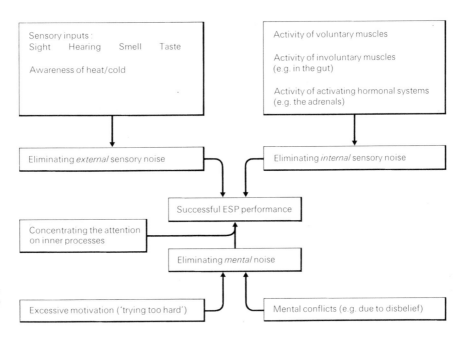

The noise-reduction theory of ESP functioning.

OBJECTIVELY SCORING A PICTURE-GUESSING ESP EXPERIMENT

TEN CONTENT CATEGORIES

	Present (1)	**Absent** (0)
01	COLOUR	NO COLOUR, BLACK-AND-WHITE
02	ACTIVITY	NO ACTIVITY, STATIC QUALITY
03	MYTHICAL CHARACTERS	NO MYTHICAL CHARACTERS
04	ANIMALS	NO ANIMALS
05	HUMANS	NO HUMANS
06	ARTIFACTS/IMPLEMENTS	NO ARTIFACTS/IMPLEMENTS
07	FOOD	NO FOOD
08	BODY PARTS	NO MENTION OF BODY PARTS
09	ARCHITECTURE	NO ARCHITECTURE
10	NATURE	NO NATURE FEATURES

minutes – the receiver is retrieved from his reverie and given four pictures, one of which is the target, to look at. He is asked to say which one most closely tallies with his experiences. Chance will give an average of 25 per cent correct choices (target placed first of the four against the report).

Honorton's first GZ study gave 13 out of 30 (43 per cent) correct choices. The statistics tell us this cannot be due to chance; the odds are around 60 to one against that being the explanation. Just as important as that figure is the size of the ESP effect; 18 per cent over the odds. This is a powerful effect, although not as good as the performances of a Bessent or an Erwin. On the other hand the 30 volunteer subjects were not selected as being particularly psychic.

In retrospect this first experiment had one flaw. Honorton used the *original* target picture in the judging, retrieved from the sender. Now since the sender looked only at that one picture, he could, quite unintentionally, have left some kind of cue on it – a fingerprint, perhaps. A cue like this could have helped the receiver to guess, during the judging, which picture was the target. This possibility could have been eliminated by using independent judges to match pictures with reports from the receivers after the whole experiment had been completed. For this reason, the results cannot be taken at face value. Nonetheless, Honorton has pointed out that the quality of the target/response matches was sometimes quite phenomenal, and that this could not possibly have been due to conventional sensory information since at this stage the GZ subjects would not have seen the target picture.

In any case, some later experiments by Honorton and his colleagues, using a beautifully subtle technique, eliminate this cueing possibility.

In the book *The Content Analysis of Dreams* the present authors give 10 different categories for scoring dreams according to the presence or absence of certain factors. Honorton borrowed this scoring system for use in his GZ work.

Above left: Honorton's binary scoring system for matching reports from Ganzfeld subjects with target pictures. The system gives a consistent 50 per cent chance of any category being present. Higher scores than that are good evidence for ESP.

Taking all the possible combinations and permutations of these 10 categories, there are 1,024 possibilities. Honorton built up a pool of 1,024 possible target pictures covering all these, from a blank slide (no category present) to the 10-category-present possibility. These can be coded in a binary form: the first is 0000000000 and the 1,024th is 1111111111. Every one of the 1,024 possible pictures could therefore be coded as a 10-bit binary digit. Under this system the receiver is tested in the usual way but, instead of getting him to judge his experience against four pictures, his running commentary is coded into a 10-digit number. If he reports people, and colour, the code is 11 for these two categories; but if he does not at any time talk about animals, the code is 0 for that category, and so on. Finally, the 10-digit number which represents his reported experience is compared with that of the target.

For the targets, then, there is exactly a 50 per cent probability of any particular category being present on it and that is true of all 10 categories independently. The method thus ensures that the target pool is indeed randomly sampled, for all possibilities are present. When you match the commentary with the target, chance alone will give you five correct 'bits' – there are 10 dimensions and a 50/50 chance of any of them being present. So, 10 times $\frac{1}{2} = 5.0$. Honorton found in experiments using this procedure that receivers consistently averaged above 5.0 'bits' per session – above the chance level, and indeed too far above it to be attributed to chance fluctuations. These results cannot possibly be ascribed to any sensory cue from the target, for the receiver never sees it, not even during the judging.

The first experimenter, other than the Maimonides workers, to get to grips with this work was Bill Braud of the Mind Science Foundation in Texas (although at the time he did this work, in 1972, he was still at the University of Houston). Braud introduced two innovations: first, he made a systematic comparison of the ESP scoring of a Ganzfeld group and a no-Ganzfeld group, to see if GZ made a real difference; second, he took into account partial hits, since these had been found quite frequently in the dream work. So, in judging, the subjects were faced with six pictures, and if they placed the target first, second, or third, this was a 'binary hit' (binary because you have a 50 per cent probability of placing it first, second, or third by chance alone). The results of this experiment were dramatic. All ten GZ subjects put the target in the top three whilst the no-Ganzfeld subjects – just talking off the top of their heads – scored right at chance. This shows that GZ specifically improves ESP performance.

At the present time, after contributions from 20 experimenters reporting 55 experiments, 27 of the experiments we know of have given evidence of significant positive ESP scoring. Only two of the experiments have gone the 'wrong way', significantly *below* chance. Once again, this massive majority in favour of positive ESP effects suggests that we are dealing with a 'lawful' phenomenon. Significant and positive ESP scoring in the Ganzfeld has been reported by 12 different experimenters.

Why does GZ work? John Palmer at John F. Kennedy University in California, together with Bill Braud, Rex Stanford of New York, and Sargent, have done the most work on this question. They have shown, for example, that the big ESP effects in GZ come from those receivers who are most strongly affected by it – the 'shift in state' effect noted by Honorton in his sensory deprivation work. Palmer's findings, though, are a particularly subtle variant on this and we will need to reflect on them and his central ideas about why GZ works at the end of the following chapter.

Again, these four have done the most to show that certain key correlates of being strongly affected by GZ tend to relate to ESP performance, providing some support for the Honorton model.

Sargent and his colleagues have suggested that there is a particular kind of person – the extravert – which is most likely to be affected by GZ, and as a consequence is most likely to score well in an ESP test with the Ganzfeld. In the Cambridge experiments, extraverts consistently showed significantly superior scoring to introverts, the difference being too large (and too consistent!) to be attributed to chance. However – and here we get into subtle notions – this effect disappears with experience. The extravert/introvert difference is very sizeable on a first testing but then shrinks and vanishes. This suggests that the difference may be due to social, and not to biological, differences between the two.

Honorton's original model makes some particularly clear predictions in the area of effects of *time*. Consider:

(1) GZ works because sensory noise is eliminated;

(2) Sensory noise is eliminated because the brain ceases to attend to the unchanging fields of sensation; attention is *habituated*;

(3) Habituation grows greater with time;

ergo:

(4) The effects of GZ should also grow greater with time.

The (4) prediction can be broken down into two parts. One prediction is that relatively long durations of GZ should be much more successful in boosting the ESP signal than short periods (within limits). Secondly, the ESP signal should be stronger later on in the GZ session rather than early on in the session. For the second prediction, there's a vital 'other things being equal' clause – one thing which may make a big difference is the time at which the sender looks at the picture! Examining the role of the sender comes after looking at the effects of the time factor on receivers, and it is relatively unexplored territory.

Sargent and his colleagues have explored these two predictions in a series of experiments.

First, the effects of length of time. The Cambridge group devised two methods for looking at this. The first was to allow people to stop GZ when they wished to, and to examine ESP scoring in relation to time using the normal picture-testing procedure. In this method the sender

RECEIVER REPORT

A fish. (Not unusual)

Clouds in the sky. (Very common)

These clouds get close. I'm looking right up at clouds in the sky. (More detail now)

Clouds of white gas. (Specific detail)

TOTAL SCOR

ORDER OF CHOIC

CORING SCHEME IN A GANZFELD PICTURE-GUESSING EXPERIMENT

rgent's scoring system for a picture-guessing experiment during nzfeld. Actual pictures and scores are shown. The receiver ored four pictures on the basis of his impressions during nzfeld. In this case he correctly decided that the sender's target s picture D.

POINTS SCORED (0–10)			
A	B	C	D
5	1	0	0
1	0	0	2
1	0	0	4
0	0	0	8
07	01	00	14
econd	Third	Fourth	First

looked at the target almost throughout the whole session. The results showed a clearly improved ESP score with longer times and the researchers were able to show that, as far as they could detect, this was not an artefact (a misleading inference caused by some untraced fault in procedure).

There is one subtle kind of problem here which one might encounter; what determines how long someone takes? The kind of thing which might happen is that the receiver arrives in a bad mood, and wishes to cut the session short. As a result, the score is poor. It might look as if the time factor is important, but it could well be the mood which really counts. Careful examination of the results showed that nothing of this kind could be detected from the battery of questions given to receivers consistently before and after the test sessions.

A better way of doing things is to make a direct comparison between two durations, say of 15 and 30 minutes. Fifteen should not be enough to get a strong ESP effect but 30 should do the trick. The Cambridge group ran this comparison – and found no difference. However, the overall scoring was at chance for both 15 and 30 minutes in this experiment! So it is hard to draw firm conclusions about Honorton's prediction. Certainly the experiments reported which have used short durations (20 minutes or less) of GZ have been very unsuccessful.

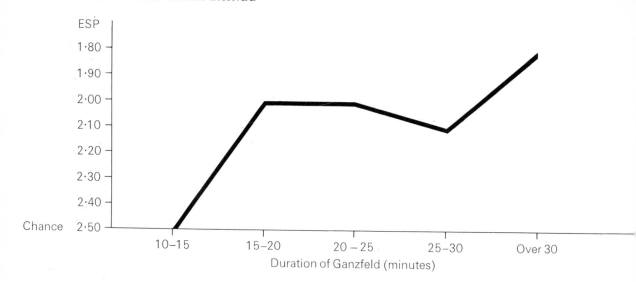

Next – the strength of the signal. The Cambridge group explored this by using a system of judging more complex than any previously employed. Simply, the receiver was asked – after the session – to give a score to each of the four pictures based on each separate element he had reported at timed points during GZ. The total score per picture for each half of the 35-minute session provides the basis for a comparison between ESP 'hits' in the first and second halves of GZ. For example one can look at the difference between the score for the target and the average for the others. If there is good ESP signal, this difference should be positive and large. If the scoring is chance, there will be no difference, and the score will be zero. In a first experiment, the researchers clearly found that in the first half of a GZ session little happened: zero. In the second half, there were big positive differences – strong signal. Honorton's prediction was supported.

In the second and third experiments on this theme, one thing was pointed out. In the first experiment, one experimenter – Sargent himself – had been present at all the sessions. He had particularly wanted this improved signal effect to be present: had this influenced subjects? So, for the second and third experiments, the results were checked for the sessions in which he was present, and those for which he was absent. In fact, in both experiments, the effect only showed itself when he was *absent*, which is the exact reverse of what one might expect! This is a first whiff of the problem of the *experimenter effect*; but for now it can be said that these results again gave some support to Honorton's prediction.

What is the overall picture here? First, GZ works in that it does fairly consistently generate positive and strong ESP well above the chance level. There is a lot of evidence (Bill Braud's control group, the state-shift effect, the effects of time) to show that it produces a specific advantage and that it works for the reasons that Honorton's model claims that it works. In all respects, the child of the dream paradigm has grown up to cut a more impressive figure than its father.

Results of a Cambridge study on ESP scoring relative to the length of time spent in the Ganzfeld condition. The experiments were of the picture-guessing type described on the previous page. Perfect scoring would be the figure 1.00 – one out of four pictures.

6 ALTERED STATES II: HYPNOSIS, RELAXATION AND MEDITATION

Hypnosis and ESP

In some scientific quarters, parapsychology is deemed a disreputable business. Now that hypnotic treatment is regularly given for obesity, smoking, and other problems, it is worth recalling how disreputable hypnosis was in its first form, as 'mesmerism'. Franz Anton Mesmer – who graduated in medicine at Vienna in 1764 – believed that the planets affected human beings through an influence like that of magnetism. After some attempts to treat patients with magnets, he decided that what was important was a force, which he called 'animal magnetism', emanating from the hands and nervous system of the physician or mesmerist.

The demand for Mesmer's idiosyncratic treatment grew and in Paris he treated many people for almost all ailments conceivable. Mesmer, dressed as a magician, prowled around in the background to an accompaniment of soft music while his patients were treated with the *baquet* – a wooden tub full of water and iron filings which supposedly stored the panaceal magnetism originating from Mesmer himself. The medical establishment was not impressed and declared that the reported cures – which were accompanied by convulsive fits – were due to 'imagination'.

Right: Franz Anton Mesmer. His theories about hypnotism were pseudoscientific nonsense – but hypnotism still worked!

Far right: Mesmer's 'patients' draw on the animal magnetism stored in the famous baquet. Hypnotism, like parapsychology, has outgrown the charlatanry of its beginnings.

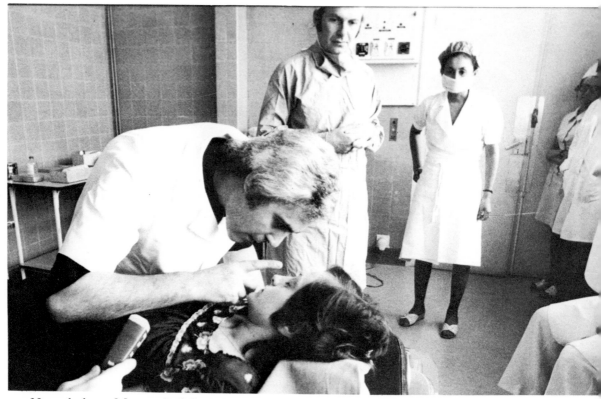

Nonetheless, Mesmer's followers carried on the work, in a more scientific manner. In England, John Elliotson and James Braid used hypnosis to anaesthetise patients during operations. They would probably have been held in great esteem were it not for the cruel fact that chloroform came on to the scene and rendered hypnotic treatment unnecessary. The medical establishment drove Elliotson from his teaching post and, on hearing that Braid had successfully amputated limbs using hypnotic anaesthesia, informed him that his patients were simply pretending not to feel any pain.

In Europe, however, Mesmer's formidable pupil de Puységur – who disliked the convulsions and the air of lurid sensation which accompanied Mesmer's treatments – found that the 'somnambulic' or trance state induced by the mesmerist seemed to be the important therapeutic instrument. In this state, he considered, the magnetic influence could act on the nervous system of the patient. Gradually what we know today as hypnosis – the soft-voiced, repeatedly-given instructions to relax, to sleep, to drift away – evolved.

Although the magnetic theory of hypnosis is in disrepute, one spin-off from it is important to us. Continental hypnotists made many claims about a so-called 'community of sensation' between the hypnotist and his subject. The magnetic force flowing between the two seemed to produce paranormal effects, especially telepathy. The hypnotised person seemed able to 'read the mind' of the hypnotist, even

John Elliotson, the nineteenth-century surgeon hounded by the medical establishment for using hypnosis to anaesthetise his patients.

Hypnosis is now a recognised medical technique: here a medical hypnotist 'anaesthetises' a patient.

carrying out suggestions before the hypnotist had given them. Mesmer himself gave demonstrations of 'hypnosis at a distance', in which a hypnotised person would react to the thoughts of the hypnotist although some distance away from him and out of the range of orthodox sensory communication. Hypnotised people were also reported as being able to sense distant events when so instructed by the hypnotist.

Before examining the evidence on this, again we must ask: why should we expect hypnosis to be ESP-favourable? Can we explain it in the terms of 'noise-reduction' and 'inner awareness' that seemed to produce such good results in sensory deprivation and GZ work?

Hypnosis presents one major problem: it cannot be pinned down by objective recording. Many attempts have been made to measure some kind of special brain-wave activity during hypnosis, without success. The idea of some special 'hypnotic state' seems to have no validity – or at least no measurable basis.

Fortunately there are some features typical of hypnotised persons which are not peculiar to hypnosis, but which can tell us something about hypnosis in relation to the noise-reduction idea.

Relaxation, reduced attention to external events – a familiar list. There is considerable argument about why hypnotised people show these features, but such considerations can come later. The important thing at this stage is that hypnotised people do show relaxation and reduced attention to the outside world. So, on the noise-reduction model, we would expect hypnosis to be favourable to ESP. Is it?

There are three major types of experiment we need to look at: those with ESP cards, those with picture targets (the hypnotic dream and hypnotic daydream work), and the Russian researches.

There are no objective measures typical of the hypnotised individual – each one of this hypnotist's volunteers may be reacting in a different way.

A review of all the published experiments using hypnosis with ESP card-guessing has been given by Charles Honorton and, adding some recent work to that survey, we find that a total of 23 *comparisons* of card-guessing ability with and without the benefit of hypnosis have been reported. Of the 23 hypnosis experiments, 14 – over 60 per cent, a huge proportion – have given significant evidence of ESP. Of the 23

experiments conducted in the normal waking state only one gave such evidence. Again, 12 of the comparisons showed a significant superiority for the hypnosis condition – and never has an ordinary waking-state experiment, in a direct comparison, given significantly better evidence of ESP than the hypnosis condition. Once again, then, we see that all results point one way: hypnosis is favourable for ESP and much better results are obtained with it than without it.

There is another effect of interest here: it seems, in some cases, that hypnotised people in card-guessing experiments *know* when they have made a correct guess. A study reported by Karlis Osis, Director of Research of the American Society for Psychical Research, with Jan Fahler, showed that when hypnotised people made 'confidence calls' in card-guessing, they showed exceptionally high accuracy in scoring.

Other experimenters using hypnosis have reported the same thing informally and the Ganzfeld work, too, supports this. Carl Sargent, in most of his experiments, requested subjects to give a rating between zero and 99 to the pictures shown: zero meant no correspondence between what a person had experienced in Ganzfeld and 99 a perfect match. Sargent looked at the cases where people had made very confident judgements, giving 90 points or more to a particular picture. The chance probability of success in this task is 25 per cent. In Sargent's work the overall 'hit-rate' was around 40 per cent; but for the 90-point judgements, the hit rate was over 60 per cent. Again, the really confident 'guesses' tended to be correct very often, an effect further confirmed by Ian McLaren, working in Cambridge on dream-ESP.

Now this is important. The noise-reduction model predicts that Ganzfeld and hypnosis should be ESP-favourable – and evidence confirms this – but there could be other reasons for the success, such as a strong expectation of success on the part of the experimenters. However, the noise-reduction model states that these procedures will not only increase the scoring rate in ESP experiments but will increase the detection *and recognition* of ESP signals. The ability to recognise correct signals is shown by the Osis work with hypnotised subjects and the Sargent–Ganzfeld work. This is a strong piece of support for the noise-reduction model – but, as ever, we need more evidence before we firmly accept this new piece of the experimental jigsaw.

The correct guesses in the card-guessing experiments may have been detected because of some role of mental imagery in hypnosis (as in Ganzfeld). Examining this idea more closely takes us on to the second type of ESP hypnosis experiment – the hypnotic dream with picture targets. The ESP part of the experiment is similar to the dream and Ganzfeld experiments – a sender examines a target picture whilst the receiver tries to detect it. Here, the receiver is hypnotised and then told to dream.

Again, Honorton has rounded up all the experiments of this type. From his collation we find that of the ten experiments with hypnosis and picture-guessing, seven have given significant evidence of ESP. Further, in his own experiments, Honorton has shown that the best scoring comes from people who score high on a 'suggestibility' measure (susceptibility to hypnosis) and who report being strongly affected during the hypnotic state. Specifically, in Honorton's experiments the best scores came from hypnotised people who reported that their attention was directed inwards rather than externally. This, of course, is exactly what one would expect from the noise-reduction idea. These picture-guessing studies show the same pattern as the card-guessing experiments: the results are consistent.

Parapsychology in the USSR

Finally we come to the work of the Russian L. L. Vasiliev.

Although Russian parapsychology is largely a closed book to Western scientists, we do know that the Russians have always had an interest in hypnosis and ESP. As early as 1926 the Experimental Commission on Hypnotism and Psychophysics was formed to examine the problem with the approval of the Russian scientific authorities. In 1928 Vasiliev visited parapsychology centres in France and Germany; in 1932 the Soviet Institute for Brain Research received an assignment to commence 'an experimental study of telepathy' – and Vasiliev headed the effort.

Vasiliev – the father of Soviet parapsychology.

Before looking at Vasiliev's work, it is interesting to note that lively interest in hypnosis and ESP still continues behind the Iron Curtain. One of the authors of this book has direct experience of this. In 1977 and 1978 Sargent published several research papers in parapsychology journals, including one in the *Journal of Parapsychology*. The response from the Soviet Bloc was a single request for a copy of one of the papers. In the December 1978 *Journal of Parapsychology* Sargent published a paper on the effects of hypnosis on ESP. Within two months over a dozen such requests for copies of this paper had been received, including one from the Lithuanian Republic's Council for Trade Union Health Resort Management!

Vasiliev's most interesting work, for which he claimed highly successful results, involved attempts to hypnotise subjects at a distance. In these experiments susceptible subjects were allegedly put into hypnotic trance, or in some cases awakened from the trance state, at distances of up to 1,060 miles. The times at which the suggestion would be given were randomly chosen; sometimes, a control – using unhypnotised subjects – was employed. There are, regrettably, major flaws in the experiments.

For example, although the times between giving suggestions and their effect on the subjects were allegedly measured with stopwatches, some 40 per cent of the times given are reported only to the nearest minute – rather poor accuracy. Again, in those experiments in which hypnotic induction of sleep was attempted, all the subjects – hypnotised or not – eventually went to sleep anyway. Vasiliev's 'results' showed that some subjects fell asleep more quickly than others. But for these results to mean anything, it is essential that the subjects should either have been put into the hypnosis or no-hypnosis category at random, or tested an equal number of times in both. This is a technical point, but the logic is clear if one considers a possible problem: what if all those subjects who tended to go to sleep quickly *anyway* were put into the group to be hypnotised, while all those who naturally stayed awake for a longer time were not? Of course the hypnotised group would show a faster onset of sleep – but that would have nothing to do with the effects of mental suggestion at a distance!

These problems – and others – force us to the conclusion that, like so much Russian work, Vasiliev's research efforts were probably too flawed for anyone to make much out of them.

After Vasiliev's death in 1966 we know little of any work by his pupils. So the research effort may have died away. Or has it? The response to the publication by Sargent in 1978 shows that the interest must still be there. Further confirmation for the continued Russian effort in the area of hypnosis and ESP comes from an unlikely quarter. The 1978 World Chess Championship was held in the Philippines between champion (by default, since Bobby Fischer would not defend his title in 1975) Anatoly Karpov of the USSR and Russian exile Victor Korchnoi. Korchnoi claimed that a member of Karpov's retinue, the mysterious Dr Zoukhar, was hypnotising him at a distance.

Sargent and British International Master chess-player Bill Hartston interviewed Korchnoi and Michael Stean (his second in the match). Further conversations between Hartston and Boris Spassky, another Russian exile (defeated by Korchnoi in 1976 on the way to his match with Karpov), suggested that Russian chess masters are instructed in hypnosis and ESP as a matter of routine. It could, of course, just be a coincidence that the Russians describe Zoukhar as a 'psychiatrist and neurologist' when some of the first scientific papers on mental suggestion in Russia were presented at the Second All-Russian Congress of *Psycho-neurology* in Petrograd in 1924.

Back to firm data: the results from experiments with hypnosis show a clear effect on ESP scoring in experiments. Honorton's judgement, after painstakingly reviewing all the published reports in 1977, is this: 'I believe the conclusion is now *inescapable* that hypnotic induction procedures enhance (ESP).' It *does* seem inescapable, and provides yet more support for the noise-reduction model.

Progressive relaxation – the key to ESP?

Relaxation of the body is a key factor in the noise-reduction story. A relaxed body has little activity in the voluntary muscles of the body and this activity can be easily, and reliably, measured using the EMG (electromyograph). In view of the key importance of relaxation, and the ease of measuring it, it is surprising that systematic research on relaxation and ESP has only begun very recently. In the case of the dream research, parapsychology had to await Kleitman's discovery of REM sleep and dreaming activity. On the other hand Jacobson's classic work *Progressive Relaxation* had been in print for nearly 35 years before Bill and Lendell Braud at the University of Houston put it to use in para-

The great Karpov–Korchnoi psych-out. Victor Korchnoi felt sure that the Soviet camp had brought in telepathy experts to affect his concentration. Paranoid fantasy – or a scientific possibility?

Right: Extracts from the Brauds' taped instructions based on Jacobson's techniques of deep relaxation. Using these techniques the Brauds' subjects were able to improve ESP scoring.

PROGRESSIVE RELAXATION

(From a tape of the PR exercises): Begin by tensing the muscles in your legs, hold that tension as the count goes from 10 to 1 to zero, feel how uncomfortable that tension is. Tense the muscles now... 10, 9, 8... 3, 2, 1. Relax now. Relax those muscles completely, exhale, feel the relief of relaxing. Relax all your muscles and feel how good it is. Now, tense your stomach muscles fully, really tense, hard, tight, 10, 9, 8,... 3, 2, 1, 0. Relax, relax those muscles, feel the relief of that, fully relaxed, let your body sink into a state of deep relaxation now, relax...
... Now we begin mental relaxation... hold your head quite straight and lift your eyes upwards to strain them... don't blink... your eyelids become heavy, tired, heavy and tired... take a deep breath in, exhale slowly, feel how your eyes become more tired as each second passes, really tired and heavy... now close your eyes. Again feel the relief of relaxing, relax your eye muscles, relax. Relax all the tension, release all the pressures... it feels good to be so relaxed. Noises and sounds around will not distract you now, but just help you become more relaxed... now relax your mind, no mental efforts... visualize something natural and pleasant, a favourite landscape or scene you love, see it in your mind's eye, without any effort, the image just comes to mind. See yourself relaxing in this place, relax. With each breath imagine yourself becoming more completely relaxed...
Now relax completely, completely, relax completely, relax. Rid your mind of any mundane worries and tensions, they don't matter now, just relax. Think of a circle of blankness keeping out any stray thoughts. Now your mind is clear, stilled...

---

psychology. Would the measurable *physiological* effects of relaxation be matched by any variation – improvement or otherwise – of performance in ESP tests?

In 1969 the Brauds began experiments using a modified version of the Jacobson deep-relaxation technique. Their first subject, a 26-year-old university teacher, was instructed to relax his body by alternately tensing and relaxing his muscles, then encouraged to relax his mind by first concentrating on pleasant imagery (peaceful countryside scenes) then, so far as possible, letting his mind become blank and passive. Meanwhile in another room more than 20 yards away a sender randomly selected a target picture from a pool of 150 postcard-sized images. The sender attempted to transmit elements – shapes, colours, even tastes and smells – present in or conveyed by the picture. Work proceeded at the rate of one session and one target per day. At the end of each session the subject was asked to write down impressions received during the relaxed state. After six sessions the six written reports and the six targets were given to an independent judge, who was asked to match each report to a picture. In the event, the judge matched targets and reports *perfectly*. The most conservative statistical test tells us that the chance probability of this happening is over 700 to one.

In seven preliminary experiments with a total of 22 subjects – singly and in groups – the Brauds were able to report an overall success rate of 86 per cent against a chance expectation of 50 per cent. In some cases

the correspondences were very striking. In the Brauds' first test, for example, the subject vividly 'saw' a glass of Coca-Cola. The target: a Coca-Cola advertisement. 'Direct hits' like this were recorded in 59 per cent of cases against a 17 per cent chance expectation. In these tests the maximum distance between sender and receiver was 1,400 miles. All in all, on the most pessimistic analysis of their results, the Brauds could claim odds against chance of 1,000 to one on experiments conducted over a two-year period. In later experiments, they compared results from deeply relaxed groups with those from groups who had undergone muscle-*tensing* exercises. The difference between the states was objectively measured with an EMG. The conclusions amply confirmed the earlier experiments.

Rex Stanford, then at the University of Virginia, was able to repeat the Brauds' experiments and confirmed their results. This, together with other work, has provided firm evidence that deep relaxation is favourable to ESP performance. Intriguingly, however, later research, even by Braud himself, has not had anything like the spectacular success of the early work.

One reason for this may be the absence – except in the Braud experiments – of any general standard for the degree of relaxation achieved by the subjects. It is quite possible that some researchers are better at relaxing their subjects than others. Without a precise measure of the depth of relaxation we are prevented from making a direct comparison between experiments – even those using exactly the same procedures – conducted in different places by different workers. Despite the disappointing results of latter-day research, however, enough evidence remains to suggest that – as with dreams, the Ganzfeld and hypnosis – progressive relaxation is favourable to ESP because it reduces the distracting noise of normal sensory input.

Meditation and ESP

Historically, the practitioners of various techniques of meditation have made considerable claims for enhanced powers of the mind during meditation itself. From earliest times, for example, the yogis of ancient India claimed to be able to subject bodily processes, such as breathing and heartbeat, to acts of will. As we have already seen, too, an early yoga master, Patanjali, states quite clearly that the discipline of withdrawing the mind from the external world can produce psi effects, albeit unwanted ones. And, at all times in history, mystics of every culture have announced truths revealed only in particular states of consciousness. These revelatory states are conventionally attained through the practice of some repetitive ritual act – the exercises, physical and spiritual, of the yogis, dancing, chanting, and so on. Is it possible, then, that the altered states of consciousness achieved by these mystical practices might be favourable to ESP?

Our first problem in answering this question is that, even if we confine ourselves to the field of yoga, there are many schools of meditation and parapsychologists have often lumped them together in reports.

Right: Meditation calms the mind, and so, theoretically, should be conducive to psi . . .

Far right: Demons attempt to break into the perfect meditation of a Buddhist master. Ancient Sanskrit texts tell us that ESP and PK events are likely to happen during meditation but that they should be regarded as distractions from the correct meditational state of mind.

One result of this is that the work on meditation and psi is remarkably disordered. We can take heart, though, from other types of scientific investigation into meditation. In medicine, for example, serious testing of the claims of diverse meditational methods have brought strong results that would have been ridiculed by medical science of only 15 years ago.

One school of meditation, Transcendental Meditation (TM), claims to be radically different from all others. TM practitioners claim to be able to achieve profound states of meditation rather rapidly by the repetition of a *mantra* – a meaningless sound which, constantly repeated, leaves the mind free to approach the deepest levels of concentration. TM subjects have been used in a number of ESP experiments. Before looking at some of them, a general conclusion can be given which will serve to prepare the reader for what is to come: it does appear that meditators can exert remarkable psi effects, but their control over them seems extremely poor. Now this is both very unexpected and very intriguing. It is unexpected because experienced meditators have astonishing powers of voluntary control over their bodies; but it is intriguing because, through their strong but inconsistent psi powers, some law of psi effects might be glimpsed.

It is worth relating briefly just what kinds of effect meditators can exert on their bodies by a simple act of will. Heart rate and respiration rate can be dramatically reduced, for example. One researcher who has studied an Indian yogi, Swami Rama, has stated that the swami stopped his heartbeat for so long that a member of the medical team examining him almost had a coronary from worry! TM researchers also claim tremendous coherence in the brain-wave spectrum during the practice of TM, coupled with low heart rate and respiration rate. These effects are very well attested, and many of them can be learned through *biofeedback* techniques. It has even been established that a human being

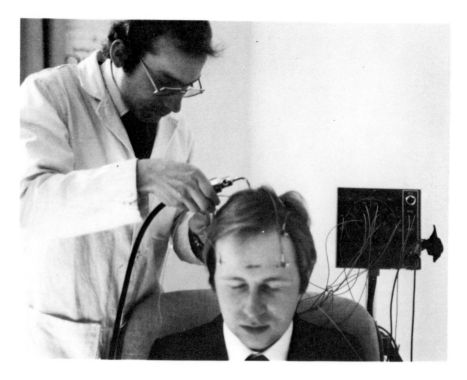

Meditators such as this TM adherent certainly produce strong ESP, but find it difficult to control its direction – positive or negative.

can learn to wish for an effect on the firing rate of a *single cell* in the spinal cord – and achieve it. This astonishing discovery was reported in *Science* in 1969.

Yet, despite this impressive record of an ability to control the activity of the body, meditators seem very bad at controlling their psi effects. In the case of the dream work, the Ganzfeld work, the progressive relaxation work – the typical ESP score is well *above* chance. Reversals – the ESP score being well *below* chance, the strange psi-missing effect – are very rare. Yet these experiments used pretty ordinary people for the most part; why is it that meditators are so bad at control? For they are. In an ESP Ganzfeld experiment with 20 TM practitioners as receivers, John Palmer found that the scoring rate – measured by two pairs of judges – was comfortably above the chance level (as in most Ganzfeld experiments). Yet the TM people themselves – judging their own material – scored their results well *below* chance. What the four judges could see as positive ESP, the TM people could not; they saw it as psi-missing. Very odd. It's true that the experiment was run in California and Californians are strange people; but the judges saw the correct picture. Why not the meditators?

Charles Honorton has reported a three-stage experiment with a TM instructor, not on ESP but rather on PK with a Schmidt machine (Chapter 3). Before meditation, the instructor tried in some tests to get above-chance results and, in others, to get below-chance results. In fact, he managed to score above-chance all the time. PK results obtained when the EEG showed the meditator to be in a deep state of meditation were almost significantly *below* chance. After meditation, he did at last show positive scoring and negative scoring when he wished to show one or the other. Despite the success in the final, post-meditation stage, the earlier results are very unstable and no coherent picture emerges from the tests.

Some work with a TM practitioner conducted by Sargent gave similar results. Unfortunately it was not possible to complete the full schedule of testing, but the preliminary results showed that the person scored above chance on an ESP test when he was trying to score below chance and below chance when he was trying to score above chance!

There have certainly been successes with TM, and some exceptionally strong evidence of ESP has been collected. Ramakrishna Rao, testing meditation students in India for ESP, found very high scoring in an ESP test after meditation – but, before meditation, he found almost equally powerful scoring – *below* chance! The difference between the low scoring before meditation and the high scoring after was massively significant – this could not possibly have been due to chance. One can understand the positive scoring after meditation, but why the low scoring before it? This is strange.

Some years after this research – and in another context – Rao suggested a possible principle, what he termed the *principle of conservation of order*, which may be just romantic mysticism – or it may be a crucial insight. Nature, Rao suggests, is ordered, and psi breaks that order. Somewhere the effect must rebound on us. If an experiment somewhere yields a fabulous above-chance result, then in the very order of the Universe we must pay for that somewhere else, with a reversal. At some time we must observe an equally below-chance result to pay off the debt. The two cancel each other out; order is maintained. The meditators obtain powerful – but opposed and inconsistent – effects because they are truly in harmony with the principle of conservation of order. This, according to Rao, is why their effects on psi are so powerful but so unstable.

This notion has a lot in common with the old notion of karmic law – and indeed with twentieth-century physics. It is a new thought in that Rao cannot yet produce detailed predictions from it and admits the idea is speculative; yet it is very old at the same time. In another way, John Palmer's views on the effects of the gamut of noise-reducing procedures on psi are similar. It is time, then, to summarise our findings.

Alternative views of altered states

We hope that we have given enough detailed examples to show that the study of altered states of consciousness has provided parapsychologists with important new insights into the operation of psi effects. In particular, Honorton's development of the Ganzfeld technique has provided researchers with a powerful method of producing strong reliable psi and of measuring its effects. As an experimental method the Ganzfeld has the advantages of being relatively straightforward, flexible and economical in operation. From an aesthetic point of view, as well, the

Ganzfeld environment, although strictly controlled, is satisfyingly similar to the 'real-life' conditions in which spontaneously occurring psi is most often reported – dreaming, reverie, states of extreme bodily relaxation. This could hardly be said of the card-guessing experiments of Rhine and his followers.

Equally satisfying is that Honorton derived his novel experimental technique from a particular analysis of the way in which ESP might work. Parapsychology has often been accused of being a science with a lot of facts but no theories. By treating ESP in the traditional way as something like a weak human sense, but one normally swamped by the distracting noise of the conventional senses, Honorton and others have been able to predict that ESP will work more strongly when normal sensory input is reduced – a prediction successfully confirmed in practice. The greatest strength of the noise-reduction theory is that *it works*.

Californian parapsychologist John Palmer takes a different, and more complex, view of events than Honorton. For Palmer, the 'altered state of consciousness' (ASC) induced by hypnosis, the Ganzfeld, or whatever, tends to produce an ESP score which is far away from chance. The ASC affects the *magnitude* of the effect. The *direction* of the effect, however – whether one scores above chance or below chance – is affected by other factors so far as Palmer is concerned. This distinction is not explicitly present in Honorton's model, which seems to suggest that the ASC tends to produce a high *positive* score.

Palmer's model has two major weaknesses. The first weakness is that Palmer cannot specify which factors control the direction of scoring. Personality seems *not* to be one of these factors: that is clear from some of Sargent's studies. Presumably *social* factors – what an old researcher studying mediums would have termed the atmosphere – are more important. The second weakness in the Palmer model is that the very large majority of significant results obtained using the dream state, Ganzfeld, and so on are above chance rather than below. While this does not conflict with Palmer's model, Honorton's model would have predicted this state of affairs and Palmer's would not.

However, there is one key method for testing the two models against each other. Honorton's model states that there should be a *positive* relationship between ESP scoring in, say, a Ganzfeld experiment, and the subject's report of how successful the Ganzfeld was in inducing an ASC in him. People who experience a radical shift away from their normal state of consciousness should score best in the ESP test. The ESP success which occurs under these conditions should, in theory, *always* be positive. For Palmer, this is not so. Palmer's argument is that this will be true if and only if the overall ESP score is positive for the group of people being tested; if, overall, the ESP score is negative, then the relationship between ESP success and the alteration of consciousness should also be negative. Why should this be?

Palmer argues that this is to be expected because the people who are most strongly affected by the Ganzfeld will be most sensitive to the social atmosphere around, which will reflect itself in a *strong positive* ESP

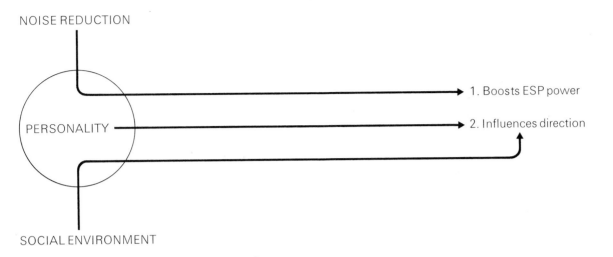

NOISE REDUCTION

PERSONALITY

SOCIAL ENVIRONMENT

1. Boosts ESP power

2. Influences direction

The strength and direction of scoring in ESP tests are affected by the interaction of three factors: reduction of external noise, personality type, and the social environment in which tests are conducted.

score if the atmosphere is right and a *strong negative* ESP score if the atmosphere is uncomfortable, formal, unpleasant, or tense.

For Honorton, people who are strongly affected by the Ganzfeld should score very *high* (i.e., well above chance) – but for Palmer they should score very *strongly* (i.e., a long way from chance – but this could be positive or negative).

The results from 14 studies which have reported measures of the success of Ganzfeld in changing the state of consciousness all support Palmer's model. Every time the score overall is above chance (11 experiments) the relationship between the two has been positive: for the three experiments in which the overall score was below chance, the relationship was negative. Palmer's model appears to have the edge at this time. But, no matter how one chooses to interpret the results, the strength of the evidence remains clear.

So the strength and direction of ESP are influenced by three factors, a calm inner awareness, undistracted by external noise, personality (extravert-introvert, believer-disbeliever), and the effect of atmosphere between people.

The position remains complex, certainly. But the broad outlines of the picture have been sketched in, and the three-factor model (noise-reduction/personality/environment) provides a satisfying and intuitively appealing basis for further work. Nor should we forget that, under the right conditions, the effects can be devastatingly simple. Bill Braud's receiver, trying to get impressions of a target picture unknown to him, talks of Coca-Cola – the target picture shows Coca-Cola bottles. Chuck Honorton's receiver, doing the same, talks of Las Vegas casinos; the target shows Las Vegas casinos. Carl Sargent's receiver 'sees' William Blake's 'The Ancient of Days' and the target is ... of course it is. There are enough key facts like these to reassure those who want to

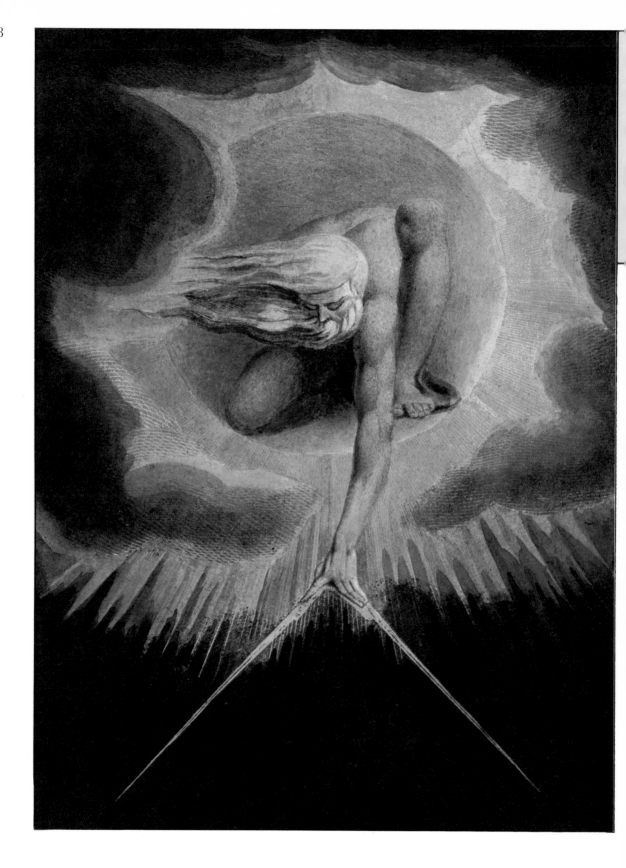

A GANZFELD PICTURE-GUESSING EXPERIMENT

Experiment 12 Session 16.
10 December 1979.
Target picture:
The Ancient of Days by William Blake

Receiver report:

Picture of the night sky with a planet or some unnatural golden oval. Glowing object, fire coming off it. Clumsily-drawn picture of woman in white nightdress . . . ragged hair, torch in one hand. The hands and feet are too large . . . Close-up picture of Sun, can see the red flames on the surface. Sun looks black . . . Blake's picture of God with the dividers, creating the world.

be presented with simple, impressive results. One could probably say: the results are relatively simple, but explanations are relatively complex. The explanations are what we must seek. The facts are there for us to understand if we can, and we must now examine more of them to get a fuller picture of just what psi can achieve. Paranormal sensing of distant events is interesting enough, but the power to influence those events would be even more interesting. We must ask the question, what *can* be achieved by an effort of Mind?

Up to this point we have dealt mainly with evidence for the existence of paranormal perception – telepathy, clairvoyance and precognition. The weight of this evidence is such as to convince a majority of scientists and the general population that ESP is now either proven or a likely possibility – an opinion revealed by a number of surveys. In the case of PK (psychokinesis: literally 'movement by the mind'), however, similar surveys show clearly that most people do not believe that it is possible for the human mind alone to cause or influence events in the real world. We have already given two examples of PK effects: the untestable, but reliable, reports on the extraordinary career of D. D. Home, and the challenging experimental results of Helmut Schmidt's work. It is now time to examine in much greater detail the systematic research that has been conducted on PK, and we have chosen four areas in particular in which to do so. These are poltergeists ('noisy spirits'), faith healing, experimental work with machines before and after Schmidt, and metal bending. If the reported examples of PK in these areas are true, then we find ourselves in a very strange world indeed, one in which perceived and measurable events take place which have no known cause. Yet if, on a critical evaluation of the evidence, we find that such events really do seem to take place, how can we ignore them?

The noisy spirit

Although *Poltergeist* is the German for 'noisy spirit', the Germans themselves now prefer the word *Spuk*. Whatever we call them, poltergeists are associated with inexplicable physical manifestations over a period of time. Often, the manifestations take the form of strange noises, and the even stranger movement of objects. Sometimes, although not always, the manifestations can be violent.

Poltergeists are very old indeed; cases are to be found in Italy as early as the sixth century. While it is hard to evaluate these reports now, investigators in the sixteenth century and onwards did make attempts to document their cases with some care, and in one sixteenth-century demonology the author, discussing poltergeists, says, 'I shall pass over examples, since the thing is exceedingly well-known . . .'

Thus, when we come to look at attempts to track the poltergeist down with the sophisticated apparatus available to us today, we have to bear in mind that the noisy spirit has been with us a long time.

The poltergeist is the one type of spontaneous psi effect which an experimenter can usefully investigate. With spontaneous ESP, as we noted earlier, we are reduced to looking at events after their occurrence.

The conventional notion of poltergeist manifestations involves violent effects focused on a young child – like this nineteenth-century haunting at Guillonville, France.

Even with laborious survey work, there is always the problem of accounting for the possibility of coincidence. The poltergeist, however, differs in one vital respect from spontaneous ESP in that it is generally *recurrent*. Poltergeist cases go on for weeks, even months, and possibly, in a few cases, for years. This means that the experimenter can go along to the scene of the action, set up his observers and his recording apparatus and wait for it to happen again – he can, potentially, catch the poltergeist red-handed.

Two modern poltergeists

Ask any knowledgeable parapsychologist which single poltergeist case he would offer the rational sceptic as the best evidence for the phenomenon, and he would refer you to the Rosenheim affair. During 1967 and 1968, in the small West German town of Rosenheim, exceedingly strange things began to happen in the office of a reputable and prominent lawyer.

Among the earlier manifestations were persistent and mysterious telephone 'calls', and the random detonation of main fuses. The lawyer was extremely angry about things, suspecting sabotage, or perhaps a disturbance in the power supply to the building. The local Post Office and power station maintenance staff were called in to research the problem. They brought in monitoring equipment, automatic counters, and even (eventually) an emergency power unit. The baffled engineers found that the monitoring equipment registered large and inexplicable power transients, while the Post Office equipment registered impossibly high frequencies for the number of calls to the local Speaking Clock service.

Matters were now completely out of hand and specialist help was called in. Professor Hans Bender, a parapsychologist from the University of Freiburg, started a full investigation, helped by two physicists from the Max Planck Institute for Plasmaphysics in Munich. The physicists brought in their own monitoring equipment and Bender himself installed cameras and recorders.

The first thing Bender tracked down was that the strange events only occurred when one particular person was in the building. This was Annemarie Sch., a 19-year-old girl. When she walked along a corridor, lamps hanging from the ceiling would begin to swing, with increasing force, a phenomenon which would persist for some little time after she had gone. Bender was lucky enough to get this on film, and checked scrupulously for any trickery – hidden wires and the like which could have produced the effect.

Meanwhile, the two physicists had been puzzling over the results from their equipment, which was monitoring the electrical effects in the building. They found the same strange electrical surges as the power station workers and the Post Office people had done. Systematically, they eliminated possible causes such as fluctuations in the mains power supply, or interference from X-ray equipment owned by a dentist who occupied part of the same building as the lawyer's office. Their conclu-

Right: Alleged poltergeist disturbance at the offices of the Air Keating Co., Leeds.

Far right: The destructive effects of poltergeists are no joke to the victims!

sions were, in essence, quite simple – something extremely strange was
going on. They had exhaustively checked for normal mechanisms of the
interferences their equipment had detected, and could find none that
would explain the anomalies.

As soon as Bender realised that Annemarie was the apparent poltergeist *focus* (the person around whom the effects seemed to centre), he
watched her like a hawk. By the end of the case (when Annemarie left to
take another job) Bender calculated that some 40 witnesses – all
thoroughly interrogated – testified to seeing a variety of inexplicable
effects. These included the swinging lamps Bender had filmed, swinging wall pictures (which Bender also got on film) and many others. The
witnesses were certainly interrogated, for the lawyer at one stage
brought a legal accusation against persons unknown for maliciously
causing the effects!

To refute these findings, we have to assume that all these people
(among them technicians, people *trained* to observe, psychologists,
physicists, and initially sceptical journalists) were deluded to the point
of idiocy. If there had been fraud, the culprit(s) was (were) facing
public exposure, humiliation, and probably a gaol sentence. Certainly
the lawyer was not immensely popular with his staff – but much less
dangerous practical jokes could have been arranged, and this one went
on for months. Despite the fact that many people – highly trained in

different disciplines – were looking for evidence of fraud all the time, no hint of it was ever sniffed. *And this is just one poltergeist case.*

There have, of course, been attempts to discredit the evidence after the event (the sceptic is always safe here, since his explaining-away cannot be checked against the facts as and when they are observed). These attempts have come to naught.

When Annemarie left, the poltergeist effects, as generally happens, followed her to her new place of work for a time, and then died away.

Evidence as strong as the Rosenheim case is rare. That is not surprising, for Bender's intensive research effort involved a great deal of time and money. In general, research funding for parapsychology is pretty low, and most researchers lack the sophisticated equipment needed to investigate poltergeist manifestations in the proper way. Still, there is good evidence from acute and detailed observations made, systematically, in other cases. In 1967, for example, Gaither Pratt (who worked with Stepanek) and William Roll, Director of Research at the Psychical Research Foundation of North Carolina, were able to observe poltergeist effects associated with a 19-year-old boy, Julio. The boy worked as a shipping clerk, a job which, among other things, involved working in a warehouse. When he was in the warehouse, objects would fly off shelves, and Roll noted that there were certain objects which seemed to do this much more frequently than others. He experimented by putting certain objects which moved frequently in particular *places* from which levitations appeared to occur very frequently, and observing them. Roll and Pratt were able to log ten incidents in which the 'target objects', as they termed them, moved when they had the area in their scrutiny both immediately before and immediately after the event. In seven cases one or other had his eyes on the boy. Strangely, however,

---

OBSERVING THE POLTERGEIST

Bill Roll's observation of one incident in his Miami case :

'At 11.27 A.M., a Zombie glass from the target area b on Tier 2 broke in the middle of Aisle 2. This glass had . . . been 12 inches from the edge of the shelf and there was a spoondrip tray, a water globe, and some notebooks in front of it. During this event there were three people in the warehouse aside from myself. Miss Roldan, who was at her desk. Mr. Hagmeyer, who was in the south-west corner of the room, and Julio. At the time of the event, Julio was sitting on his haunches at the north end of Aisle 3, placing a plastic alligator on the bottom shelf of Aisle 3. I was between five and six feet from him and facing him when this event happened. He had no visible contact with Tier 2. The position of the glass was four feet from his back. It moved away from him. None of the objects in front of the glass were disturbed. It therefore must have risen at least two inches to clear these.'

(Note : Copyright source : Journal of the American Society for Psychical Research, 1971. Paper by Roll and Pratt, vol. 65, pp. 446-447)

they never actually saw an object in motion. The descriptions made by Roll and Pratt are accurate and detailed; it seems impossible to maintain that these experienced observers were deluded.

Pinning down the evidence

This is the *type* of evidence which must be taken seriously in trying to evaluate the poltergeist phenomenon. There is such a wealth of it from observers and experimenters all over the globe that it seems very difficult to dismiss it all. Nonetheless, there are some problems which must make us cautious.

The first problem any poltergeist researcher faces is simply that 95 per cent of reported cases are not worth a second visit. Reports of strange goings-on come from lonely old ladies who really only want to have someone to talk to, or from cunning fraudulent families who would like a new council house. Often, too, people do not tell anybody of their experiences until after the poltergeist activity has ceased, so that the researcher cannot observe it directly. This has to be said to counteract any impression given that poltergeists are lurking around every corner. Poltergeists are unusual – and *good* poltergeist cases, where some worthwhile evidence can be collected, are very rare.

The second problem is fraud. William Roll, in analysing an (admittedly small) sample of cases reported, showed that for 82 cases reported before 1949, fraud was detected in just 9.8 per cent of them. For 34 cases reported after 1949, the percentage had jumped to 32 per cent. One-third! This is a high frequency of fraud, and the true figure is probably higher than that. For, if a researcher detects fraud, he may be less likely to publish his case than if he doesn't find it. Again, sometimes – given an amateur researcher and a cunning fraud – fraud may go undetected. An estimate of a 50 per cent prevalence of fraud in poltergeist cases in the last 30 years is probably a safe one.

Fraud, though, is a harsh word. For most poltergeists centre around children, and children do not possess the same moral sense as adults. While most 'exposures of fraud' do concern children, it is often the family background, rather than malice, that prompts the deception.

One alleged poltergeist case which, in the course of three visits by a researcher, produced no observable PK effects – but one instance of fraud – brings the point home. The family home had no father, and the children liked the visits of interested strangers. In particular, they took a liking to the present author-visitor. After a first visit, when nothing untoward had happened in his presence, one girl grabbed him by the arm as he was leaving and said 'You will come back again, won't you?' Towards the end of a second visit – when again nothing remarkable had been witnessed – the author was lucky enough to see, out of the corner of his eye, the boy of the household throw a kitchen brush in the air and then pretend the poltergeist had been active.

On the one hand, this means that the sceptic can point to the high rate of incidence of fraud and sniff disdainfully. It also means that the researcher going in for the study of poltergeists is putting his head in the lion's mouth – and also has to learn to develop peripheral vision as a natural way of perceiving! On the other hand, to cry 'Fraud' at the boy (eight years old) is missing the point. The child doesn't see what he did as wickedness, and he has a good motive for doing what he did. Exasperating, but the psychology of the poltergeist and the psychology of the 'fraudulent' child may be all too similar: the cry for attention. We suspect strongly that in many cases children who are focuses in poltergeist cases resort to fraud because the poltergeist won't perform to order in the presence of the desired, attentive, witness.

So, the sceptic has good reason for demanding particularly stringent controls against fraud in the case of poltergeist research. Sceptical suspicions about a high degree of fraud in poltergeist cases have been confirmed – after a fashion. It is, however, dishonest of the sceptic not to accept the evidence in cases – like the Rosenheim spuk – where this possibility seems remote.

Testing a theory

Sometimes, parapsychologists are able to refute sceptical arguments with a completeness that amounts to total devastation. It is a rare thing to find a sceptical counter-argument which is actually *testable*. Most sceptical comments on experimental work are vague, sometimes defamatory, or no more than assertion in the absence of any corroborating fact or logical derivation. Guy Lambert, the propounder of the 'geophysical theory' of poltergeists, cannot be accused on any of these counts. Lambert proposed that underground water channels – such as streams and sewers – may create poltergeist effects if they run beneath or close to the foundations of buildings. Specifically, when a head of water builds up in such channels, the building(s) may be subjected to spasmodic upward thrusts of physical force (known as water hammers). These in turn could produce, for example, strange movements of objects, as well as creaks and groans in the fabric which might be taken for poltergeist rappings. If Lambert were correct, we could expect to find a higher incidence of effects following abnormally high tides, downpours, or flooding. Later, Lambert suggested a second idea, that small local seismic disturbances – too minor to register on ordinary seismographs – might also contribute to poltergeist activity.

Such theories are not new: concern about underground water, in particular, goes back at least 200 years. Lambert's contribution was to collect evidence in a systematic way which allowed him to test these theoretical explanations. He found no difficulty in showing that *some* cases of poltergeist effects could be directly accounted for by subterranean events. In some other cases appearances *seemed* to support his geophysical theory (which is a quite different thing). There were, however, some mistakes in his logic. For example, Lambert showed that poltergeist cases tend to be clustered around coastal and tidal areas, where tidal effects would be strongest. Unfortunately, as critics pointed out, these are often regions of high population density (think of

When children are the centre of poltergeist activity, the presence of interested adult investigators like these can provide a tempting opportunity for a child to invent suitably dramatic effects.

London, for example). Of course there are more poltergeist cases in these areas – there are more people!

The first all-out attack on this theory was mounted by Dr Alan Gauld, a psychologist at the University of Nottingham, and Tony Cornell, a Cambridge graduate with many years' experience of poltergeist study. First, they attacked Lambert on *theoretical* grounds. Gauld and Cornell were prepared to accept that a very few, and minor, poltergeist effects – such as small-scale rapping noises and groans – could be the results of water hammers or subsidence. But, they pointed out, there were many problems with Lambert's theory, most notably the physically peculiar trajectories of objects moved by poltergeists – this could not be any simple vibratory force – and the seemingly purposive and intelligent nature of many poltergeist effects. Moreover, Gauld and Cornell argued, most houses were incapable of withstanding subterranean forces of the kind which would move objects around.

On this last point in particular, Gauld and Cornell were able to demonstrate physically that Lambert's theory did not work in practice. In 1961, they were lucky enough to get their hands (and instruments) on a number of structurally sound terraced houses in Cambridge which were scheduled for demolition. After extensive discussions with the Cambridge Borough Surveyor, members of the University Engineering Laboratories, and others, they were given permission to do what they liked with the houses. Equipment was brought in to produce physical forces of the kind which Lambert stated were responsible for poltergeist effects – except that the forces which Cornell and Gauld produced were far greater in intensity than the ones to which Lambert appealed to explain away poltergeist effects.

Even when producing vibrations in a house which were so strong that they could be felt two houses away by placing a hand on the wall, no movement of objects even remotely resembling poltergeist effects were observed at any time. Both horizontal and vertical vibratory effects were generated, and at the end they were so strong that Cornell commented 'You could actually hear the houses singing with the vibrations.' Despite this, nothing like a 'paranormal' movement was

Below: This machine is designed to measure PK effects associated with poltergeist activity.

Below right: Automatic cameras and recorders, vibration detectors and thermometers are all part of the poltergeist researcher's equipment.

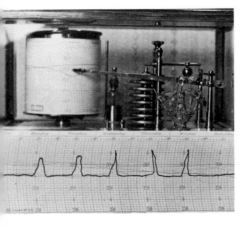

observed. Eventually, with the real risk of the houses collapsing or the equipment disintegrating, the researchers decided to conclude that Lambert's theory had been given a decent burial, and that if they went on any longer they would probably get one too.

The psychology of poltergeists

In discussing how parapsychologists investigate poltergeists we touched on psychological factors – like the desire for attention – which can make thorough investigation difficult. We now turn to a more detailed examination of the psychology of the individuals at the centre of well-attested poltergeist hauntings. For, with rare exceptions, poltergeist effects typically accompany a *focus* person, such as Annemarie Sch. or Julio in the cases we have already described. Does a focus person have a typical psychological profile? Is he or she more likely to be male, or female, extravert or introvert, neurotic or well-adjusted?

On the question of the sex of focus individuals, we can turn to the survey work of William Roll. At once, an intriguing fact emerges. In cases reported before 1900 some 80 per cent of focus people were female. But in this century the distribution has changed dramatically, and figures show that both sexes are equally afflicted by poltergeist activity. Roll also found that the average age of a poltergeist focus is 16 years. Here again, however, there has been a change for, in recent years, this average has climbed steadily until it now stands at 20 years.

Increasingly, the old as well as the young are found at the focus of poltergeist activity. Can this be related to the growing social isolation of old people?

'ESTHER COX, YOU ARE MINE TO KILL' AN ILLUSTRATIVE POLTERGEIST CASE

Just over 100 years ago, 18-year-old Esther Cox was the centre of a poltergeist case in Amherst, Canada. A plain and (allegedly) psychoneurotic girl, Esther lived at home in conditions of poverty, sharing a bed with her (attractive) sister Jane. When Jane's beau attempted to rape Esther, an outbreak of poltergeist effects ensued.

The Cox family had to cope with disturbances in the sister's bedroom : boxes were levitated and flew around, the bedclothes were flung from the bed, to an accompaniment of loud banging noises. A doctor was called to attend to the feverish Esther, and was confronted with the sight of writing appearing on the wall before his eyes : 'Esther Cox, you are mine to kill.' Later, as he stood in a doorway, plaster broke off another part of the wall and landed at his feet, having travelled *around a corner* to land there. The doctor also noted sounds which were so loud that they seemed like the pounding of the roof-shingles with a sledgehammer.

Esther started going into trances, and a minister who offered his services was greeted by a bucket of water becoming agitated and appearing to boil in Esther's presence. Fire-raising now entered the range of reported poltergeist effects and the Coxes' house was nearly razed to the ground.

A visiting magician, Walter Hubbell, visited the house several times and observed seven chairs falling over when he entered one room, and later suffered a number of abortive poltergeist assaults (knives were thrown at him). Hubbell's book about the case was a best-seller. Although the book is not fully reliable, the testimonies of the family, doctor and minister are difficult to ignore completely, and the case illustrates many of the 'classic' poltergeist effects.

This is largely due to an increasing proportion of focus people who are old – 70 years or more.

Nevertheless, it is still the case that most of those at the centre of poltergeist phenomena are children at or around the age of puberty. This fact may seem to support the traditional notion that sexual tension and frustration are the underlying cause of poltergeist manifestations – a notion fully exploited by the commercial cinema in such vulgar shockers as *The Exorcist* and *Carrie*. It was perhaps natural for early researchers to consider that puberty, sexual tension and the poltergeist were linked. So many poltergeists focused around girls at the age of puberty; sometimes, too, the effects included attacks with clear sexual, or masochistic, overtones. In fact, increasingly, poltergeist cases have come to involve boys and girls in more or less equal numbers, evidence which dilutes any possible link with frustrated *female* sexuality. Moreover, in many early reports (and today) it is the case that activity ceased spontaneously or after a few visits from a doctor or priest. Unless we assume gross professional malpractice on a grand scale, it is hard to see how such visits could resolve frustrated sexuality, although they might do much for a neglected child – a theme which we will need to develop.

First, however, we must deal with another popular explanation for the link between poltergeists and children. In many cases, poltergeist-afflicted children have been professionally examined by psychiatrists or

Below: The nineteenth-century Esther Cox case, with its violent and frightening effects, reads like a script for modern occult melodramas such as The Exorcist.

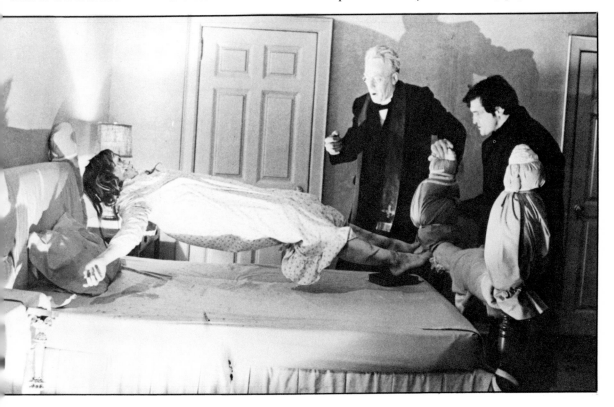

psychoanalysts, who have duly pronounced them to be suffering from one or more psychiatric ailments – hysteria, depression, over-aggression, under-aggression (leading to repression), neurosis and so on. A major problem with such diagnoses is that the consultant is likely to know why the child has been referred for examination – and is thus predisposed to find something wrong. Conversely, if the consultant is ignorant of the reason, he may diagnose the child as neurotic – but the child might be neurotic because of persecution by a poltergeist! The only clear way of telling would be to have a personality profile of the child before the outbreak of poltergeist activity. Examples of this are so rare that no coherent picture emerges of any psychological factors which might predispose children to poltergeist activity.

Much firmer evidence suggests that poltergeists are linked, not with sexual frustration or mental illness, but with a desire for attention. In a survey of young persons aged 18 and under who had been the focus of poltergeist events, William Roll made a remarkable discovery. No less than 62 per cent of them were living away from home when the outbreak began. Of the others, 17 per cent had only one parent living, or present in the home, at the time. These figures really do seem high – although we have no comparable figures for children in general. But this unstable/absent family background certainly lends support to the idea that poltergeists may be devices for gaining attention. Additional support may be provided by the sudden increase, since 1950, of poltergeist attacks focused on old people. Society's attitude to people of this age is notoriously more callous today than in earlier times.

Much work in this field needs to be undertaken. But for a possible psychological explanation of poltergeist effects, we think that the most fruitful approach would be to look at the need for attention against a deprived background. In the case of adolescents, the need for attention might be reinforced by the period of adolescence, itself a time of crisis and uncertainty. Obviously, however, this cannot be the complete explanation. Many children seek attention, but few generate poltergeist effects.

So, what can we learn from the poltergeist? It would be surprising if we got a neat, reliable, coherent story. For we deal here with PK at its most anarchic. We deal with uncontrolled environments in which we may be able to measure what is going on, but in which we cannot hope to control, predict, or manipulate events. This is spontaneous psi! The one thing we *do* learn is that there is a core of cases in which the evidence for PK is very strong (like the Rosenheim case). But the PK effects observed in these cases are too wild, too uncontrolled, too violent for us to be able to learn anything *systematic* about PK from poltergeist manifestations.

Nonetheless, we find in the poltergeist evidence for an effect of mind on matter which we might hope could be more positively used. We find affirmation of that hope when we look at the role of PK in faith healing.

The healing mind

The tradition of faith-healing is an ancient and persistent one. Claims

Right: The healing miracles of Jesus suggest powerful PK forces at work – stronger, it seems, than death itself. Far right: In modern times the shrine at Lourdes offers the hope of miraculous recovery to the sick and the dying.

Casting out devils: priests are still called upon to perform the ceremony of exorcism. Is this a form of faith-healing for mental rather than physical illness?

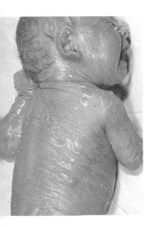

Crocodile skin (icthyosis), an incurable condition that has been successfully treated by hypnosis. It is difficult to disentangle the role of hypnotic suggestion from that of alleged PK in the cures brought about by faith-healers.

for 'miracle cures' are extravagant and hard evidence difficult to obtain. In essence, however, believers in faith-healing are certain that some individuals have the power to cure the sick purely through an act of will, without using medication, or even medical knowledge, of any sort. From the point of view of a parapsychologist, any power of the mind which claims to produce a direct effect in the physical world – in this case on the human body – is a candidate for the possible operation of PK. But can the alleged powers of faith-healers be tested scientifically? And, specifically, can we show that PK does, or does not, play a role in the cures wrought by faith-healers?

Even in the best-documented accounts of 'miraculous' cures, we cannot be sure that the initial diagnosis was correct, or that cures were not the long-term result of orthodox medical treatment. Moreover, we know that suggestion alone can have powerful – but certainly not paranormal – effects on the human body, as the following example shows.

In the *British Medical Journal*, Dr A. Mason reported the successful treatment by hypnosis of an intractable genetic illness. His patient was a boy suffering from a debilitating condition known as 'crocodile skin'. In such cases the skin is hard, brittle and breaks easily, causing suppuration and infection. There is no effective physical treatment known for this illness, and people who suffer from it generally die as a result of the perpetual infections they contract. Many different treatments had been tried on the boy, without success.

Before he began his treatment, Mason was well aware that, should he succeed, sceptics would wish to account for the cure in any way other than as the result of hypnosis. Accordingly, Mason arranged to hypnotise the boy and give the suggestion that the hard skin should disappear from *one arm only*. Remarkably enough, this is exactly what happened – strong evidence that hypnotic suggestion can work therapeutically and, even more important, specifically. Mason went on to clear up some 90 per cent of the affected areas of the boy's body in this way. Hypnotic suggestion had effectively cured an 'incurable' and crippling disease.

Testing a healer

How, then, to dispose of these problems – of diagnosis, evaluation, the long-term effects of previous treatment, the role of suggestion? For until we can rule them out, it will be very difficult to isolate an effect which we can be sure has been brought about by faith-healing and by no other cause. Bernard Grad, Professor of Psychiatry at McGill University, proposed an ingenious solution to the problem. He designed an experiment whereby relatively painless wounds were inflicted on laboratory mice which were then 'treated' by a faith-healer, Oskar Estabany.

Grad took a number of mice and, under anaesthetic, removed a small portion of skin from the back of each animal. The mice were then divided into a control group (whose wounds were allowed to heal naturally, without treatment) and the experimental group to be treated by Estabany. During the treatment, Estabany was allowed to do no more than touch the cages in which the mice were held. This is important, since it is known that handling and stroking will influence the physical processes of healing in wounded mice.

Under carefully controlled conditions – including a 'blind' measurement of the rate of recovery of both groups of wounded mice – Estabany's mice recovered notably faster than the control group. In another experiment, however, in which the cages were insulated under heavy bags, Estabany had no significant effect on the mice.

So far the evidence for any special powers possessed by Estabany was inconclusive – although the experimental method showed that it was, theoretically, possible to test for psi (PK) in a way that eliminated any psychosomatic factor in faith-healing. Much clearer results emerged from other experiments in which Estabany's effect on plants was tested. Grad prepared two groups of plants which were to be grown in chemical solutions. The control batch of plants was grown in a solution which was favourable for growth. The other batch was planted in a saline solution which might normally be expected to inhibit natural growth.

The plants were watered at regular intervals. In the case of the plants in the saline solution, Estabany 'treated' the water by holding the sealed flasks which contained it. The object of the experiment, of course, was to find out if the plants in the adverse growing medium would grow faster than might otherwise be expected. Grad was able to show, quite conclusively, that this is indeed what happened. Interestingly, Grad analysed samples of the 'treated' solutions and found no chemical changes which could explain the results: yet, clearly, Estabany *was* boosting the growth of plants in an environment which would normally be hostile to such growth. Here was sound evidence for a PK effect – not on the solution itself, but on the plants, *with which Estabany had no direct contact.*

Top to bottom: Day 10 and Day 14 of Grad's experiments with plants treated by Estabany. The batch marked with X contains the treated samples, the Y batch is the control.

Oskar Estabany, a faith-healer who demonstrated PK effects under laboratory conditions.

Estabany was again involved in a remarkable series of experiments conducted by Sister Justina Smith, head of the Chemistry and Physics departments at Rosary Hill College, Buffalo. These were designed to find out if Estabany could exert a PK effect on a very simple physical system, the activity of human enzymes. Enzymes are a category of proteins which, in the human body, subserve many vital functions. Essentially, they influence the rate of certain chemical reactions. Many enzymes speed up such reactions, while others are inhibitors: in general the system is one of delicately poised checks and balances. Enzymes are not themselves broken down by chemical reactions, but act as catalysts. To give an idea of how important enzyme activity is, if a few key enzymes stopped functioning in your body NOW, you would be dead before you finished reading this page.

Smith tested Estabany on his ability to influence the activity of one enzyme in particular, *trypsin*. This is a gut enzyme, involved in breaking down food: it is fairly easy to study since it can readily be prepared in a pure form, and the biochemical measures (*assays*) needed to evaluate its activity are relatively simple. Smith found that Estabany was able to influence the trypsin solution by increasing the activity of the enzyme. This was the case even though Smith had been careful to monitor the immediate environment of the trypsin for changes in temperature or magnetic field, both of which are known to affect the operation of the enzyme. No such changes took place, although Smith found that the PK effect on the trypsin was similar in power to that of a 13,000 gauss magnetic field.

Further evidence

In view of the clear-cut results obtained by Sister Smith, it is odd that there is only one reported attempt at replicating her experiments. This was by the American researcher Hoyt Edge, working with a faith-healer called Anne Gehman. In a series of rigorously controlled experiments, Edge obtained results that, while varying from experiment to experiment, nevertheless showed a definite, positive overall PK effect. As in Smith's experiments, Edge made careful comparisons between the effect on the trypsin solution of an artificially induced magnetic field, with that of the healer. He found, like Smith, that both magnetic fields and PK effects could influence the activity of an enzyme, a crucial chemical in the metabolism of the body. His healer did not produce results as strong and reliable as those Smith had obtained with Estabany, but they were still too strong to be attributed to chance alone.

As a footnote to Edge's work, it is interesting to note that on one occasion he found that the magnetic field he was using as a controlled effect completely failed to influence the trypsin activity. In other words, the normal effect of a simple physical variable was not repeatable on demand. When sceptics allege that findings in parapsychology are 'not repeatable', results like these are worth bearing in mind!

Of mice, fungus...

Another experiment, similar in some ways, was reported in 1971 by Graham and Anita Watkins, working in North Carolina. They anaesthetised mice, two at a time, and asked a person – viewing the sleeping mice from behind a thick glass screen – to concentrate on waking *one* of them, the left- or right-hand mouse, before the other. The 'target' mouse was decided upon at random. Their ten volunteer human subjects were either faith-healers or else had been successful in other PK experiments done in the laboratory. The results were very clear: the 'target' mice awoke notably earlier than the other mice. The odds-against-chance for the total result were some 100,000 to one.

This experiment was subsequently replicated by two other researchers, who did not find effects as remarkable in terms of power as the Watkins had. Nevertheless, their results, too, showed an effect which could not be put down to chance.

The Grad/Estabany experiments with plants, and the two experiments using anaesthetised mice, do show that humans can use PK to influence the activity of plants and animals. This is clearly very relevant to understanding faith-healing.

Other researchers have looked at such phenomena as PK effects on fungus growth, and have found that people can accelerate this growth by a simple act of will. One very recent American study found this to be the case even when the people concerned were at some distance from the laboratory where the samples of fungus were kept. In this experiment, volunteers at home simply concentrated on the idea of the fungus growing. There is a parallel here with 'absent healing' in the faith-healing tradition, where a healer concentrates on 'sending' healing 'energies' to a distant person. This study was divided into two parts, the first part of which was very highly successful, and the second part of which gave poor results (rather like Edge's experiment).

So, taking Grad's work, the experiments by Smith, Edge, the Watkins (and their replicating colleagues), and the fungus studies, we have a reasonable amount of evidence which points to an ability possessed by at least some people: the ability to influence organic systems by efforts of will. In other words, PK. Our survey hardly exhausts the evidence: for example, recent research in Texas with Matthew Manning has suggested that he may be able to slow the rate of disintegration of blood cells in weak salt solutions. Slowly but surely the evidence is building up.

... and men

It seems that human beings can exert measurable PK effects on simple systems such as bacteria, enzymes, yeasts and plants. Even mice, biologically far more complex, have responded to human PK. But what of human beings themselves? As we have seen, it is difficult to assess the possible role of PK in faith-healing. So researchers have tried to create a more simplified experimental framework by which to test the effect of human PK on other human beings.

Above: A PK experiment in progress. The woman in the background is trying to influence the choice of card by the receiver.

Below: Pet owners
crowd the waiting-room
of a faith-healer who
specialises in healing
animals. This power has
been demonstrated in the
laboratory.

Working in Tel Aviv, H. and S. Kreitler have tried to establish a possible PK effect on human perception. In their experiments a subject was presented with a well-known optical illusion, the Muller–Lyer arrow. At a different location a sender was shown slides of different aspects of the illusion in which either the top or bottom arrow seems longer. The slides were shown for only a very short period of time. Meanwhile the receiver was asked to report on which version of the illusion he was seeing. Could the sender influence the receiver to see the version presented on the slide? Evidence from this and other experiments indicates that, under certain conditions, this did occur.

Even more interesting results have been reported by Elmar Gruber of Freiburg University. His subjects (the receivers) were told only that they would be taking part in an experiment relating to movement under stress conditions. Each one was fitted with opaque glasses and headphones through which filtered white noise was related and invited to walk at random around a suitably padded room. Gruber had arranged for a light beam to be projected down the middle of the room so that every time a subject crossed the beam a click would be heard in a set of headphones to be worn by a sender. The sender was instructed to concentrate on getting as many clicks as possible (that is, to make the subject move around the room as much as possible). This took place only for a randomly decided 50 per cent of the experiment: during the other 50 per cent, no clicks were delivered and the sender was asked to cease attempting to influence the subject in any way.

Meanwhile a machine registered *all* crossings of the beam. If PK was operating, the subject might be expected to make more crossings in the PK condition than in the control condition – which is exactly what happened.

There are not many experiments of this type available for us to examine, but the ones we can look at do provide encouraging evidence for the proposition that one human being can influence the behaviour of another by PK. We can go on from there to ask if one person can affect another's *physiology*, the operation of the physical processes of the body, by PK?

Brain waves

Researchers have approached this question by testing possible PK effects on a single human physical variable such as heart rate, skin conductance or brain activity. Targ and Puthoff, best known for their remote-viewing (ESP at a distance) research and their work with Uri Geller, have investigated the last possibility. A receiver, who knew nothing of the true purpose of the experiment, had his brain activity measured by an EEG. In another place a sender, also connected to an EEG, was subjected to a flashing stroboscopic light set at a particular frequency which had the effect of altering his brain activity. With two people in particular Targ and Puthoff found evidence to suggest that the brain waves of the receiver altered to resemble those of the sender.

As yet there is little evidence from other workers to show that human measurable body activities can be influenced by PK. A really massive effect was reported by a pseudonymous Canadian researcher known only as Lloyd, who received much publicity in the fringe press. He claimed that, in a similar experiment to that of Targ and Puthoff, his receiver's EEG had altered as though he had actually *seen* the flashing light. Unfortunately for 'Lloyd' his experimental methods were totally discredited by Brian Millar of the University of Utrecht. No evidence of the effect was found when Millar repeated Lloyd's experiment under sound conditions.

Nevertheless, there is room for hope. So far, much of the research in this area has been crude in nature, while different research methods have been used by different researchers. When more standardised and correct methods are adopted we might realistically hope for something different.

PK and organic systems: a summary

What conclusions *can* we draw at this stage about PK effects on organic systems – be they humans, mice, bacteria, plants, or enzymes? So far as humans are concerned, the evidence, such as it is, is equivocal. The experiments reviewed above (except Lloyd) have shown results – but we cannot be sure the effects observed are due to PK. They might equally be the result of ESP whereby the receiver unconsciously detects the intention of the sender and responds to it.

In other cases – such as the experiments on enzymes – we can be more confident about asserting a purely PK effect. Based on the evidence we have, then, the following conclusions seem reasonable:

1. At least some people can influence the rate of growth of (at least some) plants by PK.
2. At least some people can influence the behaviour, and possibly the physiology, of (at least some) animals by PK.
3. At least some people can influence the activity of organic molecules by PK.

If PK does seem to be able to affect organic systems, what of its possible operation upon the world of inanimate matter. The work of Helmut Schmidt has already given us one example of human PK action on inert matter. We now need to explore this further, for most PK research has concentrated on this area.

Tumbling dice

In the course of his pioneering work on ESP, J. B. Rhine met a gambler who started him off on PK research. The man told Rhine that dice throwers who played craps and similar games occasionally felt capable of influencing the fall of the dice by an effort of will. Rather than dismissing the possibility as a gambler's fantasy, Rhine, an open-minded man, decided that it merited serious investigation. He and his colleagues spent nine years in testing for PK effects on thrown dice before they published their results. Rhine was fighting enough battles to get ESP accepted without rushing into print on the PK front as well!

Influencing inert matter by PK: a volunteer attempts to affect the random fall of marbles into numbered slots.

The essence of Rhine's experiments was very simple. One or more dice were thrown, while the subject was asked to concentrate on making them fall so that a particular face or faces would be uppermost. With any one die, the normal odds of this happening by chance are one in 6, since there are six faces on each die. As time went by, Rhine tightened up his experimental procedures. He was aware that the commercial dice that he used were not true. The hollowed spots on the faces biased the dice slightly in favour of the 6-face. Rhine countered this with the 'Sevens Method'. Subjects were asked to try to influence *two* dice at a time to produce a total score of seven on the two faces uppermost. To do this, the subject must score one low face and one high face: $1 + 6$, $2 + 5$, or $3 + 4$. No dice bias could explain higher-than-chance success in this experiment – but several such successes were recorded by Rhine and others.

Another source of bias in the early work was that subjects were allowed to throw the dice manually. Rhine later developed machines which projected the dice into ribbed chutes. Subsequent workers introduced photographic recording of the dice tests as a way of eliminating human bias and error.

Surveying his first 20 experiments, Rhine found that, despite possible flaws in the early work, many of them had produced scoring rates higher than 16.67 per cent, the 1-in-6 chance level. However, it was a second pattern of evidence that triggered the publication of his work. The standard record sheets used by Rhine and his colleagues were divided into quarters: first, second, third and fourth, from the beginning to the end of a dice PK session. A subsequent analysis of these sheets by Rhine and Betty Humphrey showed a progressive decline in scoring rates from the first to the fourth quarter which held true for 18 experiments. The odds against this 'quarter decline' being the product of chance alone were over 100 million to one! The picture was absolutely clear-cut: the odds far exceeded any possible effect due to bias in the dice, or any distortion caused by the analytical method used. The quarter-decline (QD) factor, alone, presented fairly strong evidence for the operation of PK in this work. In 1962 a hostile survey from the psychologist Edward Girden pointed at many weaknesses in the early dice-PK experiments. Although not entirely justified, Girden's criticisms had the effect of discouraging work in the field for some time.

More recent experiments have concentrated on examining the effects of such variables as the number of dice used, their size, and the distance of the subject from the dice. Some of these will be reviewed in Chapter 9. At this point, however, it is worth asking whether factors known to have an effect on ESP – belief, personality, the reduction of sensory stimulation – have similar effects on PK.

We have some evidence on these matters from dice-PK research conducted sporadically over the years since Rhine's work. Further evidence, some confirmatory, some contradictory come, together with new information, from research into PK using Schmidt REG machines and their successors. How do the findings from PK research compare with the strongest and most stable findings from the ESP experiments we have reviewed in this volume?

Belief and PK It must be said here that evidence is thin and contradictory. Two recent experiments have found that successful performance in PK tests *did* correlate positively with a belief in ESP to an extent too great to be ascribed to chance. On the other hand, four other experiments (three of them over 20 years old) which examined PK performance relative to belief in PK found no positive correlation. Further work here depends on more reliable ways of measuring the strength of subjects' belief, or disbelief, in PK.

Personality and PK The paucity of experimental work in this area gives us very little to go on. In Argentina, Mischo and Weis have recorded one series of PK tests which gave a strong indication that successful scoring was positively linked with sociability – a characteristic of the extravert personality. Another series of tests, however, produced no positive results. Two experiments conducted by Sargent found no relationship between extraversion and scoring. On the other hand, these experiments, in which a Schmidt machine was used, produced a rather odd result. As long as the machine ticked over alone, or only Sargent was present, the machine delivered random pulses to its four channels, as it was designed to do. When it was being used to test subjects, on the other hand, it delivered many more pulses to channel 3 than chance would predict. And, interestingly, this effect was most marked when extravert subjects were being tested.

Three experiments, one by Mischo and Weis, two by Sargent, have shown a correlation between a negative PK effect and neuroticism. On the whole, though, there really is very little evidence as to links between personality and performance in PK experiments. What there is tends to confirm that factors such as extraversion and neuroticism, which are known to affect success in ESP experiments, also play a part in PK. At least, no findings point clearly the other way.

Altered states and PK Rhine himself found no evidence that hypnosis had any effect on PK. Only three experiments on sleep-PK have been carried out and, again, they found no clear effect. As far as we are aware, no Ganzfeld experiments have been conducted in this area. On the other hand, work by Schmidt, William Braud, and Honorton has shown reasonably clearly that the action of meditation does appear to generate successful PK performance. At the same time, however, even meditators who are good PK subjects seem unable to control PK effects. Sometimes, when asked to produce a PK effect above chance, meditators have in fact produced results significantly *below* chance. The picture here, then, remains a confused one.

An important experiment by Honorton seemed at first to suggest that muscle tension in subjects favoured above-chance scores, while relaxation produces below-chance results. Interestingly, though, Honorton himself, when tested, duplicated his subjects' results, but showed a much stronger effect. Honorton has suggested that perhaps *all* the results were due to him. Did the subjects cause the PK effects, or

Rhine's PK work with dice started out as testing a gambler's intuition and ended up putting experimental PK research on the map.

Baffled TV presenter David Dimbleby examines a less-than-useful doorkey on the programme which introduced Yuri Geller to British television audiences.

was the experimenter responsible for them? (The implications of this question, which Rhine termed the *indeterminacy problem*, will be discussed in detail in Chapter 9. In essence, the central concept of the indeterminacy problem is that, in psi experiments, one cannot be *absolutely certain* where the psi came from, even when significant psi effects are present.)

In addition to Honorton's experiment there is evidence from William Braud and Rex Stanford. Braud found that subjects produced superior PK effects while in a passively relaxed state, than when asked to concentrate on doing mathematical and logical tasks. Stanford and others have reported an intriguing variation of this comparison. Subjects were asked to try very hard to bias a Schmidt machine. They were then told to stop, as if the test was over. In fact, the Schmidt machine was left running. In these experiments the PK effects were generally poor when the subject was trying, but were good immediately the effort had stopped. This 'release-of-effort effect' certainly tallies with the states of mind known to be favourable to ESP, in which self-consciousness and tension are reduced to a minimum. The Cambridge psychologist Robert Thouless has gone so far as to say that the perfect state of mind for getting successful PK is summed up by 'I want to succeed but I don't really care whether I do or not.'

To summarise, then, we can say that the bulk of the evidence from 'altered-state' experiments suggests that conditions which favour successful ESP performance also favour successful PK performance. The effects on PK of personality and belief, on the other hand, are much less clear, owing largely to a shortage of experimental work on the subject.

Jean-Paul Girard, the French metal-bender, has reportedly bent metal bars sealed in glass tubes.

Metal-bending: fact or fiction?

Finally we have to consider the most controversial of all alleged PK effects – the paranormal bending of metal by acts of will. As we shall see, the term metal-*bending* is something of a misnomer since other effects – churning, fracturing, and hardening – have been reported.

On 23 November 1973, BBC Television, in Britain, screened a programme featuring Uri Geller, a young Israeli plucked from the obscurity of second-rate amateur conjuring shows by a maverick American scientist/inventor, Andrija Puharich. Watched by a large studio audience (including John Taylor, Mathematics Professor at King's College, London, who was invited along to be the 'scientific hatchet man', as he put it), Geller appeared to bend keys and cutlery paranormally and, seemingly inexplicably, restarted watches which were said to be broken. Viewers wrote in to say how, when Geller was on television, cutlery had bent in their own homes, long-stopped grand-father clocks burst into fits of chiming, and objects moved around seemingly of their own accord. Media men rushed in to sign Geller up to participate in (travesties of) experiments on ESP with the general public. The Geller craze was born.

There is a vast smoke-screen of irrelevant and obscuring events surrounding Geller and his career. These include accusations and counter-accusations, rumour, innuendo, 'confessions' by members of the Geller entourage (who were well paid for this), assertions by Puharich that Geller's powers are controlled by super-intelligent beings lurking in UFOs, as well as magicians who claim they can duplicate all of Geller's feats, other magicians who deny this, and on and on and on. What is in very short supply is data from controlled scientific experiments, and the handful of these offered for scrutiny by Geller's acolytes are not impressive. Which is why we shall leave Geller in the world of the circus and look at some infinitely more impressive research from a number of sources. Some has been conducted by Professor John Hasted at Birkbeck College in London, some by Drs Crussard and Bouvaist in France, while very recent Japanese research, too, has added to the picture.

First, we might examine some reported metal-bending effects which on face value look to be strong evidence for PK. Later, we can examine some very subtle effects which would appear to reduce the possibility of fraud or error to vanishing-point.

A selection of metal-bending effects produced by children at Professor John Hasted's laboratory, Birkbeck College, London. The scale in the foreground is in centimetres.

(1) *Sealed-tube bending*: Crussard and Bouvaist have been able to record bending of metal strips in *completely sealed* glass tubes with the French metal-bender Jean-Paul Girard. Hasted and others have examined the French experimental methods and have concluded that all chance of fraud could be eliminated.

(2) *PK action at several locations simultaneously*: Hasted, working with (generally juvenile) metal-benders, has attempted to detect any PK 'force' by using strain-gauges. These, mounted in metal strips, will produce electrical signals (linked to a chart recorder) if there is any bending of the metal strip. On frequent occasions, using several such gauges, set up considerable distances apart, Hasted has been able to record synchronous signals from two, three or more of them. This would not be possible to effect fraudulently without some mechanical contrivance (which would hardly go unnoticed by observers). As to other possible causes, one of us has verified that vibrations, whether distant or close by, have no effect on the strain gauges, and no electrical problems would appear to be capable of producing these effects.

(3) *PK action beyond the limit of human physical strength*: Hasted and the French workers have both been able to obtain bending of metal rods which would require a force in excess of physical strength. Crussard was able to videotape one session in which Girard can be seen to be simply gently stroking the metal – yet the deformation produced was found to require *three times* the limit of physical strength.

(4) *'Impossible' PK effects*: Hasted has reported two devastatingly simple tests for 'impossible' PK. One test employed a brittle alloy bar which *cannot* be bent to a particular angle of deformation in less than a certain known time: if any excessive force is applied it simply breaks. The only way to bend it is by applying a small load continuously over

time, which produces a bend by a process known as 'creep' (which, as the name suggests, is a slow business). Yet Hasted reports bending of such alloys in well under the minimum time thought to be possible using a 'creep' process.

Another apparently 'impossible' PK effect is the so-called 'plastic deformation'. Hasted has reported a case in which a metal-bender gave him a spoon after gently stroking it, and 'It was as though the bent part of the spoon was as soft as chewing-gum', which Hasted verified by gently manipulating the spoon. Hasted states that 'I do not think there can be any question of fraud when a really plastic bend is produced under close scrutiny.' Such an effect could occur if corrosive chemicals (such as mercuric salts) were applied to the metal. These, however, are not only highly poisonous, but had they been applied, would have discoloured the metal. There would also have been a loss in weight due to the corrosion. Hasted weighed this spoon before and after bending and found no weight loss.

Such evidence as this cannot be dismissed easily. When we consider the techniques of the French researchers, we realise that we are no longer in Gellerland. Crussard and Bouvaist are funded by a French metals company and, when examining metal-bending effects on any particular strip or rod of metal, the following experimental measurements are taken of the hallmarked samples:

(i)   All dimensions are measured, before and after bending.
(ii)   The micro-hardness of the metal is measured at several points, again both before and after bending.
(iii) Residual strain profiles (a measure of crystalline structure) are examined.
(iv)   Electron micrograph analyses of fine structure of ultra-thin foil specimens are often made.
(v)   Analyses of chemical composition at various places along the strip or rod are made.

The results of plastic deformation in metal cutlery produced by one of Hasted's juvenile subjects.

Now this is a formidable battery of tests and some very subtle effects, virtually impossible to fake (perhaps even completely impossible for the metal-bender to fake alone), have been recorded. A few of them can be mentioned here.

(1) Both the French researchers and Hasted have reported local hardening of areas of metal specimens, even in some cases where no bending has taken place. Japanese researchers have also reported a few such occurrences. In one of these cases of 'anomalous hardening', the properties of the metal strip are stated by Hasted to be like those of 'a strip exposed to crushing by a weight of five tons'. However – and this is intriguing – the pattern of strain and local dislocations in the metal are *not* what one would expect from application of a large external force. It appears that what is going on here is some *internal* stress in the metal.

(2) Crussard and Bouvaist have reported an astonishing case in which a metal strip was bombarded with radioactive cesium atoms, and – after bending – was found on examination to have a *different distribution*

of the cesium within the strip to that originally observed. It is as if the very atoms of cesium were translocated within the strip.

(3) Work with Girard has also produced particular changes in aluminium strips which are typical of high-temperature ($625\,^{\circ}C$) reactions, and can only be detected by careful metallurgical analysis.

Other remarkable effects could be mentioned, but are also rather technical in nature. As a parting shot, it is worth noting that for most of the findings reported, the metal samples employed were identifiable by hallmarks so that no substitution could have been effected.

What are we to make of this? Certainly, we are not metallurgists and we cannot appraise the more subtle of the reported effects. There may be differences of opinions amongst metallurgists concerning the techniques, or the interpretation of findings, or both, and we cannot judge the results as presented. Other effects, however (most notably the use of the brittle alloys and the use of several strain-gauges) appear to be extremely simple research techniques which have produced quite clear-cut evidence of PK. Certainly some researchers have (usually without ever having seen Hasted's apparatus) hummed and ha'd about the possibility of equipment error, but we are not aware of any explanation of the strain-gauge readings in terms of artefacts of measurement. The ball is firmly in the critics' court at this time.

PK: a summary

The evidence for the existence of PK (although there remains some yet to be examined) is not as strong as the evidence for the existence of ESP, but at least in part that is because less research has been done on PK. Nonetheless the evidence that does exist is extensive and some of it of a very high quality. It would be difficult for a reasonable man, looking at all the evidence, to reject the view that PK does exist.

So far as the psychology of PK goes, the evidence is weak, again because of a lack of research. What one might hope for is that PK effects would tell us something about the *physics* of psi and the kinds of forces involved. Hasted and others, in their research on metal-bending, have something to say about this, and the recent research using Schmidt machines for examining PK is also relevant. However, before examining the physics of psi – ways in which these effects might work – it is necessary to examine one final area of parapsychological enquiry of great interest and importance. So far we have been concerning ourselves with studies on psi which have used individuals and groups making some kind of *conscious effort* to use psi (D. D. Home and poltergeists apart). However, in real life people do *not* make any effort to use psi: it simply happens. Research in the last decade has bridged the gap between these two areas by examining the ability of individuals to use psi in laboratory settings without making any effort to use it – simply because they are unaware that they are being tested for psi! Such experiments have yielded challenging evidence of spontaneous psi, as we shall now see.

Metal bending at a distance. This single large crystal of aluminium was twisted out of shape at a distance of more than 30 feet by Andrew G., a 12-year-old subject in the Hasted experiments. The strain gauges attached to the crystal provide an extremely accurate measure of the degree of twisting involved.

New directions in psi-testing

A problem which worries many people who have had what they feel to have been psi experiences is this: although they see the scientific research, and intellectually accept the findings which go to support the existence of psi, they feel that 'laboratory psi' is somehow different from their own spontaneous, emotional experience. For example, in most of the experiments we have described so far, people have been asked to use any psi abilities they might possess to perform particular tasks. This conscious use of psi contrasts sharply with reports of spontaneous psi experiences in which individuals were definitely not consciously seeking to exercise psi powers. The objection is an important one, and we would want to answer it at both a general and a particular level. The general point is that there has always been a close relationship between scientific study and spontaneous cases. In fact it is precisely because of the power and strangeness of such cases that scientists have felt a responsibility to investigate psi scientifically. More particularly, there have been experiments in which people have been tested for psi without their knowledge that this was being done. Under these conditions, we argue, workers are getting closer to testing spontaneous psi in the laboratory.

Coincidences happen to everyone. But are we unconsciously engineering them by our own psi abilities?

Psi for everyone

The American parapsychologist Rex Stanford has expressed a particularly interesting view on this issue. He suggests that *everyone* may have psi powers which operate below the threshold of normal consciousness. Even more startlingly, he has proposed that people may be unconsciously using these powers all the time in order to search the world for information which is to their advantage. For example, most people have experienced unexpected but useful coincidences. Might it be, Stanford asks, that the 'coincidences' are due not to chance but to the individual's psi abilities gleaning information and manipulating events so that all parties to the coincidence will be in the right place at the right time? He refers to this kind of process as the Psi-mediated Instrumental Response (PMIR). And, since the heart of his argument is that the psi activities take place without the conscious intention of the individual concerned, he calls them *non-intentional* psi.

Stanford suggests that, through non-intentional psi, individuals unconsciously meet certain important needs (which he calls *dispositions*). ESP, for example, might be used to sort out relevant information: other aspects of psi – PK perhaps – might be deployed to do something with that information which would satisfy some need. Strange as it may seem, it is perfectly possible to test Stanford's theory scientifically. More strangely still, the results of such experiments, far from disproving the theory, go some way to support it!

'Seven hours to go . . .': experiments show that people can use psi to escape from tedious tasks.

For example, in 1971 James Carpenter, a psychologist at Duke University, performed the following ESP experiment. He divided his subjects into two groups according to whether, in a preliminary test, they showed high or low levels of anxiety. They were told that they were taking part in a standard ESP test for clairvoyance, in which they would be asked to guess at ESP cards presented to them in sealed envelopes. What the subjects did not know was that, for half the test material, the ESP cards weren't the only objects inside the envelopes. Carpenter had put in a selection of pornographic pictures as well! Analysing the results, Carpenter found that the high-anxiety group of subjects scored better when the envelopes held only the ESP cards, while the low-anxiety group scored better when the pornographic pictures were included. Surprisingly, the subjects had responded quite clearly, and in quite different ways, to information of which they could not possibly have had any knowledge.

Other researchers, notably Martin Johnson, Professor of Parapsychology at the University of Utrecht, have been able to repeat Carpenter's findings in similar experiments. Yet, it can be argued, the subjects knew that they were involved in ESP tests, even though they didn't know about the particular aspects for which they were, in fact, being tested. An even more convincing case for non-intentional psi could be made if similar results emerged from experiments in which people have no idea at all that they are being tested for ESP.

Stanford himself reported just such a study conducted in 1970. In this experiment, volunteers were asked to listen to a tape-recorded account of a dream and then, later, to answer questions about it. The camouflaged, ESP component of the experiment was that there were certain target answers and certain non-target answers. That is, Stanford wanted to see if non-intentional ESP would help his volunteers to answer the target questions *correctly* and the non-target questions *incorrectly*. For this to happen ESP would have to affect the memories of the subjects in such a way as to, where necessary, suppress an accurate recall in favour of an incorrect answer, just as, with other questions, it would have to boost flagging memories in order to provide the correct answer. The results showed very clearly that the way in which memory worked was affected by ESP even in conditions where people had no notion that they were being tested for ESP at all.

Many experiments of this kind have been published, enough to lend strong support to the first part of Stanford's PMIR theory. In the form of a proposition the theory has three main planks:

1. PEOPLE CAN USE ESP IN EXPERIMENTS WITHOUT ANY CONSCIOUS AWARENESS THAT THEY ARE DOING SO, AND WITHOUT ANY INTENTION OF USING IT.

2. ESP CAN BE USED, WITHOUT INTENTION OR AWARENESS, TO FULFIL NEEDS.

3. PK, LIKE ESP, CAN ALSO BE USED, WITHOUT INTENTION OR AWARENESS, TO FULFIL NEEDS.

ESP and human needs

A crucial component of Stanford's theory is the question of need – a term that he deliberately leaves undefined. For most people 'needs' are synonymous with bodily needs – for food, drink, warmth, shelter, sex and so on. But individuals make far more complex demands on the world than this narrow definition allows for. In more recent writings, Stanford uses the word 'disposition' – a term which takes account of needs arising from life in society as well as from the demands of the physical organism.

Some extremely interesting work has been done on the question of the relationship of human needs to the operation of non-intentional ESP by Martin Johnson, Bill Braud, Ramakrishna Rao and Ephraim Schechter. All used various refinements of one type of experiment. In it, students are asked to sit an academic examination for which some of the answers are provided in sealed envelopes attached to the answer papers. The object of the experiment is to see whether the examination candidates do significantly better on the questions for which the sealed answers were provided. In all the experiments for which rigorous criteria have been observed, these researchers have discovered that the students do indeed score higher on these questions.

Rex Stanford, American parapsychologist, argues that everyone has psi ability.

Bill Braud's 1975 experiment is a particularly satisfying and elegant demonstration of these results. Braud put students through a three-part examination, thus:

Part 1: 16 questions about definitions.
Part 2: 14 short essay questions. For seven of these (randomly chosen for each student) 'hidden answers' were supplied, so that the information could have been acquired by ESP and used in a good essay performance.
Part 3: A conscious, intentional ESP test.

The possible marks for parts 2 and 3 were 76 points and 12 points respectively, so that the motivation for success in the non-intentional ESP test was greater than in the open ESP test. Braud's findings confirmed that average marks for the target questions significantly exceeded those for the others.

Sex and money

Given that experiments suggest that ESP can be linked to specific needs, we will certainly want to know whether the strength of the ESP effect varies in proportion to the strength of the need. Regrettably, few experiments of this type have been conducted, but one conducted by Stanford himself is worth mentioning. He selected a group of men and subjected them to a word-association 'test'. If any of them produced a particular (very fast or very slow) response to a randomly chosen 'key' word, he was invited to take part in another experiment. Naturally, the subjects did not know this when they took the word-association test: nor could they know that in the further experiment they would be invited to rate photographs of a number of young women in various stages of undress in order of sexual attractiveness. Moreover, Stanford iced the cake by having half the group tested in the word-association section by a male experimenter while the other half were tested by a woman. He reasoned that, if tested by a woman, the men's sexual needs might be encouraged and that the ESP effect might be correspondingly stronger. In prospect, non-intentional ESP would work in the following ways: in the first place, the subject would gather unconsciously that there would be a pleasant reward for choosing the 'right' response in the preliminary test. Secondly, ESP would furnish the right response to make in order to get the reward. In the event, the results were exactly in line with Stanford's expectation. Men generally did produce a very fast or very slow reaction to the key word much more often than chance would have predicted, and they did especially well when tested by a woman.

This, and other experiments of the same type, support the second part of Stanford's proposition, that

2. ESP CAN BE USED, WITHOUT INTENTION OR AWARENESS, TO FULFIL NEEDS: THE STRONGER THE NEED, THE STRONGER THE ESP.

Passing exams might be a lot easier if psi were working for you all the time. In ESP tests disguised as academic examinations, candidates did significantly better on questions for which hidden answers were supplied – answers which they could only have got through ESP!

If all of us have psi abilities, why don't we win every time we go gambling? Stanford suggests that competing motivations – the fact that everybody else wants to win as well – may be the problem.

However, there are limits. We know from work in experimental psychology that if the strength of need is very high, behaviour becomes disorganised and performance breaks down. Parapsychologists would generally think it somewhat difficult, and almost certainly ethically wrong, to conduct experiments under such conditions. What we can do, however, is to look at needs which conflict. For Stanford makes the important point that where needs are very strong, but accompanied by feelings of conflict or guilt, the ESP effects may be reduced. We may even find negative effects – psi-missing. Interestingly enough, the only case of psi-missing with a non-intentional test comes from an experiment by Sargent in which monetary reward was used as an incentive. Taken overall, the group of subjects scored strongly *below* chance – a comforting result for those who take an optimistic view of human nature! There is also some work by Stanford that suggests that non-intentional psi can be used in the service of altruistic needs.

Non-intentional PK

So, to the third and final aspect of the core of Stanford's theory. The first two parts hold up well. ESP *can* be used without awareness or intent, and it seems particularly likely to do so in the service of some need. The final aspect is the involvement of PK, the notion that if nothing else can do the job, PK can be deployed.

In all the previous PMIR experiments, a simple motor action – writing the right examination question, making the right kind of response in a word-association test – could do what was needed. In the most elegant of Stanford's experiments, such an action would *not* be enough, only PK would do.

Forty people – all males – were tested in this experiment. The first thing they were asked to do was a test of conscious PK for three minutes, working with a machine rather like a Schmidt machine. Next, they were told they would be doing a psychology experiment on the co-ordination of movement. This, technically known as a *pursuit rotor tracking* experiment, involved keeping a small pointer or some similar instrument in the middle of a track which moved slightly from side to side. Stanford set the movement of the track to be very slow, so that the task would be very tedious. The unfortunate volunteers were told to expect 45 minutes of this misery.

Meanwhile, unknown to the volunteers, and at some distance from them, Stanford had set up a random event generator (REG). This produced ten pulses every ten seconds, divided between six different channels. The machine ticked over whilst the people were doing their pursuit rotor tracking. Now, if at any time the machine produced at least seven out of ten pulses on just one of the six channels, which is a pretty unlikely thing to happen (and we know exactly how unlikely it is), the man doing the rotor tracking was stopped and taken to another room – to look at erotic photographs instead.

Now we must look at what's behind this. An experiment has been set up in which people are being bored out of their wits. If a machine, in some distant place, does something very unusual and strange, they will escape their boredom and do something pleasant instead. If they do not, they are condemned to stay with the boring experiment.

So: the primary need is to escape. They *can* get out if the machine does something odd but, since they're not told about that, they must use ESP to find out. Finally, since the probability of the machine doing that something odd by chance alone is pretty small, the only real chance of escape they have is to use PK to make the machine do that something odd. So, the complete formula: need-related ESP and PK, all without any awareness or intention.

The results of the experiment were completely clear-cut. The subjects performed only slightly above chance on the first stage – the conscious PK test. On the non-intentional PK test, though, they scored well above chance. If chance alone had been at work, only 7.20 per cent of the volunteers would have escaped; in fact, 20 per cent did so. This experiment is a clear demonstration that people can use ESP and PK together, without any conscious intention of doing so, in order to satisfy some need.

There is evidence, then, for the third and final proposal of the PMIR notion, namely:

3. BOTH ESP AND PK CAN BE USED, WITHOUT AWARENESS AND INTENTION, TO SATISFY NEEDS.

What limits are there?

A common-sense question would be, 'If non-intentional psi really works, why aren't we getting what we want all the time?' The first problem, surely, is that of competing motivations. Generally, if some-

A man might use spontaneous psi to bring about a meeting with a woman who attracts him.

thing is desirable, many people pursue it, and therefore one person's PMIR may be in competition with that of another.

The second problem – already mentioned in passing – is that if a need or desire is very strong, rather than enhancing performance it destroys it: the organisation of behaviour becomes weak and integration is lost. True, the evidence for this happening in parapsychology experiments is absent, but most researchers would have considerable ethical qualms about inducing need to such an extent in the laboratory. Psychologists, however, have amassed plenty of evidence to show that behaviour is disrupted by very high levels of need.

The third point is that certain attitudes, and personality characteristics, are known in the case of intentional ESP in particular to generate poor performance, even negative scoring (psi-missing). Stanford argues that it is extremely likely that the effect of these factors will be the same for non-intentional psi as it is for intentional psi. Sceptics, introverts, and neurotics may deliberately inhibit or distort psi. As an example, Stanford suggests that a neurotic man might well use PMIR to engineer an encounter with a pretty woman, but not so far as to bring about a real possibility of sexual involvement, since he is too anxious about sex to wish for that to happen in a wholehearted way. If there is a conflict, anxiety, guilt, repression – then PMIR is likely to be systematically distorted.

In addition to all these points, Stanford pulled together many different research findings and, together with Bill Braud, has developed a line of thinking which may promise to link over into the physics of psi. We know that situational factors (such as competing motivations) may inhibit PMIR and that personality problems (like neuroticism) may even produce systematic distortion of PMIR. But there are also certain features of the human brain and the way we typically perceive and respond which may also tend to inhibit PMIR fairly strongly. We need to look at these, since they show some fine-grain detail of the way ESP and PK interact with other mental systems and will produce some intriguing analogies with the approaches physicists are taking to the whole problem of psi.

Psi and the de-structured brain

As part of his overall psi research, Stanford looked again at the favourable effect on ESP detected during altered states of consciousness. As we have already seen, Honorton, by treating ESP pragmatically as though it were some sort of weak sense, was able to develop the Ganzfeld technique. In the Ganzfeld environment ESP seemed to function more reliably when external 'noise' was reduced to a low level. However, whether those ESP effects are positive (above chance) or negative (below chance) may depend on other factors such as personality and environment. Stanford suggests that the reason that the Ganzfeld and other ESP-favourable states work is because they encourage brain activity to become less predictable, less coherent and structured.

Stanford was led to his position by a number of experiments that he and other workers conducted in the 1960s using the Rhine card-guessing technique. He found that there was a distinction between those people who tended to balance the number of different guesses, and those who made their guesses in a more uneven and spontaneous manner. The distinction can be difficult to draw because people do tend, on the average, to balance out their guesses between the possible alternatives. But an extreme version of this would be to call each of the five different card symbols five times each – something that happens more often than chance would lead one to expect. Stanford and other researchers found that people who balanced their guesses as symmetrically as this, tended to show extremely weak scoring in terms of the power of the ESP effect. Less-balanced guessers showed stronger ESP effects: sometimes above chance, sometimes below.

From these results, it seemed that people who guess according to a strongly constrained, fixed type of sequence show weak ESP effects. Might it be that those states which favour ESP do so because they break up patterns of responding? In other experiments, Stanford and others looked at a second type of bias that occurs when people guess at cards. For those who don't balance their calls perfectly, there is usually a tendency to make some responses more than others: 'Circle', for instance, tends to be a popular guess. If playing cards were used instead, for example, the Ace of Spades is likely to be guessed rather more than one time in 52. In picture-guessing, as well, there are certain rather popular themes and others which are much more rare. Guesses, then, can be divided into two types: common and rare. Technically, they are often referred to as high-bias and low-bias responses. Drawing on his own experiments, together with published and unpublished work, Stanford found that people scored higher when they made a

low-bias response than when they made a high-bias response. This finding has held up very well indeed over the years. The most recent review of the evidence, reinforced by more recent experiments, has confirmed the consistency of the pattern identified by Stanford.

This pattern is a commonplace of psychological testing. It has long been known that responses which people make very readily are more prone to error than ones they make rarely. It is as though in order to make an unusual response one actually needs more information – and is, in the event, less likely to jump to false conclusions.

Now, we noted that certain altered states of consciousness – hypnosis, Ganzfeld and the rest – do generally produce results well above chance. Stanford suggests that this might be because these states influence the brain away from normal, structured activity towards an increasing unpredictability and randomness. In altered states, then, the low-bias response might actually become more common – resulting in better performance. If so, we would have a satisfyingly complete account of why altered states are ESP-favourable.

Earlier, we told a quite different story about these states. Isn't this a contradiction? Seemingly, perhaps, but in fact not so. Honorton's account of why these states are ESP-favourable was couched in terms of the noise from the outside world and the body itself. Stanford's way of talking about this is to say 'Yes, but that noise is not *any* noise. It is systematic. We see and hear definite, coherent, structured things. Those things impose an organisation on the brain, on the mind. They produce certain types of responses and reactions; they engender biases in thinking and doing. On the other hand, brains without strongly structured activities going on all the time are more likely to generate psi effects.'

So, Stanford's bias model explains why the ESP-favourable states are so favourable, and can also explain some other findings. For example, we noted that ESP tends to improve during a test session in the Ganzfeld. According to Stanford this is because with increasing time the activity of the brain gets less and less predictable as the constraints imposed on it by the outside world gradually diminish.* Moreover, using similar logic, Stanford's ideas could easily be applied to, say, the beneficial effects of hypnosis on ESP. The model is complete and neat; it may be an alternative way of talking about things to the one Honorton offers, but we suspect that it is more than just an alternative description. For the whole idea of psi being strongest in systems which are relatively random, unconstrained and unbiased is one very much in keeping with recent research in PK and physics. As we shall see, Stanford's psychological story carries over into physics rather persuasively. Honorton's story, however, has some unfortunate pitfalls in this respect, in that it is a *pretence* that ESP is a weak sense. We know that it almost certainly is not a form of sensing, for reasons we will come to shortly; we just pretend that it is *like* one because that 'As if . . .' is useful in generating experiments which work rather well.

It is time now to leave the area of research into the psychology of the Unexplained – although that will be returned to later – and ask what is perhaps the most fundamental question, 'How might psi work?'

A de-structured world: Salvador Dali's surrealist paintings brilliantly evoke a dream-like state of consciousness in which familiar images are transformed by a process of drifting association.

---

* Indeed, very recent studies by Sargent, Heidi Bartlett and Sue Moss – as well as by Stanford himself – have given direct support to this notion.

Sceptics often maintain that psi is impossible because it is incompatible with known physical laws. This view, of course, rests on the belief that physical laws are true, and true for all time. This belief, set against the history of scientific thought, is a vulnerable assumption in itself. Moreover, as we shall see, exciting theories have recently been proposed which suggest how psi might work in terms of known physics. First, however, it is useful to review what, from the point of view of physics, we know about psi.

At the heart of our knowledge is a mystery – we do not know how psi works. On the other hand, experiments have produced effects which cannot be explained as chance and which therefore, according to conventional scientific criteria, are real effects. We can measure the strength of these effects, as well as the influence on them of other measurable factors, psychological and physical – personality, distance, time. We find that the effects can be boosted as though they were a signal (as in Ryzl's majority-vote experiments with Stepanek) and that they can also be treated as a weak human sense (as with Honorton's Ganzfeld experiments). Psi can be affected, positively and negatively, by human intention: on the other hand, equally significant effects can be generated non-intentionally, as we have seen from Stanford's experiments. Yet, in other cases, psi behaves quite unlike any human sense. And, if psi is like a signal, what known source of energy could be responsible for transmitting it?

The cybernetic model of human perception presents the brain as a super-computer, processing coded information from the outside world and formulating appropriate responses

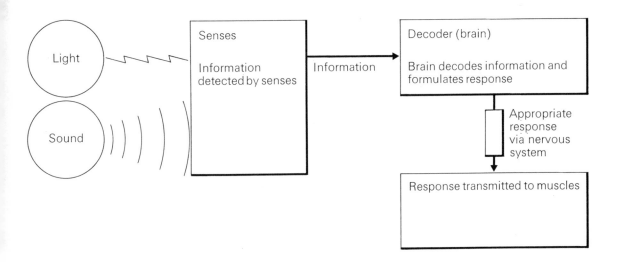

The cybernetic model

A working model which scientists have used to describe human perception and action is one we can call a *cybernetic* model: the Human Machine, the Brain-as-Computer. In such a model, information reaches the brain through the senses: this information is conveyed to us by some physical carrier signal (such as light-rays conveying information to our eyes). The brain decodes that information. If we need to act on that information, our brain will send messages along the nerves appropriate to the action we want to undertake: information flows from the brain to the muscles. In short, the human organism is a receiver of information – conveyed by a physical transmission medium – which processes and decodes that information and acts on it when appropriate, with this action involving physical information transmission (nerve impulses travelling to muscles).

Now, is it possible to examine psi as a function of the Human Machine? Whilst Rhine always claimed that psi was 'non-physical' – meaning that one couldn't examine psi as part of this robot organism – it was he who coined the term '*extra*-sensory perception', and what value judgements *that* term involves! For we are conditioned by our language to think of ESP as some special, extra, kind of *perception*, and to a lesser extent to think of PK as a special, extra, kind of *action*. Our first instinct is to look for some kind of physical transmission medium for ESP – something analogous to the light-rays which convey information to our eyes. This is perhaps a natural enough tendency, but it's based less on sound scientific reasoning than on habitual patterns of thinking.

Rather than start by examining specific types of physical transmission medium experiments (like the fruitless pursuit of electromagnetism) one might start by reflecting on the issue of whether it is actually possible for *any* known physical carrier to mediate ESP effects. There are both theoretical and sound experimental reasons for thinking that this could not be the case. Take, for example, experiments on what is termed 'blind-PK'. In these, the subject wishes for a high score on the target face of a die – but is not told which the target face might be. The physiological explanation for psi suggests a cybernetic process by which the subject uses ESP to find out the target face to aim for, then uses PK to influence the fall of the dice. Since ESP is not a perfectly reliable system for acquiring information we would surely expect a lower scoring rate in blind-PK experiments than in ordinary PK experiments, in which the target-face is known by the subject. In fact, blind-PK experiments have been notably successful, and their overall success rates are certainly no lower than those from ordinary PK experiments.

Indeed, it will already have occurred to the thoughtful reader that the experiments covered in the last chapter go even further. For in the 'non-intentional psi' experiments, subjects do not even know they are being tested at all. We must therefore consider the possibility that they may be using ESP to find out that they are participating in an experi-

An electrically screened room, or Faraday cage. When the wire mesh is electrified it screens out a wide range of electromagnetic radiation. With apparatus such as this, physicists have tried – and failed – to find an electromagnetic basis for psi.

ment, and ESP again to know what to aim for in the PK task, and then PK to change things in a desirable way (to escape from a boring experiment, or to succeed in an examination, and so on). In many cases, a great deal of information would have to be obtained by ESP to make success in these experiments possible, yet performance in these experiments appears to be *superior*, if anything, to that in conventional ESP experiments. This appears very puzzling.

There is a possible escape route here if we want to retain the cybernetic view of psi. We might consider that some other factor compensates for the fall-off in blind-PK and non-intentional psi experiments which would surely result from relying on ESP alone to get information about what to do. It may be that, in the blind-PK and non-intentional psi experiments, the fact that subjects do not consciously know what they are doing helps to reduce anxiety and apprehension about being tested. And we know that anxiety is unfavourable for psi success.

This is a weak argument and can readily be shown to be wrong by a neat experiment completed by Schmidt. Schmidt conducted a PK experiment in which people had to try and bias the action of a REG, the output of which was visually displayed (on a screen). However, there were actually *two* REGs being used, and their outputs intermixed, although the subjects were not told this. One of the machines was a 'simple' REG. This machine simply generated one electrical pulse randomly on each trial. The other was a 'complex' REG. This machine generated 100 pulses for each trial, counted the number of positive and negative pulses, computed which had arisen more frequently – and offered it as the target, displayed as a *single event*. So, if the complex machine generated 53 positive and 47 negative pulses, it took the positive pulse as the generated one and displayed that.

Surprisingly, scoring rates on the two machines were the same. The scoring rate was quite independent of the complexity of the system PK was affecting. This is unexpected from any cybernetic model, and since the psychological conditions were the same for the two machines, we cannot suppose that 'anxiety' operated with regard to one machine and not the other.

Having set out, in general terms, the cybernetic explanation of psi, with its problems, we must also mention some particular aspects of psi which cause further difficulties in accepting it.

Psi at a distance

In the popular mind ESP is thought to be completely independent of distance. This impression is probably the result of sensationalised accounts of spontaneous ESP experiences. But is there any scientific basis for this impression? In passing, we can mention the remarkable ESP experiment conducted a decade ago by Apollo astronaut Ed Mitchell. Scores of thousands of miles from Earth, Mitchell 'sent' telepathic messages back to acquaintances on Earth. In fact, the results did show evidence of ESP, although too few tests were completed for the experiment to be conclusive.

Karlis Osis, of the American Society for Psychical Research, has conducted the most impressive experiments in the effects of distances between senders and receivers on ESP. Reviewing previous work in 1965, he found that other researchers had noted a clear decline in ESP scoring as distances increased. In his own experiments Osis made sure that the receivers had no knowledge of the location of the sender – a precaution not observed in the earlier work – and found a small but clear-cut fall in scoring rates relative to distance.

This decline, however, must be put in perspective. Osis noted that it was much less marked than the tendency for receivers' performances to decline during a test session – probably a psychological effect. The decline over distance, moreover, was nothing like inversely proportional to the square of the distance, the relationship being nearer to two-fifths of the distance. This fact alone probably puts paid to any simple energetic basis for ESP.

John Beloff: how, he asks, can psi work on a sealed pack of cards, of which the sequence is unknown until after the subject's guesses have been made?

Physical properties of ESP and PK targets

Research has shown that psi works on all types of targets, regardless of their size or physical properties. It has been modestly well established that ESP can be used to detect targets on microfilm, which suggests tremendous accuracy. Very few comparisons of microfilm and conventionally sized targets have been made, but those which exist point to no difference in scoring between the two types. A similar paradox has been pointed out by John Beloff, an Edinburgh parapsychologist, in connection with a standard type of ESP test called a 'Down Through' (DT) test. A shuffled pack of 25 ESP cards is sealed *before* the subject begins his guesses. After the 25 guesses have been completed, the pack is broken open and the guesses compared with the targets. Significant ESP results have been reported from DT testing. What possible kind of sensing or radiation could convey information over such a wide range of target sizes on the one hand, and on the other from a closely packed pile of symbols?

Turning to PK experiments, there are similar problems. In dice PK tests, for example, scoring rates remain unaffected by the weight of the dice used, and by the materials from which the dice are made. Evidence such as this adds up to further damaging arguments against the notion that psi may be physiological in nature or, alternatively, be mediated by some form of radiation.

The time barrier

Of all the psi phenomena, precognition is the one which causes most theoretical headaches. If an event precedes its cause in time – if the information exists in the future – then it really does not seem reasonable to look for any kind of physical radiation or energy which could be transmitting information back in time. There are extremely few comparisons of precognition success over a variety of time periods in experimental conditions. However, the very fact that success has been obtained in experiments on ESP in which the guesses were made even a few hours before the targets were generated is a major problem for physical theories of psi.

Unless . . . unless what appears to be precognition might actually be PK (the guesser biasing the targets). Rhine, in his own precognition research, was aware of this problem, and devised a 'weather key' – a random production of targets which would be triggered by a temperature variable at a distant location some time after the guesses were made. Sceptics suggested that perhaps the subjects in the precognition experiments were using PK to influence thermometers hundreds or thousands of miles away, at which point Rhine more or less gave up on the theoretical problem.

It could possibly be maintained that all laboratory studies on precognition have actually been tapping PK, which would remove the problem. However, what of the spontaneous cases? What, for example, of the numerous precognitions of the Aberfan disaster? One could dismiss them all as coincidence and avoid the problem (and we would

Apollo astronaut Ed Mitchell (left) is the only person ever to perform an ESP experiment in deep space.

have much sympathy with that approach), but to explain them away in terms of PK would be swallowing the camel whilst straining at the gnat.

If one does consider that precognition exists then indeed it presents insuperable problems for any model of psi which involves energy transmission.

Towards a new definition of psi

All the evidence we have noted raises fundamental doubts about the way in which we think of psi. We now have to consider new theories which not only account for many of the difficulties we have pointed out for the cybernetic/physiological explanation of psi, but actually predict that some of them should be present. These theories – which suggest many ideas for precise experiments – have been worked out by physicists and they lean heavily on quantum physics. The ideas behind them are strange and often contrary to common sense. There are two points to make about this. Their oddness is not intrinsic to the fact that they deal with psi events, but rather to quantum physics itself. The second point is simply this: bizarre events are not likely to have simple explanations!

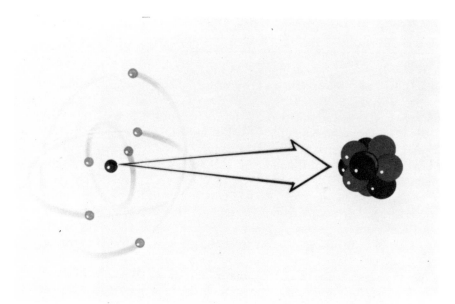

The classical model of an atom. The central nucleus (enlarged in the foreground) is composed of negatively charged neutrons and positively charged protons. The orbiting particles are electrons.

A fuzzy world

In order to understand the latest attempts to set psi in the context of physics, the reader is asked to bear with a brief explanation of how physicists now think about the Universe. For a very long time the *atom* was thought to be the basic building-block of matter. In historical terms it is only recently that we have realised that this is not so and have begun to explore the *subatomic* realm. The evidence of that is all around us – in nuclear power stations and nuclear weapons.

If all subatomic particles had a fixed velocity and precise position, it would be possible to imagine the Universe as a giant billiard table.

At school we were taught that the atom is composed of a number of subatomic particles. According to this account, the atoms of the different elements are composed of varying numbers of *neutrons* (particles with no charge in the nucleus of the atom), *protons* (positively charged particles in the nucleus of the atom) and *electrons* (negatively charged particles orbiting the nucleus). Neutrons and protons are of approximately the same size, whereas electrons are much smaller (around $\frac{1}{1800}$ of the size of the proton).

The neat diagram of the atom with its constituent particles is easily visualised as looking rather like a miniature Solar System. Unfortunately, the truth of the matter is that it is by no means as simple as this.

Improbably, certain features of the ways in which electrons behave show that to view them as *particles* leads to some terrible absurdities. It is now an accepted view that the electron sometimes behaves as if it were a particle and sometimes as if it were a *wave*. To put things more precisely, sometimes it is more useful to think of the electron as a particle, and sometimes more useful to think of it as a wave.

The next problem we have is that in the old 'classical' physics, particles had *definite* properties. They had precise velocity and precise position – rather, to use a famous analogy, as if the Universe were a giant billiard table. However, from the viewpoint of quantum mechanics (which, with Relativity theory, is the basis of modern physics) this is not so. Before a measurement is made – an *observation* of the system – the properties of a particle are *indefinite*. It is the case that the particle covers, or fluctuates over, a *range* of positions (or velocities) simultaneously. The particle's properties are fluctuating or *fuzzy*. The useful analogy given by physicist Evan Harris Walker is that of a person standing in the doorway of a house with one foot inside and one outside: he is both inside and outside the house at the same time. Similarly, our electron is in many places, and has many velocities, at the same time.

At this point one might well consider the proposition that, compared with this notion of a fundamentally fuzzy Universe, the concept of telepathy (for example) is remarkably unobjectionable as an affront to common sense. However, there is worse to come.

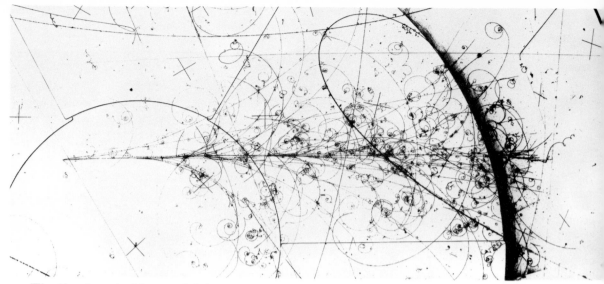

The 'fuzziness' of the particle in quantum mechanics is described by a *wave function*, which is a function of time and the particular property of the particle to be measured. The wave function is basically like the normal distribution we considered in a very different context in Chapter 1. If we deal with a particle which has a velocity fluctuating around 3 centimetres per second (3 cm/sec.), then the wave function looks like that shown opposite.

What this wave function means is that, when we observe the particle (make some measurement of its velocity) we are *most likely* to observe the value of 3 cm/sec. But as we get further away from that average value we are correspondingly less likely to observe it, so that 4 or 2 cm/sec. are more likely measurements than 1 or 5 cm/sec. We deal here with the principle that, the further away from the average one gets, the less likely one is to observe that extreme value – the same principle used in statistical evaluations of psi experiments. Indeed, quantum physics might be said to be fundamentally statistical in character. Just as statistical theory provides precise equations with which to predict the average and scatter of distributions of scores in psi experiments, using ESP cards or falling dice, similar equations can predict the distribution of values along the wave function of the particle.

Now we might consider making measurements on a large number of particles, which have the same wave function. If we make velocity measurements for a large number of such particles we find that our distribution of values looks like that of the wave function for the single particle we noted before.

Our series of measurements, however, is an interesting business. *For the series of individual measurements is random.* What we *do* know about our system is the probability of making certain observations: we know that if we measure the velocity of a single particle, there is a certain most probable value, and others of less probability (the normal distribution again). What we do *not* know is exactly *which* value we will find for the velocity of any particular particle. We cannot predict this: in this respect the system is truly random. This, of course, is the principle of

The trajectories of subatomic particles photographed in a bubble chamber at the CERN particle accelerator, Geneva.

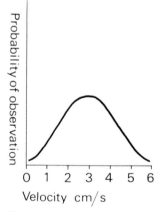

The range of possible velocities for any particle observed at a precise velocity is expressed as a distribution curve.

nature which Schmidt exploited in building his machines around the radioactive decay (and electron emission) of Strontium-90.

A further key point to grasp is that the particle we measure only acquires a *precise* velocity when we measure it. Before that time it has no precise velocity at all, but fluctuates over a range of velocities. Now we have to examine how we make our measurements, and matters get extremely interesting.

The velocity of a subatomic particle A is about to be measured at point B. But, since the velocity of A is indeterminate, and the detector B and meter C can be seen as a collection of subatomic particles – with indeterminate features – how can we record a single, definite measurement? This is the measurement problem.

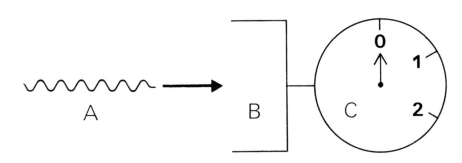

The measurement problem

We might now consider an electron travelling in space, which we are about to measure for velocity using a recording meter. Common sense tells us that when we make a measurement, the meter needle shows a precise value. Unfortunately this is not so. The detector and the meter are themselves composed of large numbers of atoms, and can thus be considered in terms of a *many-particle* wave function. This odd way of looking at the problem follows inexorably from the logic of physics. From this view it can be shown easily that if the velocity of the particle is indefinite (an axiom) then the *position of the meter needle must also be indefinite*. That is, the needle must fluctuate over the different measurements in just the same way as the velocity of the electron is 'fuzzy', that is, fluctuates. Yet this is absurd. Observers see a discrete value: the needle is in one place.

Evan Harris Walker paraphrased a famous paradox invented by the physicist Schrodinger to express just how acute this problem of measurement is. With our meter we are trying to measure the velocity of an electron particle. Now, imagine the meter needle is attached to a hammer which is just above the head of an unfortunate rat, so that if the meter needle moves, the hammer hits the rat. The velocity of the electron is indeterminate, which means that the position of the meter needle is 'fuzzy', i.e. the needle occupies many positions simultaneously. Our only conclusion can be that the rodent is simultaneously both dead and alive! This is quite absurd, yet this 'measurement problem' follows inevitably from the most basic concepts of modern physics.

So, the measurement problem in quantum physics is this: how does a 'fuzzy' system become a discrete measurement when observed? Several solutions have been proposed, and some of them are of great interest to us.

We should say at once that the most popular of these does not appear to offer much hope for explaining psi phenomena. Nils Bohr and associates have proposed the so-called 'Copenhagen interpretation' of the problem, which asserts that macroscopic systems (such as measurement devices) cannot be considered in the same way as microscopic (subatomic) systems. In short, one cannot discuss them in quantum terms. There are two problems here. The first one is that this interpretation appears to say that measurement simply happens; it cannot be analysed further, and must be accepted unquestioningly. Our original wave function has collapsed into a discrete value. An objection to this is that certain physicists (notably von Neumann) appear to have made rather a good job of describing measurement devices in quantum-mechanical terms, and there is no doubt that under certain conditions macroscopic events are very readily describable in quantum-mechanical terms (especially at low temperatures).

An alternative suggestion, made by Princeton physicist John Wheeler and others, is the truly staggering one that collapse of the wave function does *not* happen, but that all the possible measurements are actually observed, somewhere. In our universe only one possibility is observed: but in an infinite number of alternative universes, an infinite number of doppelgangers of ourselves are observing all the other possible outcomes. We cannot know of them, but they exist, and the infinite number of universes is growing, multiplying by an infinite (or incalculably large) number at every second.

Danish physicist Nils Bohr argues that measurement simply happens, and must be accepted.

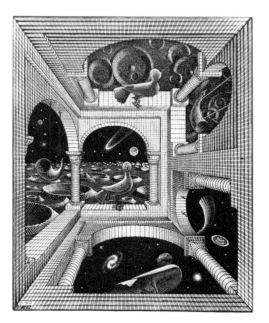

In the multiple-universe theory of measurement an infinite number of identical universes allow an infinite number of identical observers to measure all possible values of a single subatomic particle.

Remarkably (one might have thought) this notion is taken seriously enough to be debated in learned journals of physics and discussed at top-level conferences of physicists. Admittedly, few physicists opt for it as the solution to the 'measurement problem'. As one critic has said, 'Although this is a complete and consistent picture, it is a rather unsettling one, with no means to test its validity.' Nonetheless, John Hasted has argued that the many-universes interpretation of quantum physics may help us to explain psi, and we shall return to his arguments later in the chapter.

More interesting, however, is a line of argument proposed by several highly respected physicists who have suggested that there must be certain 'hidden variables' in the quantum system which are required for a full description of it. It is these variables which cause the collapse of the wave function. What are they? Many years' search for them proving unsuccessful, the suspicion began to be entertained that they might comprise the operations of human consciousness itself. In 1961 American physicist Eugene Wigner proposed this in a speculative form and in 1967 proposed the idea more seriously. Since that time other physicists have arrived at the same conclusion. This school of thought remains a heterodox one in physics, but it is a point of view which is proposed by a reasonable minority of theoreticians.

There are certain reasons for thinking that there might be a link with parapsychology here. They are certainly speculative, but they lead to testable ideas. In this connection we can now look at a further strange aspect of measurement. Let us consider two particles, bound together by an inter- or intra-atomic binding force. Now, imagine this dyad being split up by an explosion. The two particles will fly off in opposite directions, and we can imagine detectors set up to measure their velocities.

Action at a distance: the two-particle dyad AB is split by an explosion. A and B fly off in opposite directions. Yet if the velocity of A is measured at a point X, the value is the same as for particle B at an equal distance from the explosion even though B has not been measured.

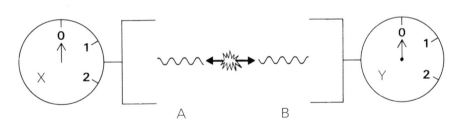

When particle A is observed we will 'see' a finite velocity, say 4 cm/sec. The wave function for particle A has been collapsed. But the law of conservation of momentum states that, under these conditions, particle B will have a velocity equal and opposite to that of A. Thus an observation of A collapses the wave function of particle B. *This is action*

at a distance. This 'distant collapse' of the wave function of particle B by an observation made at a spatial distance from it illustrates the problem that the quantum-mechanical wave function is *non-local*, i.e. not confined to a small region of space. Such distant collapse will occur when an observer deals with two (or more) systems which have interacted with each other in the past – and are thus said to be *correlated systems.* In our example the correlation was caused by the particles having been at one time bound together.

This is the famous Einstein–Podolski–Rosen paradox and the implication is simple: an observer can affect an event taking place at almost any distance away from him. Thus collapse of the wave function can be *spatially* invariant. In certain treatments of this paradox the collapse can have features of *temporal* invariance. We are dealing with observation effects which are not limited by space or time constraints. These look very like psi events.

Now this is perhaps as far as many physicists sympathetic to parapsychology would be prepared to go. They would suggest that quantum physics is an uncertain enough business to prevent anyone calling psi events impossible. and that the intellectual framework of quantum physics can cope with psi events. Certain physicists, however, have gone further. Nobel laureate Brian Josephson has stated that if psi events had not been reported, an imaginative theoretician could have predicted that they should occur. Olivier Costa de Beauregard goes yet further: he states categorically that the most fundamental axioms in quantum physics demand that psi events *must* occur as a result of the spatial and temporal independence aspects of the EPR paradox. This alone would be interesting enough, but Evan Harris Walker has taken matters further and produced a theory which is part good physics, part plausible intuition, part wild speculation, and which makes some clear predictions about psi phenomena. Already we have seen that certain aspects of psi events (independence of time and almost complete spatial independence) are easily thought about in quantum mechanics, since effects just like these occur in this realm. Other difficulties, too, disappear if we pursue Walker's line. We shall see exactly how this happens.

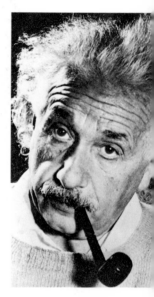

Albert Einstein: his theories imply that an observer can affect an event far away. Psi, then, is at least theoretically possible.

Consciousness and the physical world

Walker's theory can be said to deal with the three crucial variables in the psi experiment: the observer, the observation, and the observed system. In his theory, they become Consciousness, Feedback, and Randomness. How?

First, Walker has a theory of the interactions between the physical brain and the (physically unmeasurable) Mind, or Consciousness. Randomness enters the picture because the brain, with its staggering complexity, contains many random or quasi-random processes. Consciousness is capable of producing powerful effects on the function of the brain by collapsing the wave function of these processes. Thus the Mind/Brain interaction is, for Walker, symmetrical to the Mind/Quantum system interaction. It's just that one occurs within the body, and the other outside it.

Now this might seem bizarre – we are not accustomed to think of our brains as random operators. In the Walker model, however, a first point is that the brain only contains a few random processes. The second point is that Sir John Eccles, winner of a Nobel prize for his work on central nervous system function, has very similar ideas. By affecting just a few random processes in the brain (which will trigger off a cascade of subsequent effects through neural connections), Consciousness can create powerful changes in brain function. We are not certain that Walker says anything more about this process other than the fact that it happens, but we can ask if this theory has implications for psi.

It is essential to the Walker theory, for technical reasons, that Consciousness should be capable of operating non-locally: that it can interact with a physical system which it is observing, rather than be confined to the brain itself.

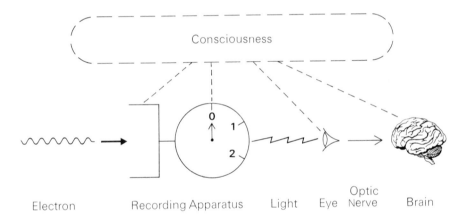

Consciousness and the physical world: the act of observing a measurement may not be confined to seeing the value registered on the meter. Random processes in the brain may also interact with the subatomic events in the measuring device, as well as with random events to be measured.

This is the *basic* nature of the model: that Consciousness can influence random events directly, both within the body and outside of it, by collapsing the wave functions of those events in the act of observation. This notion alone, however, doesn't tell us much. We need to examine the model piece by piece to extract firm predictions. The first variable we can look at is the observation itself: the coupling of Consciousness to the physical system

Observing and influencing

The first prediction made by the model, which is simple but devastating in its implications, is this: If you do not observe a system, you cannot affect it. In the case of psi experiments, this means that if you never see the results of the experiment you could not have used psi in it. This prediction leads to a re-interpretation of many old experiments, clears

up many apparent problems about psi, makes exciting predictions, and also generates some paradoxes worthy of *Alice in Wonderland*.

Re-interpretation: Just who does produce the psi in successful experiments? The obvious answer, of course, is that the subjects do. The Walker theory says that this may be so, but if the subjects do not see the results, then they *cannot* have produced the successful results. Take the example of Osis' long-distance ESP experiments. Since Osis observed the results (got *feedback of results*) and the subjects did not, then it *must* have been *Osis himself* who produced the results by his own psi powers. According to Walker, the apparent dependence of ESP on distance revealed by Osis's experiments is an illusion. It was not the subjects but Osis himself who produced the successful results. He *wished* to see a fall-off in score as a function of distance between the subjects and the targets, so he observed one. Osis's own psi could have created this result, either by his consciousness collapsing the wave-function of the random target production or by collapsing the wave functions of the semi-random guessing of his subjects. As Walker says, '[Consciousness] could cause collapse of the total wave function of its own brain and another person's brain (telepathy), or another person's body (psychic healing) or a distant object (PK).'

Let's take some other experiments and re-interpret them. In some of Sargent's studies he has found positive relationships between ESP scoring and extraversion. However, since the subjects never observed their scores, this must be put down to that relationship's being created by Sargent's consciousness influencing the nature of the results as *he* observed them!

This is heady stuff and not easy to grasp, but two points begin to emerge. The first is that, at last, Walker's theory places *a limitation on psi*. This is crucial: without feedback of results, there can be no observation, and therefore no psi. If psi really could achieve anything, transcend all boundaries, it would defeat any attempt to explore it. For example, take the ESP/extraversion correlation: could we be sure that it was real, or was it perhaps just our subjects using ESP to learn about what the experimenter *wanted* and complying with it? All we could ever know about psi would be that it existed. Walker offers a clear opportunity to pin psi down once and for all. This is the great virtue of his model.

The second point which becomes clear is that we may have been

When does PK happen? At the moment when the subject tries to influence the dice – or later, when the results are checked?

looking at the wrong people when examining psi. We may have obtained much more repeatable findings if we had looked in the right places – that is to say, at the people who observed the results. So Walker's theory holds out the hope for more repeatable experiments.

Two pluses for the theory so far: the hope of limiting psi and of obtaining it more reliably. Next, the value of the theory in dealing with some anomalies.

Explanations: In three classic ESP experiments, Sarah Feather – Rhine's daughter – and philosopher Bob Brier observed a *very* strange feature, namely that the *person who checked the results strongly affected the scores.* In none of the cases did the subjects know anything about the results.

Now, how can a checker – in some cases a checker who never even met the subjects – influence the results of an experiment? In terms of our conventional way of thinking about psi, we have to go into *ad hoc* mental contortions to explain it. In Walker's theory, though, the position is simple. Walker's theory would not just explain this result: *it would predict it.* In observing the scores, the checkers collapse the wave functions; of course they affect the scores obtained! Moreover, they can do it without any contact with the people who produced the guesses – indeed those guessers are utterly irrelevant to the whole affair.

This type of 'difficult' ESP experiment result, and others, are immediately transformed by Walker's model into obvious and predicted effects.

Predictions: Walker's theory predicts, first, that psi should be space-time independent (unless, amusingly enough, the observer does not wish this to appear in the results he observes!). This follows from the space-time independence of observation effects in quantum physics. The time independence, in particular, has spawned some beautiful experiments from Schmidt and others which would never have been conducted by simply holding the older ideas about psi, and one prime virtue of a theory is its ability to generate new and incisive enquiry.

Schmidt arranged for an REG machine to be triggered so as to generate a series of binary random numbers which were stored on magnetic tape and not observed by anyone. Hours or days later, Schmidt arranged for subjects to listen, over headphones, to series of clicks which appeared either in the left- or the right-hand channel, and to wish for a high frequency in one ear rather than in the other. The nature of the clicks was determined by the numbers recorded on the magnetic tape: that is, to succeed in their task the subjects had to use PK to affect the activity of a Schmidt machine some time *in the past.* The experiment was highly successful and the results showed clearly that subjects could do this. Others, notably Elmar Gruber in Germany, have successfully repeated this experiment. These results are quite astonishing – but they offer a way out of the problems associated with precognition, as we shall see later.

In addition, Walker's theory predicts that if the *psychological* states of the subjects were measured when the REG was actually producing the

The prophecies of Nostradamus, written down in the 16th century, seem to have predicted events from the rise of Napoleon to the death of Pope John-Paul. New theories as to how psi works may explain the phenomenon of precognition.

clicks, and again when they were observing the results, only the latter measurement would correlate with their scores in the experiment: a clear prediction, testable and falsifiable. Research urgently needs to be done on this prediction.

In addition to predicting that, without any feedback of results, you cannot use psi, Walker's theory predicts that the amount of psi a person *can* use is limited by the amount of feedback he gets. To a certain extent, the more feedback received, the more psi can be used. Thus, a subject who gets feedback for every guess can produce (potentially) a strong psi effect, if he gets no feedback he cannot produce any effect, while if he is told only something vague like 'The experiment went well' then he will be able to produce only a small effect.

Paradox: Now for the difficulties. First, Walker's theory predicts that the existence of more than one observer can affect an observation. He proposes an addition rule for combining the effects of different observers. We cannot find any compelling logical reason for that solution, but it is the case that if an observer can influence an event then we have to postulate that all observers can.

When this proposition is combined with the space-time independence factor, some mind-boggling problems arise. The upshot of matters is this: *any* observer, at any time or place, can influence the outcome of a random process. As has been pointed out, this could mean that in a philosophical sense, no experiment is ever finished, since any number of observers may yet observe the results and influence them. There are two rejoinders here. The first is that almost all of these later observers will receive only a little feedback – probably in the form of a table summarising the results of the experiment. Under these conditions they cannot exert much of an effect. Secondly, the outcomes they wish to see will differ, probably randomly, across the whole population of later observers.

Schmidt himself has produced evidence which supports this prediction of the effects produced by many observers. In one particular PK experiment – using pre-recorded targets on magnetic tape as before – he played some of the targets *four times over* to the subjects without their realising this. They scored much higher on those targets than on those they only observed once. Multiple observation effects do appear to exist.

Evan Harris Walker (centre) has proposed radical new ideas as to where and when psi events take place.

This really does lead to hideous paradoxes. The so-called 'divergence problem' – the difficulty that having more than one observer will influence the results – is the key area of theoretical debate within Walker's theory, and others related to it. Yet the problem is intrinsic to the theory: if we have effects caused by observations (which clears up many difficulties) and space-time independence (which we must), then the divergence problem follows logically. Yet this very problem has led to some intriguing experiments, such as that by Schmidt described above.

Ghost and machine: the machine

Randomness: this, for Walker, is the key feature of the Human Machine. He argues that Consciousness creates psi events by influencing the collapse of the wave function of random processes. For Walker, all macroscopic pure-chance processes are quantum processes. This is a brave and contentious step but, again, predictions follow from it.

The first prediction is simple: so long as a system *is* functioning randomly, the structure, complexity and details of function of the system are completely irrelevant. Thus Schmidt's finding that, whether his testing machine was simple or complex (page 135), the results were the same, is just what Walker's theory would predict. As long as there are no psychological differences in the way that subjects react to different test systems (and Schmidt got round that problem in the best way, by making them indistinguishable) then no differences in psi performance will be expected. No results contradict this view whilst many support it.

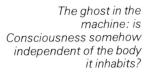

The ghost in the machine: is Consciousness somehow independent of the body it inhabits?

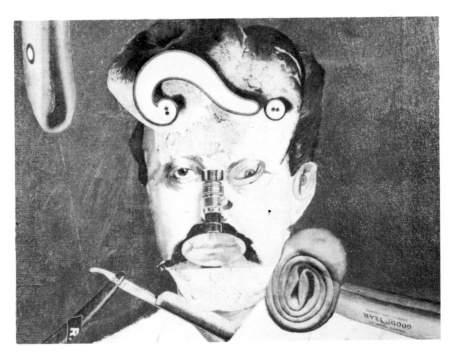

Walker has provided some further support for his theory by looking at dice-throwing PK experiments. His theory predicts not only that the nature of the random system is irrelevant, but that the amount of randomness *is* important. The more random function in the system, the more opportunities there are for consciousness to influence the random events and succeed in the PK task. Thus, while the physical nature of the dice does not appear to be of direct importance, Walker has predicted that the *number of times the dice bounce is important*. The more bounces, the more randomness; the more randomness, the bigger the possible PK effect. Ergo, the more bounces, the bigger the PK effect. Walker has shown that this does appear to happen.

Incidentally, this randomness postulate helps to dispose of an old sceptical argument about PK, most frequently voiced by Hansel. Why, Hansel asks rhetorically, did Rhine not test for a direct effect of some PK 'force' on a chemical balance and measure it directly? Why use dice? The answer, according to Walker, is obvious: the dynamic system (dice) would be much easier to affect than the static system (balance). Dynamic systems, with their inherently greater randomness, will be much easier to affect than static systems. Indeed, this may be why levitations, if indeed they happen at all, are so rare. Needless to say, Hansel's 1980 book contains no reference to Walker's arguments.

A further series of predictions relates to the state of the brain as a random system in ESP experiments and they are probably the best supported of all, but we shall return to them later.

Ghost and machine: the ghost

And so to Consciousness itself, once ridiculed by Gilbert Ryle as the 'ghost in the machine'. And so it is, but Walker claims that it is a highly effective ghost.

The first important component in Consciousness, for Walker, is the desired goal: What does the observer want to see, what does he wish for? This parameter will influence the collapse of the wave function. This is a purely psychological level of inquiry, since one can only find out by asking the observer (or by manipulating his desires).

However, Walker states that there is some limitation on the ability of Consciousness to influence physical systems. It is suggested that Consciousness can only do so much per unit time, that there is a limit on the amount of *information* (in a mathematical sense) which Consciousness can 'feed into' a random physical system to bias the outcomes of random processes. He has made a computation of what this limit might be, but the actual values he suggests are less important than the notion that there is some limit. This postulate, which looks reasonable, produces some further, quite clear, predictions which differ markedly from those made by other models of psi.

To see how these predictions can be tested, let us consider some of the many psi experiments we have looked at already, but in a different way. In PK testing with dice, a person has a 1-in-6 chance of getting a hit with each throw of the dice. In ESP testing with Rhine cards, a

Patterns of randomness: do random events in the brain, in the world at large, and in the subatomic realm, generate the phenomena we call psi?

person has a 1-in-5 chance of scoring a hit with each guess. In Ganz-feld–ESP testing, since four pictures are generally given to the person to choose from, he has a 1-in-4 chance of selecting the correct picture with each guess. Stepanek was guessing in an ESP test in which he had a 1-in-2 chance of being correct with each guess. Different kinds of experiments utilize different *chance probabilities* of success: from 50 per cent (1 in 2) to 25 per cent (1 in 4) to 20 per cent (1 in 5) to 16.67 per cent (1 in 6) down to 10 per cent (1 in 10).

Walker's theory produces a startling prediction: if one has a good subject, the odds-against-chance for his scoring will be *exactly the same* no matter whether we have a chance probability of 50 per cent, 25 per cent, 20 per cent, or 10 per cent – or even 70 per cent or 90 per cent for that matter. This prediction arises because the statistics used to assess the odds-against-chance value measure information, and Walker states that Consciousness feeds in a constant amount of information to the system. Therefore the statistical significance of our results – the odds-against-chance – will not change as a function of the basic chance probability.

This prediction is quite different from those which would follow from other models of how psi works. Consider, for example, an appeal-ing model of psi which states that psi works on a few trials, and when it does so it is successful (all-or-none effect). How often it works – on, say, 1 per cent or 2 per cent or 5 per cent of the guesses made (in an ESP experiment) or dice throws (PK experiment) – stays more or less the same across time. Intuitively, this is quite a pleasing notion, but it makes a very different prediction to that made by Walker. For, as the basic chance probability falls to lower and lower values, the odds-against-chance should rise very sharply. Why? Because, if the basic chance probability is very high, most of the psi successes will be obscured by chance hits.

An example: we have a subject who is capable of using psi on 10 per cent of all trials, whether they be guesses in an ESP experiment or dice-throws in a PK experiment. We put him in front of an REG which has 10 channels, and it is arranged so that 90 per cent of the pulses generated will be hits. He uses PK on 10 per cent of 100 trials, so he should get 10 extra hits. However, it doesn't work this way. On the other 90 trials, chance is also operating: on 90 per cent of these 90 trials (81 of them) chance hits are scored. Total score: 91 hits, just one above chance.

Now we put him in front of the same machine, and this time the machine is programmed so that only 10 per cent of the pulses generated will be hits by chance. This time he scores 10 hits by PK plus 10 per cent of the other 90 (nine) by chance – total, 19 hits, nine above chance.

One can see now that the all-or-none model must predict that much better scores will be obtained when the basic chance probability is low. As we have seen, however, Walker predicts that the odds-against-chance for scoring will always remain the same, whatever the basic chance probability.

Mathematically inclined psi researchers have constructed precise models of how the scoring should vary as chance probability is altered for several different models of the action of psi.

Here we deal with something almost unthinkable even 20 years ago: precise mathematical statements about how psi should operate. The very few experiments which are actually relevant to these predictions tend to support Walker's theory, but they haven't controlled for psychological factors. For example, people generally tend to prefer taking part in psi experiments in which the basic chance probability is neither very low nor very high. Rhine used to recommend chance probabilities of between 20 per cent and 50 per cent for ESP studies, and most researchers have followed that lead. Why is this? Because if the chance probability is very low then so many guesses are wrong that people get discouraged. If, on the other hand, the chance probability is very high, then almost all guesses are right anyway, and a person cannot really get the feeling of success, of beating the odds. However, new technology gives us the chance to beat these psychological problems. One can employ several REGs, with different probabilities of getting a hit by chance, and use a computer to randomly mix their pulses, so that the person is seeing on a visual display a series of pulses which, *on average*, have a chance probability of being correct of around 50 per cent.

Summing up

With such a complex and difficult theory, it is vital to summarise its good and bad points.

The major points in its favour are fourfold. The theory is logically sound. The physics behind it are unusual but not absurd. The theory makes numerous testable predictions, and it makes sense out of many results from experiments which have so far defied rational analysis.

Nevertheless, difficulties remain. The theory is contrary to common sense – but, as we have seen, so is quantum physics generally. The problem of multiple observations is crucial and, until it can be resolved, remains the Achilles' heel of the whole enterprise. Allied to the common-sense problem is the fact that the theory does not seem to account for spontaneous psi events, nor even many experiments. But it remains a fruitful avenue of investigation.

Consider again an ESP experiment in which someone makes his guesses and, at a later time, sees the targets and observes his results. Walker's theory considers this in terms of the observation influencing random processes (with no space-time constraints) – one of those random events being the activity of the person's own brain at the time he made his guesses! This is certainly a pretty bizarre way of looking at things. Yet, important implications follow from it.

The first is a re-interpretation of the most successful work in parapsychology (special individuals apart) – the 'altered-states' experiments, including dream-ESP, hypnosis, Ganzfeld, and so on. Earlier, we examined the success of these techniques in terms of a 'sixth sense' analogy: the techniques reduce distraction from conventional senses and thus the weak ESP signal can be detected. As we have already noted, however, there is an alternative explanation put forward by Rex Stanford which fits perfectly with Walker's theory.

Stanford states that the altered-states techniques certainly do reduce external noise. However, they do more than this. As time goes by they increasingly produce more random functioning in the brain. The brain is no longer occupied with external events and, fairly rapidly, the responses made by someone in this state become increasingly unusual, bizarre and unrestrained. There is indeed plenty of experimental evidence to suggest that, in these altered states, the manner in which people think becomes increasingly illogical, unusual, and bizarre. We have only to consider our own dreams, in which we happily fly, become other people (or even disembodied observers) and in which we can easily move in a split second from the middle of the High Street to the Sahara desert.

Walker would deal with this by saying that it is because the altered states increasingly randomise brain function that they increase psi – because, as the randomness of the system increases, the more readily an observation can influence that system. Walker's theory takes the best psi evidence in its stride.

There is yet another issue to be considered here: the *experimenter effect*. Although differences between researchers are considerably exaggerated, it is true that there are some researchers who appear to obtain psi in almost all their work – most notably Schmidt, Honorton, and Braud – while certain others appear never to get any evidence of psi at all. Much of this is probably due to psychological factors, but another explanation can be considered (the two possibilities are not exclusive and both probably have some truth in them). It may be that the highly successful experimenters obtain such good results because they are themselves strongly psychic – or, as Walker would put it, 'strong psi sources'. The unsuccessful experimenters may simply have no psi abilities. Certainly, it is known that Schmidt and Honorton, in particular, are extremely good subjects in psi experiments. A radical implication of this notion is that most subjects, too, have no psi powers (if they did even the unsuccessful experimenters would get results). Psi is something confined to a very few people – many of them being successful parapsychologists!

To examine this issue it has been suggested that these successful experimenters should try to minimise the feedback they get in their own experiments. Under such conditions would they continue to get clear evidence of psi? For they would no longer be able to use their own psi strongly if Walker's theory is right. Brian Millar, a researcher in Utrecht and the most notoriously unsuccessful experimenter in the history of the science, suggests that they would not. He adds the provocative footnote that, to know where all the great mediums of yesteryear have gone, one need look no further than successful modern parapsychologists.

There are two broad ways of considering Walker's theory. One can look at it as a precise formulation which can be experimented on rapidly and pronounced true or false. A more sensible way of looking at it is to consider that it does have some elements which are sound, some which are more in the nature of intuitive guesses, and a few which appear very doubtful. One should ask not 'Is the theory right?' but 'Is this theory a step in the right direction?' The reason why the latter is probably true is that it suggests many possible experiments and makes clear predictions about what should happen. That is the prime function of a good theory, and what makes it superior to (say) John Hasted's speculations about multiple universes.

Hasted suggests that psi events occur when there is some communication between parallel universes (probably achieved by Consciousness operating on random processes as in the Walker model). The speculation is interesting and might make some sense of psi events. The great problem is that it is very hard to see how the idea could be tested experimentally.

New directions

We consider that many researchers will be turning their attention to Walker's theory in the near future. Already continental researchers are exploring it with fairly successful results. This may leave the reader rather cold. Just what could be the link between spontaneous, emotional psi – telepathy, clairvoyance, precognition – and this strange language of randomness, observations, wave functions and random event generators?

It is probably a mistake to contrast the two things in this way. Walker is concerned with the mechanics of psi. His theory would not pretend to claim to have anything much to say about the psychology of psi – why it works, or what its functions may be. There is no possibility of Walker's theory taking any of the wonder out of spontaneous psi events, any more than an explanation of *how* light is detected by our eyes and the neural signals are processed in the brain could ever explain *why* we see a Van Gogh as beautiful. Attempts to explore the underlying mechanics of psi should not be seen as reductionist attempts to explain psi away, nor as irrelevant to the vagaries of psi in real life. The two areas – research on how psi works, research on how it functions in real life – are complementary to one another.

Nevertheless, further questions about psi remain unanswered. Perhaps the most pressing is that which certainly preoccupied the earliest psychical researchers: survival after death.

So far, our main concern has been with the growing body of scientific evidence which tells us how psi might work, when it might work best, who uses it most efficiently, what it might be able to accomplish, and so on. Yet we have ignored the central question which fired the imagination of the first systematic psychical researchers: do human beings survive physical death? For those English researchers of the last quarter of the nineteenth century, faith alone was not sufficient. Driven by the triumphant materialism, evolutionary theory and scientific atheism of their age, they were determined to find evidence, rather than mere surmise, of survival after death.

The existence of psi suggests that the Mind can operate outside the constraints of the Body; the existence of PK also implies this. So the next step, logically, would be to seek direct evidence of detachment of Mind from Body. Our first port of call, then, is the Out-of-the-Body Experience, or OOBE, also called astral projection, or astral travelling. Here is a typical, though very brief and undetailed, account of an OOBE from an eight-year-old boy:

'Such a funny thing has happened. I was just lying in bed reading when I felt I was rising into the air. I seemed to go near the ceiling. Then I looked down and could see myself lying in bed. I came slowly down. I called out . . .'

Do such events really occur or are they just hallucinations? If Mind can leave Body in this way, can it leave it permanently – and remain conscious – after the death of the Body? This possibility is more sharply focused by one special type of OOBE, the Near Death Experience (NDE), in which people report having left their body when very close to death or having left it at the point of clinical death only to be resuscitated.

Our next step would be to look at events which suggest the operation of Mind *after* death: apparitions, communications from mediums, and evidence for 'past lives' from hypnotic regression and direct study of people who claim to be reincarnations.

Can there be a final scientific verdict on the issue of survival after death? The answer must be no. For example, a medium may give detailed information about someone who is dead. We may consult documents and interview witnesses whose testimony convinces us beyond reasonable doubt that the information is both accurate and could not have been acquired by any other but paranormal means. But this does not prove that the dead person has somehow survived to be able to pass this information on. The medium may equally have been using exceptional psi powers – Super-ESP – to gather information from

Astral travelling – in which Consciousness seems to leave the body and range at will – has been seriously studied by psychologists under the less romantic label OOBE (out-of-the-body experience). This demonic dramatisation illustrates an Edgar Allan Poe story.

living human witnesses (telepathy) or from documents (clairvoyance). This impasse, and the possibility that Super-ESP might provide an alternative explanation to survival after death, will be discussed in more detail later.

Nevertheless, even if we cannot reach scientifically watertight conclusions, we can weigh up the evidence as a judge or a jury might. Is survival the most reasonable, the most consistent, the least shaky interpretation of the findings we shall be surveying? We cannot have a final scientific verdict but we can have a provisional, rational one.

Mind beyond body

'I was very tired, physically exhausted, but my mind was rather active. I lay down on my bed to rest for a while in the late afternoon. I felt an odd prickly sensation in my limbs and then a buzzing sound . . . I was conscious of some kind of pressure around or in my head and then I felt as if I was travelling along some dark tunnel, very fast . . . this ended and I looked around me to find myself seemingly floating a few feet up in the air in my bedroom. I looked down and found my body underneath me. For some odd reason I was especially taken with an odd cobweb pattern on the top of my wardrobe . . . I got a little scared by this and I willed myself to go back to my body. I got pulled back as if along some kind of cord or thread and it seemed to me, though I'm not certain, that I re-entered my body through my head. I gave a slight jump and sat up. It was completely unexpected. When I regained my wits I checked the wardrobe top . . . the odd cobweb pattern was there alright.'

An OOBE experience. Such experiences are not uncommon. Surveys suggest that between 10 and 25 per cent of the population have had at least one such experience, while a small percentage report *repeated* OOBEs.

OOBEs: TWO SURVEYS

I How common are OOBEs?

Country	Date of survey	Sample size	% reporting at least one OOBE
Duke University, USA	1954	155	27
Oxford University, UK	1967	380	34
Southampton University, UK	1967	115	19
USA (marijuana users)	1971	150	44
Iceland	1977	902	8
Surrey University, UK	1978	132	11
University of Virginia, USA	1979	268	25
Virginia (residents), USA	1979	354	14
University of New England, Australia	1980	177	16

II Frequency of OOBEs

Percentage of people reporting OOBEs

One OOBE	60.9
Two	8.9
Three	5.3
Four	2.3
Five	1.7
Six or more	20.9

From a UK survey in 1968

Once again we must ask ourselves if ESP can be ruled out as a possible explanation for OOBE perceptions? Certainly, the report given by the woman resting on her bed in the late afternoon suggests possible ESP: she saw an odd cobweb pattern out of normal view and later found that the perception she had in her ESP was accurate. But if Mind *can* leave Body and travel outside it there is no reason why it should not be able to perceive cobwebs by ESP. Remember that OOBErs report essentially normal perceptions during their out-of-the-body trips.

Can the claim that Mind leaves Body be supported by evidence of Mind perceiving events at places distant from the body, places it may have travelled to?

There are several good experiments on this theme. Charles Tart, the Californian worker, has shown that one of his female subjects, who could induce OOBEs more or less at will, could report correctly a five-digit number placed on top of a wardrobe in the room where she lay in bed. This was in spite of the fact that her head was wired up to an EEG machine so that the leads would have detached had she moved. A rather more ingenious experimental approach to OOBEs was pioneered by Karlis Osis in New York, using a subject who repeatedly had OOBEs. With his subject in one room, Osis set up, in a different room, apparatus which would display an optical target visible only to someone standing right in front of it. The subject always reported the target correctly when he was confident that he had done so. The logic of Osis' experiment was that to 'see' the target successfully, the subject's Mind would have to leave his body. Unfortunately the logic is faulty: we know that ESP can detect microfiche symbols and that PK can influence unknown target systems. In short, Osis' results may simply show quite normal psi effects. The OOBE itself may be no more than a contemporaneous hallucination.

A similar conclusion is suggested by two experiments reported by John Palmer in which he successfully induced OOBEs in volunteers. In the first experiment he used a rotating spiral visual field. In the other he put his subjects into Ganzfeld, during which they received suggestions that they should have an OOBE in order to find out about a target picture being seen by a sender in a different room. In the first study, the overall scoring was below chance and the people who had OOBEs showed significantly strong psi-missing. In the second, exactly the reverse was observed.

The point here is that these results are *exactly* the same as those obtained by Palmer in ordinary Ganzfeld ESP experiments without any OOBE reports, the strongest ESP results coming from those subjects most strongly affected by the experiment (i.e. with the most strongly altered state of consciousness). This suggests that the OOBE experience may be irrelevant. What really counts is the relaxation and the Ganzfeld.

This possibility is reinforced by the 'remote-viewing' experiments of Targ and Puthoff in California, where receivers attempt to describe a scene being visited by a sender somewhere in the general location of the laboratory. Successful viewing has been achieved with some people who claim to travel out of their bodies to 'see' the sender, but has also been achieved with many other people who have no such experience. Might OOBEs, then, be pure illusion?

Although medicine and psychiatry have something to say about the possible illusory quality of OOBEs, too few experiments have been done to dismiss them as mere subjective hallucinations. In fairness it must be said that in Palmer's experiments subjects reporting OOBEs had a quite different quality of experience from that of practised OOBE travellers. For the former the OOBE may have been an illusion, but for the latter it may not have been. It is important to make more use of seasoned 'astral travellers' in OOBE experiments.

This is one of the provisos that clearly emerges from a study reported in 1976 by Robert Morris and colleagues in which Stuart Blue Harary, an experienced astral traveller, was tested. Morris suggested that a good test of whether something really did leave Harary's body during an OOBE would be to use a human or animal monitor which might respond to that something. Harary's pet kitten was chosen for the job. The cat was placed in an enclosed space at a certain distance from Harary, and he – during a randomly selected 50 per cent of the total duration of the experiment – 'travelled' to it. During the time when Harary was having an OOBE the kitten sat still and appeared comfortable and happy. It never miaowed. During the other half of the experiment, the cat appeared restless and miaowed 37 times. Clearly there is a difference between zero and 37; Harary does seem to have been influencing the animal. Interestingly, with another cat with whom Harary had no rapport, no significant results were found.

So did Harary really leave his body? Apart from the kitten's reaction, one experimenter monitoring the cat reported seeing an appari-

Californian psychologist Charles Tart reports that one of his subjects could perceive information at a distance while undergoing an out-of-the-body experience.

tional shape at one stage during the experiment, when in fact Harary was having an OOBE. But still the case is unproven: Harary could have been using PK to affect the cat and the experimenter. The same problem applies to more recent experiments by Osis, in which success in the ESP 'seeing the target' test was accompanied by signals coming from strain gauges (as in Hasted's metal-bending research) located nearby.

John Palmer has suggested that a stronger case for OOBEs could be made if it were shown that psi effects associated with OOBE reports were different *in type* from psi effects found without OOBEs. This is certainly an interesting line of thought. Nevertheless other researchers who have tried to track down changes in brain-wave activity accompanying OOBE reports have come up with inconsistent results.

At present we simply have no good grounds for deciding whether the OOBE is a subjective or a real phenomenon. However, since OOBE reports seem to accompany strong psi effects, the OOBE state may be strongly conducive to psi.

Near-Death Experiences

Early chroniclers of OOBEs, Robert Crookall among them, notes that a proportion of OOBEs were induced by strong fear, stress, or injury. Interestingly Crookall and others tended to avoid placing too much emphasis on stress-induced OOBEs, fearing that they might be explained away as hallucinations more easily than natural ones. In the last few years, however, great interest has been shown in the stress-induced OOBE; Raymond Moody has collected well over 300 cases of what he terms Near-Death Experiences (NDEs) from people who have been greatly stressed, severely injured, or in some cases pronounced clinically dead although they later recovered. Here is a fairly typical example of an NDE as reported to one of us (the numbers refer to some of the characteristic NDEs listed opposite).

'I find this very difficult to explain, hard to express myself ... there are certain qualities I find it hard to convey (1)

'I was in a car accident [details given]. I was dimly aware of much activity going on around, and people shouting, but I can't remember much of that (2). I felt strangely calm, very tranquil, as if little mattered to me anymore (3). I slowly became aware of travelling as if down a long chute of some kind (5), moving along, a blur around me. I don't think I had any idea of what I was. In the distance, though, I saw a light ... a globe of light. It moved towards me slowly and when it drew close it was so brilliant, pure light, but not dazzling (9) ... This light, I simply cannot describe what it meant ... it wasn't God or Christ or anything like that, but it was someone, some agent or force ... I got an astonishing feeling of the complete benevolence of this light. Behind it were what I suppose I would have to call buildings of some kind, all lit up (12) ... there were other lights around, I suppose now I would say they were spirits or something but I don't remember any of them as people I'd known ... The light suddenly made some motion to me. It

CHARACTERISTICS OF NEAR-DEATH EXPERIENCES

1. **Ineffability** Very difficult to convey all aspects of the experience in words.
2. **Knowledge of others** Some people appear to know the speech and actions of those around them when they are deeply unconscious.
3. **Calmness** Strong sense of tranquillity and peace.
4. **Buzzing sound** Auditory sensations, described as buzzing, 'ringing of a loud bell', 'a whistling sound, like the wind'. Frequently experienced as unpleasant.
5. **The Dark Tunnel** Sensation of rapid movement along a 'dark tunnel', 'a long cave', 'a valley' (origin of the term 'Valley of the Shadow of Death?').
6. **OOBE aspect** Sensation of possessing a body apart from the physical one. Frequently great surprise is expressed about this.
7. **Meeting others** Encounters with 'spirits' of people one has known who have died.
8. **'Bewildered spirits'** (unusual) Reports of seeing people who are dead and bound to some object, person, habit; they appear in conflict or torment; they appear more humanised than other 'spirits'.
9. **The Being of Light** Appearance of a personal being, composed of brilliant but undazzling light, radiating intense joy, love, and warmth. Strongly ineffable. Frequently seen as a guide or emissary.
10. **The Review** The Being of Light directs the attention to the past life, to the actions undertaken and the consequences of others, wordlessly. This is done to evoke reflection, not to 'judge' the person. "He (Being of Light) was trying to show me something in each one of these flashbacks. All through this, he kept stressing the importance of love . . . There wasn't any accusation in any of this, though".
11. **The Vision of Knowledge** (unusual) Brief glimpses of a quite separate realm of existence in which all knowledge seems to co-exist in a timeless state. Very strongly ineffable.
12. **Cities of Light** (unusual) Sometimes described in almost Biblical terms as Heaven; rivers like glass, buildings of crystal; all suffused with light.
13. **The Border** A body of water, or a line, gate, fence, door, or grey mist; to cross it means to accept Death.
14. **Rescue or reprieve** (unusual) Belief that the Being of Light or some other agency pardons one or saves one from Death. In such cases the person is frequently afraid for another person still alive on earth; a spouse whose heart may be broken, a child who may not be brought up as the person would wish.
15. **The Return** Often disappointing *at the time*, especially in cases where people have been resuscitated after clinical death.
16. **Effects on later life** Very strongly positive. Loss of all fear of death, occasional reports of acquiring greater sensitivity to people (including developing psi abilities), strong sense of purpose. Reduced anxieties about life.
17. **Telling others** Frequently met with incomprehension or dismissal; people learn not to discuss NDEs too readily.

The Christian image of Hell. Some of those who have been at the point of death claim to have experienced a form of judgement, and to have seen realms of bewildered and unhappy spirits.

pointed, or rather it seemed to orient itself in some way down ... I realised that I was going to return to myself, to my body, and live. Although it sounds bizarre I must say I'm not sure I was altogether pleased. This light was so full of everything good that I think I almost wanted to stay. But it faded ... eventually I came round (15). I had been very severely injured in the crash.'

Now this person had never heard of Moody or his work, and yet the correspondence of his experiences with many of those described by Moody is striking. The major component missing in this account is what Moody terms The Review. The Being of Light frequently directs (non-verbally) the attention of the person to his life and its past events with a wordless question such as 'What have you done with your life? Are you prepared to die?' Moody's respondents said that such questions were never accusatory; they were aware of the Being's infinite and unqualified love for them. Many of Moody's respondents claimed that they had lost all fear of death, though they did not wish to die. The huge majority of those who have a Near-Death Experience treasure it, and live and think more positively afterwards.

The case for survival rests on the meetings of such people with others known to them who have died, and on the fact that an NDE is not brought to an end by clinical death (in one case lasting for over 15 minutes). The content of the NDE may even have an imagery familiar from the visionary writings of mystics: some people report having seen a 'realm of bewildered spirits', beings whose purpose in life has not been fulfilled, or who have committed suicide. An origin for the Day of Judgement, and consignment to Heaven or Hell, is implicit in The Review aspect of NDEs, in which the person is shown the consequences of his life's actions on other people. Moody, pondering on the perpetrators of Nazi atrocities, wrote that their actions would have 'resulted in countless individual tragedies ... innumerable long lingering deaths, and fast brutal ones ... in awful degradations, in years of hunger, tears, and torments for their victims. If what happened to my subjects happened to these men, they would see all those things and many others come alive, vividly portrayed before them. In my wildest fantasies, I am totally unable to imagine a hell more horrible, more ultimately unbearable than this.'

Naturally Moody sought for 'normal' explanations of Near-Death Experiences. A severely injured or stressed person is inevitably affected by powerful physiological events such as depleted oxygen supply to the brain, and isolation of the various senses. Some of Moody's reported NDE characteristics, notably the sensation of travelling along a tunnel, are quite commonly associated with such physiological stresses. Drugs and anaesthetics could also be a contributory factor to NDEs, although Moody cites one interesting case of a woman who had twice been close to death, once with and once without anaesthetics; she had an NDE only on the occasion when no anaesthetic was given.

Psychiatrist Ronald Siegel of Los Angeles has penned an extensive critical review of NDEs. He claims that they can be explained in terms of strong psychological needs and wishes combined with medical trauma. Most of the characteristics of NDEs, he points out, are also reported by people taking LSD and other hallucinatory drugs. This may be missing the point; why should there be any difference? If there is some continuity between out-of-the-body and near-death experiences why should we expect the latter to be completely different from certain experiences of those who are living and healthy?

Further, many features one might expect to be present in NDE reports if they are no more than wish-fulfilment are *not* present. One might expect religious people to report more NDEs then agnostics, but this is not the case. Accounts of cultural stereotypes of Heaven or Hell are extremely rare: for example, angels and devils are not frequently met with. Nor do social class, education, and economic status correlate with NDE imagery. And cultural biases simply do not appear to contaminate either the frequency of NDEs or their special characteristics. To date, no convincing suggestion as to their causes has been put forward.

Moody for one is sceptical about medical 'explanations' of NDEs; his own data being insufficient to prove survival after death, he has outlined a research programme for himself and others in years to come which will probe the matter further. At present NDE research is a very young subject and only taken seriously by a small number of unbiased researchers. To those who have had an NDE, however, and who have mentioned it to others and been met by blank incomprehension or dismissive comments about hallucinations, the subject is profoundly important.

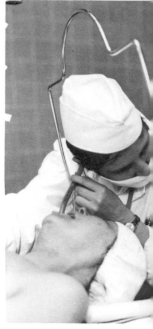

Even after being pronounced clinically dead some patients recover – having clearly seen and heard events around them during the period of 'death'.

Before leaving the topic of the NDE, it is worth considering whether there is a possible psi component in it. This possibility has been suggested by cases in which deeply anaesthetised people (or even clinically dead people) have heard and reported back to doctors what they were saying. One doctor reported to Moody:

'A woman patient of mine had a cardiac arrest just before another surgeon and I were due to operate on her. I was right there, and I saw her pupils dilate. We tried for some time to resuscitate her, but weren't having any success, so I thought she had gone. I told the other doctor who was working with me, "Let's try one more time and then we'll give up." This time she came around. Later I asked her what she remembered of her death . . . She said she heard me say "Let's try one more time and then we'll give up."'

Clearly such cases could be coincidence or even subliminal perception, but ESP is a possibility.

The importance of the NDE in the field of parapsychology as a whole is that it links the OOBE with evidence for survival from mediumship and from other areas. The similarities between OOBEs and NDEs are very considerable, as Moody's sample, much larger than Crookall's sample of stress-induced cases, shows. The few reports that exist in which people who have died are allegedly describing the death process through a medium are also similar to direct NDE reports. A similar relationship can be seen in the case of apparitions.

Apparitions: the quick and the dead

Are ghosts, or apparitions, purely hallucinatory? Many people report having seen a ghost – the experience is as old as our records of civilisation. Here is a fairly typical account of 'seeing a ghost':

'I was working in a large girls' boarding school in Kent. I was 29 years old and in excellent health, good eye-sight, and of a normal and non-excitable disposition.

'One night I was going downstairs, carrying an Aladdin Lamp [sic], turned fairly low . . . and as I reached the top of a long straight staircase I saw what appeared to be the figure of an elderly man walking down the staircase in front of me. He was five or six steps down when I saw him. His back was turned to me, his hair was grey, and one hand was on the banister rail.

'I stood still and watched him go down until on reaching the bottom of the staircase with his hand on the newel post, he disappeared. There was no sound of footsteps although the staircase was not carpeted. He seemed to be wearing a long dark garment.

'I knew at once he was a "ghost" but was only conscious of extreme interest. The house was very old, reputedly haunted, and there were of course a great many people living in it, although I suppose most of them were asleep at that time.

'Although I lived there for four years this was my only experience of the kind in that house, and although other people occasionally saw "ghosts" these were not the same as the figure of the old man.'

There are four good reasons for considering this a purely hallucinatory experience. The first is that *observing conditions were bad*, only the light of a dim lamp at night. The second is that *the house was reputedly haunted*; the maxim that we see what we expect to see has a grain of truth in it. Related to this is the third fact that *other people saw different 'ghosts'*; this very much suggests that there was nothing objective there, only subjective perceptions. Finally there is nothing about this report which suggests anything other than hallucination being involved.

So in what circumstances might an apparition not be a hallucination? We suggest there are four possible non-hallucinatory categories of 'ghost'.

1. *Collective apparitions:* cases in which several people independently see the same apparition in the same place at the same time.
2. *Hauntings:* repeated observations of an apparition by different people, at different times, in the same place.
3. *Crisis apparitions:* apparitions of the dying which appear to a living person around the time of death.
4. *Informative apparitions:* apparitions which give some information to the person seeing them which they could not otherwise have known.

The first two categories are not very common, although there are enough cases to make them worth considering. A typical example of a haunting would be the following:

'I had lived in Trondheim for four years and left the city in 1938, but

Trondheim Cathedral, Norway: the scene of a collectively experienced apparition of the figure of a Catholic nun.

have often visited the city since that time. I was much interested in the construction work done at the cathedral...

'One sunny morning I went into the cathedral. I walked along the north passage ... Looking across towards the south hall, I noticed a nun sitting quietly in one of the many niches along the wall ... I wondered what she was doing here at this time of day. I thought I would talk to her as I came closer, but when I was just six or seven feet away from her, she faded away and I saw her no more! I must say I was puzzled, but walking into the west end of the cathedral I stopped and talked to one of the women cleaning the church and said to her: "I thought I saw a Catholic nun over in the west end, sitting in a niche, but when I came near she disappeared. How could that be?" "Oh", answered the woman, "we often see her." And this I have verified by others.'

Such cases – when observations are made in good conditions, and when independent witnesses have been interviewed by researchers and the details checked – cannot easily be dismissed as hallucinations. The same can be said of collectively experienced apparitions.

Crisis and informative apparitions are rather more important, however. Crisis cases at least are fairly common and there is the possibility of verifying their accuracy. If a person reports seeing an apparition of someone at the time of their death in a distant place, unpredictably, then it is possible to verify the link by interviewing witnesses. If the link is verified, and not due to coincidence, we can at least say that if such apparitions are hallucinations they are hallucinations with added ESP.

The most important work in this area was done in the nineteenth century by the founders of the British Society for Psychical Research. These dedicated men and women produced the monumental study *Census of Hallucinations*, in which some 17,000 people were asked about their experience of hallucinations (including apparitions). The cost of doing a survey like this today would be astronomical! Some 2,300 people said that they had had at least one experience. After eliminating dreams, and experiences due to drugs, fever, and so on, some 1,700 cases were left. Of these, around 80 involved an apparitional experience coinciding with someone's death, and occurring within 12 hours of death. Extensive checking and questioning pared this number down to 32 cases where death could not possibly have been predicted, and where there were (in almost all cases) witnesses. 'Strong' cases, therefore, represented about 1.5 per cent of the total sample. From the Registrar-General's tables of the day it was found that the odds against a person dying on any given day were some 19,000 to one. Clearly the number of 'crisis apparitions' largely exceeded the coincidence rate to be expected by chance, and so the researchers concluded that coincidence could not be the explanation: at the least, telepathy must be involved. Unfortunately there were many subjective aspects to these evaluations. Alan Gauld, an expert on spontaneous psi cases, has commented that the statistical methods used would not be acceptable today. Data such as these cannot be straitjacketed into scientific

A reputedly haunted house in Cambridgeshire. Does the knowledge that a house may be haunted predispose people to see apparitions? Experiments by Gertrude Schmeidler show that psychics can identify the sites of actual reported hauntings.

analysis – there are simply too many uncertainties attached to them. However, it must be pointed out that the actual rate of coincidence between experiencing an apparition and the death of the person whose apparition is experienced exceeded the chance level by a factor of around 250. Even if the researchers' methods had been responsible for some freak results, this is still an impressive margin.

If we accept, at least for the sake of argument, that apparitions may not be explicable solely in terms of coincidence and subjective hallucination, do they appear to favour a 'survivalist' interpretation? Or can they be explained by the operation of a particularly powerful ESP – Super-ESP, if you like? There are points in favour of both. On balance, the Super-ESP hypothesis looks marginally more likely, although collectively experienced apparitions are particularly hard to explain in such terms.

An interesting recent advance, which promises greater progress in the experimental study of apparitions than hitherto, has been made by Gertrude Schmeidler and her colleagues. After investigating allegedly 'haunted' premises, they compiled lists of what 'ghosts' had been seen doing in the places in the house where they had been seen. Small groups of 'psychics' and sensitives were then asked to visit the houses and check off 'correct' actions and locations from a list which contained both true and false items randomly intermixed. Schmeidler found that some of the psychics were able to pinpoint, some to a highly significant extent, what the 'ghosts' had done and where they had been seen, claiming to have picked up this information from the 'vibes' in the building. A control group of sceptics scored uniformly at chance on this task, a particularly interesting result for rather complex reasons. If we suppose that sceptics would tend to explain 'ghosts' in terms of hallucination and tricks of the light, and if we suppose that this really is the explanation for ghosts, then one might have expected the sceptics to score well, since they would naturally select precisely those shady corners, nooks or crannies which would favour optical illusion. But they did not. The psychics may, of course, have succeeded by ordinary ESP, but their claim that they directly picked up something from the buildings themselves cannot be discounted.

Is there anybody there?

In Chapter 2 we examined the remarkable career of D. D. Home, a *physical* medium, a person who appears to be in communication with 'spirits' and in whose presence paranormal physical effects (PK) appear to happen. Where survival after death is concerned, however, our attention must turn to *mental* mediums. Mental mediums convey information which they usually claim to have obtained, paranormally, from the 'spirits' of dead human beings, now inhabiting another world. It is, of course, always possible that such information could be the result of Super-ESP. The first task, however, is to decide whether there is a paranormal element at work here at all.

The medium Mrs Leonore Piper . . .

Now the vast majority of mental mediums are inoffensive people whose sincerity it would be uncharitable to question but who produce a great deal of waffle which no seasoned researcher takes seriously. Their services can be comforting to relatives of a recently deceased person and many of them charge no fee or only a token fee. They are not commercially orientated charlatans exploiting the gullible for profit. On the contrary they are often kindly and very well meaning people.

The 'Golden Age' of mental mediumship roughly spanned the years between 1880 and 1940. During this period six female mental mediums – all of whom had high reputation – were investigated thoroughly, and in every case reasonable evidence for psi was obtained. Since that time no equivalents have been reported on (although one of the six, the flamboyant Irish-born medium Eileen Garrett, died only a decade ago). Why this recent dearth? Sceptics would say that researchers now know all about mediums' tricks and so the 'evidence' for mediumship has simply evaporated. But there is another explanation which we will present shortly. In any case the sceptic's argument would fail, and fail badly, when confronted with one man alone, the Australian researcher Richard Hodgson, the man who studied the first great mental medium and arguably the most powerful of all, Mrs Leonore Piper. In fact the details of Mrs Piper's career are far more revealing and of considerably more value than a shallower general survey of mediumship.

In 1884 Mrs Piper was a quite unexceptional Bostonian housewife, unexceptional, that is, until she visited a faith-healing medium, slipped into trance and received a 'message' for another sitter. She then began holding seances for her friends, during which time a 'control' spirit, a Frenchman calling himself Dr Phinuit, became a regular *dramatis persona*. Phinuit was the intermediary between Mrs Piper's sitters and the 'spirits' with which they wished to communicate. Rumours about these sittings reached the ears of the psychologist William James, who was curious enough to attend one of her seances in 1885. Later, James despatched other researchers to Mrs Piper, introducing them with pseudonyms. Many expressed the view that Mrs Piper had given them information, often of a quite personal and intimate nature, which they did not think she could have obtained by normal means. One however wrote to James describing her as 'that insipid prophetess' – she was not a woman of great education or erudition.

In 1887 a Richard Hodgson arrived in Boston to take up the post of Secretary to the American Society for Psychical Research. Naturally he attended some of Mrs Piper's seances. From his own letters and those of others he emerges as a fairly obnoxious human being, extremely intelligent, but also belligerent, insensitive, and vituperative – a less likely dupe of charlatanry it would have been difficult to find. Yet he eventually became convinced not only that Mrs Piper had psi ability but that her case proved the reality of survival after death.

An Australian, born in 1855, Hodgson read Law at Melbourne and Moral Sciences at Cambridge, and was a founder member of the (British) Society for Psychical Research. In 1884 the Society sent him to India to study Madame Blavatsky and the Theosophists, and to evaluate the 'paranormal' happenings which they claimed took place at their meetings. Hodgson's report was devastating; he regarded Blavatsky as a fraud and most of the Theosophists as pathetic dupes. In other investigations he zestfully destroyed the credibility of witnesses at seances held by physical mediums, in which activity he was helped by his considerable abilities as a conjuror. In short, Hodgson's forte was debunking, and there is plenty of evidence to show that in full cry he was as subtle as an air-raid and twice as unpleasant.

Working with other researchers, Hodgson approached the case of Mrs Piper in his typically meticulous manner. Complete verbatim records of most seances were kept, and signed testimonies from seance participants collected. *Proxy sittings* were also organised – a proxy sitting is one in which a sitter is sent along and told to ask about, say, Mr Alfred Robinson, even though the sitter has no idea who Mr Alfred Robinson is; this eliminates the possibility of the medium acquiring information from involuntary 'cues' displayed by the sitter.

In 1889 Hodgson exported Mrs Piper to England. There, too, many proxy sittings were held. On arrival at the house of the researcher Sir Oliver Lodge, Mrs Piper's baggage was checked for any information she might have collected on potential sitters. Indeed on one famous occasion Hodgson actually hired private detectives to follow her and her family to check that she was not secretly researching her sitters by going to libraries, talking to friends and so on. At the time Lodge had a house full of newly employed servants who could have told Mrs Piper almost nothing of value. Sittings were held with individuals chosen 'in great measure by chance' by Hodgson; in some cases he even selected them after Mrs Piper had gone into trance, precluding her from collecting any information about them in advance. In one sitting, Lodge presented Mrs Piper with a watch belonging to an uncle of his whom he had known slightly in his later years. 'Uncle Jerry' announced himself, named his brother, and claimed ownership of the watch. Lodge replied

. . . and Richard Hodgson, the debunker who couldn't debunk her!

that he would need information (not known to him) about Jerry's early life to validate this claim, which he would then check with the surviving brother. 'Uncle Jerry' obliged. As Lodge wrote:

'"Uncle Jerry" recalled episodes such as swimming the creek when they were boys together, and running some risk of getting drowned; killing a cat in Smith's field; the possession of a small rifle, and of a long peculiar skin, like a snake-skin, which he thought was not in the possession of Uncle Robert [the surviving brother].

'All these facts have been more or less completely verified ...'

What Lodge did *not* report was that these correct and sometimes very specific and unusual items of information were interspersed with generalities and erroneous comments. However, a reading of the full records suggests that quite a good proportion of correct and specific information was given in the seance. One could indeed dismiss this as coincidence, in isolation. But when an individual appears able to provide substantially correct information over and over again this argument wears thin. Though the Lodge sitting was not a proxy sitting as such, it approximated to one: information was given which was completely unknown to anyone present.

Coincidence can also be ruled out from an experiment conducted with Mrs Piper after her return to America. Phinuit had now been largely displaced by 'G.P.', ostensibly the 'spirit' of a young man, George Pellew, who died in an accident in 1892. G.P. correctly recognised, from a total of 150 sitters, the 30 he had known when alive, and only those 30. He never made a mistake. The odds against this happening by chance are astronomical. A less quantifiable, but equally important, point is that G.P. behaved in slightly different ways entirely appropriate to each individual; his demeanour and style of conversation were, his friends claimed, exactly as they had been towards them when he was alive. During G.P.'s control, Hodgson had almost complete supervision of seance proceedings, and very full and complete records were kept.

What is most remarkable about Mrs Piper is that *every* researcher who studied her at first hand for a reasonable period became convinced that she had paranormal powers. The records of her seances run to several thousand pages, and so we do no more than dip into the evidence here, but the accumulated material defied, and defies, disbelief. Hodgson, with other sceptics almost as hostile, was totally convinced by Mrs Piper. Indeed Hodgson went further than believing in Mrs Piper's paranormal powers. He believed that her mediumship proved survival after death. This belief is thought to rest on evidence he did *not* publish – it was rumoured that Mrs Piper gave him information of an intensely personal nature concerning a deceased woman. Did this influence his judgement?

What conclusions can we draw from the career of Mrs Piper? She certainly provided accurate information about persons and events she could not possibly have known about. But was this information communicated to her by the spirits of the dead? Or was it the result of

Mrs Piper's reputation on both sides of the Atlantic was enough to make front-page news. This sensationalised 'confession' should not be taken too seriously – but indicates the degree of public interest in the subject.

powerful, unconscious Super-ESP? That she had psi ability of some kind is really beyond question. And there are good reasons for not accepting that her feats demonstrated the reality of survival after death. 'G.P.', her second control spirit, was very unusual in that he had a historical existence during life: more usually, the control spirits of mediums seem much more like secondary or alternative personalities of the mediums themselves. Studies of mediums in trance – using word-association tests, EEG measurements and other instruments of enquiry – have often shown that the 'spirit' is psychologically very different from the medium. Further than that, however, it is very hard to go.

One further piece of evidence from mediumship, however, seems to tip the balance somewhat against the Super-ESP hypothesis. It comes from Alan Gauld, whom we have already mentioned. He studied instances in which the information given by 'spirits' about their lives on Earth can be verified by consulting historical sources. Gauld was fortunate enough to find an archive of material gathered 20 years before by a group of amateurs who had held seances over a period of time: detailed notes on the seances had been kept and filed away. In this archive, Gauld unearthed several cases in which 'spirits' of persons unknown to the participants gave information about their lives which, although subsequently proved to be correct, were originally published *incorrectly* in contemporary sources! In such a case there can be no question of one of the seance participants having inadvertently read about the dead person – or of somehow using Super-ESP to extract information from published material.

Here is one quite extraordinary example, involving one 'Harry Stockbridge' – a pseudonym used by Gauld for the young man in question. The 'spirit' of Harry Stockbridge (who was unknown to any of the participants) arrived at the seance unannounced, as it were, and gave the following details about his life. We give the results of Gauld's own researches in brackets:

'Second Loot attached Northumberland Fusiliers. Died Fourteen July, Sixteen.' (A second lieutenant in the Northumberland Fusiliers, named Harry Stockbridge, was killed on 14 July 1916. The date of death is *incorrectly* given in the War Office official lists.)

'Tyneside Scottish.' (Stockbridge was originally in a Tyneside Irish battalion of the Northumberland Fusiliers, but at the time of his death had been transferred to a Tyneside Scottish battalion, a fact which does not seem to have found its way into print.)

'Tall, dark, thin. Special features large brown eyes.'
(Verified by relatives and by a photograph, but not, so far as could be discovered, mentioned in any printed source.)

'I hung out in Leicester.' (True.)

Asked what were his likes and dislikes: 'Problems any. Pepys reading. Water colouring.'

(He studied mathematics and physics at university. His university career is referred to in print, but not his subject of study. Relatives could not answer for sure on the latter points.)

Asked if he knew a 'Powis Street' about which a sitter had dreamed: 'I knew it well.'
(It later transpired that there was a street of this name not far from his birthplace.)

Now, at some points we would like more detail: what more could have been said about Powis Street, for example? But the first three points – correct name, date of death, description, regiment, battalion – considering that these were sometimes unknown in print or wrongly stated, if we accept that coincidence is *not* an explanation (and the existence of other good cases from the same group makes this highly unlikely) then we are dealing here either with psi or with an extensive and extremely careful fraud.

The traditions and mathematical apparatus of astrology may disguise the fact that an astrologer is actually using ESP to discover information.

Spirits and UFOs: useful scapegoats?

An intriguing experiment, of relevance here, is that carried out by Iris Owen and others in Toronto. A small group of highly dedicated researchers wrote for themselves an entirely fictional biography of a 'spirit' they named Philip. They then held a series of seances with the object of getting in touch with him. Eventually 'Philip' did indeed begin to communicate with them through an ouija board. More interestingly 'Philip' began to levitate tables and produce apparent PK effects! The experiment has not been satisfactorily replicated, but it suggests very strongly that 'spirits' might simply be a psychological prop for the medium.

Are UFOs the 'ghosts' of the technologically advanced twentieth century?

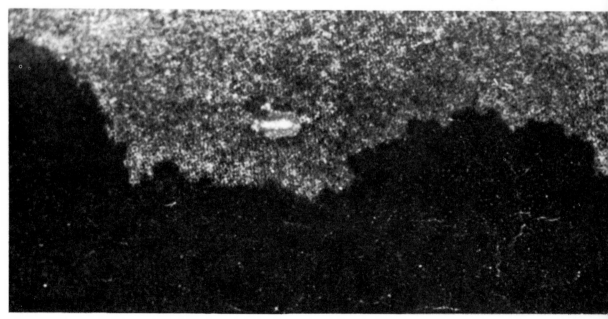

This gains credibility if we consider the point made by Rex Stanford and others – namely that psi events (especially powerful ones) are ego-alien. We are not entirely comfortable with them. Thus our chances of exerting psi effects are stronger if we can somehow blame their occurrence on someone or something else. The 'spirits' represent such a something else. This account would go a long way towards explaining the undoubted fact that great mediums are only to be found in the past. In the nineteenth and (to a lesser extent) the early twentieth century, 'the spirits' were to some extent culturally acceptable. Their acceptability has declined. Other forms of psychological prop are required. Speculatively, three possibilities raise their heads. From those who argue that it is the *experimenters* in parapsychology who generate results from their own psi, one could adduce that the *subjects* in those experiments are the psychological props! A second possibility (less worthy of study) is that unidentified flying objects might be a prop. UFOlogists have reported cases of alleged spontaneous ESP and PK among people who claim to have been contacted by UFOs, for which they believe the UFOs or their occupants may have been responsible. More in keeping with the times, certainly, than spirits of the dead. We are not impressed by the reported evidence – but the idea could be tested. The third intriguing possibility concerns astrology. Although there is little evidence to show that *traditional* astrology has any validity, there is a moderate amount to show that astrologers can give accurate information from birth charts alone. So they could be doing this by ESP – indeed, two of them have suggested this to us. The astrologer would have the best psychological prop of all – a system which is, at least in principle, based on scientific theory! One could hardly imagine a better psychological prop for the late twentieth century.

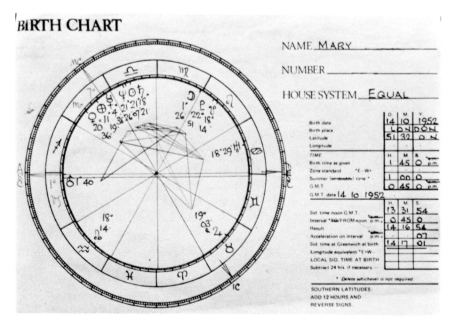

An astrological birth chart, showing the positions of the planets (symbols within the inner circle) in the signs of the Zodiac (symbols in the 12 divisions of the inner circle). From the mass of information – the planets, their links (lines within the inner circle), and the signs they occupy – some astrologers are capable of making accurate statements about people. But might they be using ESP to do this with the birth chart just acting as a psychological prop which facilitates the use of ESP?

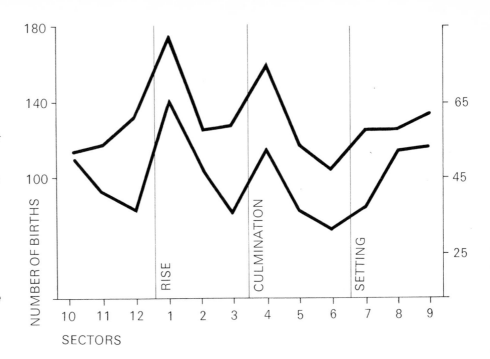

Is there any scientific evidence to show that astrology works? Research by the Gauquelins in France provides some. The chart shows the frequency of births of sports champions when Mars is in different positions in the sky: they tend to be born most often when Mars is close to the eastern horizon (Rise) or directly overhead (Culmination). Data from the Gauquelins are shown in the upper curve and left-hand scale, independent data in the lower curve and right-hand scale.

These speculations suggest that the Super-ESP hypothesis is not, after all, entirely devoid of any predictive value. However, let us speculate a little further about the survival issue. If we suppose Mind can leave the body, and survive independently of it, might it not be capable of re-associating itself with another physical body? Reincarnation is not a common belief in Judaeo–Christian cultures but it is common elsewhere. Clearly if reincarnation were established as a likely fact one would probably have to accept some notion of survival after death. The evidence for reincarnation comes from two sources of widely differing value: studies of 'hypnotic regression to past lives' and direct studies of possible reincarnation in children. It is these cases we now need to examine.

Hypnotic regression: living past lives over?

Hypnotic regression to *childhood* is a hotly debated, although 'normal', phenomenon. Hypnotised persons have been asked to recall events from their very early years and behave as they did at that age; there is much conflicting evidence, but some of it suggests that such people can act in ways very like children of the appropriate age in ways not easily simulated by non-hypnotised people. It would be accepted by almost everyone, though, that there remains a strong contaminating effect of the mind of the adult who is being regressed; it is as though a hybrid of a child and an adult is speaking to the hypnotist. This and many similar problems confront the hypnotist who attempts to regress the hypnotised person back beyond birth to a 'past life'.

In the last decade much attention has been given to two British hypnotists, Arnold Bloxham and Joe Keeton, who have conducted many such regressions and presented their findings with an admirable lack of axe-grinding. It would be fair to say that, in most cases, nothing has emerged to support the notion of survival after death. This is not surprising – a balanced view of hypnosis would be to say that 95 per cent of what happens to 95 per cent of hypnotised people is simple role-playing, response to suggestions, acting, and going along with the hypnotist. It is the other 5 per cent which is interesting. It is certainly fair to assume that the overwhelming majority of alleged hypnotic regressions to past lives is made up simply of acted-out fantasies, reconstructed from half-forgotten historical books or magazines. Bloxham and Keeton were both well aware of this, although some other hypnotists have not been so cautious.

Among the interesting minority of cases, perhaps the most impressive one could find is that of 'Jane Evans', from Bloxham's files. This woman was regressed to *six* different past lives. For at least three of them, sufficient corroborating evidence could be found for the existence of the historical character to suggest that coincidence would not be a likely explanation; the others were rather too vague. Now this does diminish the possibility of fraud: who would bother to check large amounts of historical material (at least some of it buried in obscure archives and discovered only subsequently), for *three* different characters? The motivation is missing, for the woman in question has never made any fame or fortune from her experiences. Fraud is not impossible, but it is not a *reasonable* explanation.

The 'six lives' of Jane Evans were recorded by Bloxham and later checked by Jeff Iverson, a BBC producer who made a programme on the research. By one of those strange coincidences, Iverson was born in the same Welsh town as Jane (and one of the present authors) although the two had never met.

A particularly intriguing example of Jane Evans's allegedly previous incarnations is that of Rebecca, a Jewess killed in pogrom in York in 1190. Under hypnosis, in the character of Rebecca, Jane gave a chilling account of being trapped with her child in the crypt of a small church just outside the gates of the city as a murderous mob closed in. Those who have heard the tapes testify that Jane's behaviour as she recounted the final scenes of butchery in the crypt was emotional to an alarming and distressing degree.

In other sessions, 'Rebecca' gave details of her life in York prior to her murder, naming many places and individuals whose identity could be verified, together with others that could not. The latter could be wrong or simply not recorded in the incomplete records we have for the period. However, a key aspect of Rebecca's testimony was the church in which she claimed to have died. Professor Barrie Dobson, a professor at York University and an authority on Jewish history of the time, was called in to listen to the tapes. Dobson thought that, of all the surviving churches in York, only one, St Mary's Castlegate, fitted Rebecca's description. Unfortunately, the church did not have a crypt.

Six months later, Dobson wrote to Iverson, the producer, with an extraordinary piece of news. A workman engaged in the renovation of the church had accidentally broken into what looked like a crypt beneath the chancel. It was blocked up again before archaeologists could examine it. But the workman had seen round stone arches and vaults, indicating the Norman or Romanesque period of building, that is, before 1190 rather than after. More recently still, the discovery of re-used Roman and Anglo-Saxon masonry below floor-level in St Mary's Castlegate makes it absolutely certain that there was a church on the site in Rebecca's time.

This is intriguing: a piece of evidence turns up retrospectively which supports Rebecca's claims. This could not be fraud or reconstruction from memory. There may indeed be something worthy of investigation in cases of hypnotic regression. But for every one solid case hundreds fall apart on a brief checking. Nor would it be surprising if further historical research weakened even the best cases on record. Unfortunately very few investigations of hypnotic regression have been carried out by professional parapsychologists. Ian Wilson, author of an excellent volume on the Turin Shroud, has recently examined such cases for his book *Mind out of Time?* In it, he makes many criticisms of hypnotic regression work. The value of his criticisms is lessened by his concentrating his attack on weak cases, but he is certainly correct in concluding that most hypnotic regressions provide absolutely no evidence for 'past lives'. Much better evidence for reincarnation can be obtained from direct studies of individuals who appear to be reincarnations of deceased people. Why this should be so becomes clear when we consider the different areas from which the evidence is drawn.

Reincarnation: direct studies

In 1977 the prestigious *Journal of Nervous and Mental Diseases* published two papers on the subject of reincarnation by Dr Ian Stevenson, a researcher based at the University of Virginia. That such a journal should publish on such an unusual topic is a clear indication of the esteem in which Stevenson's work is held, even by sceptics.

There are two good reasons why Stevenson's evidence is simpler to evaluate than hypnotic regression evidence. First, Stevenson's cases concern *very young children*, whereas regressions involve adults. The hypothesis of reconstruction from mostly forgotten memories of papers, books, magazines and radio and TV programmes is important with respect to adults (with many years' exposure to such sources of information) but not to children of two or three years of age. Second, Stevenson's cases mostly come from relatively underdeveloped countries where sources of communication of this kind are hardly plentiful. In short, a regression from a literate and observant Western adult will pose many more problems than cases involving very young children from semi-literate societies.

The most characteristic quality of Stevenson's work is its sheer professionalism. Through one of his many contacts, he hears first details of a case of possible reincarnation. Almost without exception, the case concerns a *very* young child (in around half the cases he investigates, two years or younger) whose utterances and behaviour suggest reincarnation. Stevenson will travel to study the case at first hand: in Alaska, Lebanon, India, Brazil, Ceylon . . . literally all over the globe. Stevenson himself speaks fluent French and German, and in other cases uses trusted interpreters to interrogate witnesses. Witnesses are almost always interviewed more than once to check for reliability. For any given case, Stevenson uses at least two interpreters, and sometimes three or four, to check testimony and the accuracy of inter-pretation. Stevenson possesses a vast library of tapes from these inter-views. Documents, registries, archives are meticulously checked for corroboration of testimonies. The care and attention to detail are remarkable.

First we may look in depth at a case of unusual evidential value, which Stevenson was able to investigate *before* the two families con-cerned (the family of the child and that of the deceased person of whom the child appeared to be a reincarnation) had met. Obviously, such cases offer the researcher the chance to check testimony unaffected by confused memory after meeting the other family.

A Druse community in the Lebanon. Belief in reincarnation is widespread among this Islamic sect.

Stevenson arrived in Lebanon in 1964 after being told by a young Lebanese, who had assisted him in a Brazilian investigation two years before, that many cases of reincarnation occurred in his home country. Among the Druse people, who belong to an unusual Islamic sect, belief in reincarnation is common: indeed, it is a fundamental tenet of their religion. However, many Druses express considerable scepticism about particular cases of reincarnation: they are not a gullible people. As Stevenson set out among these people to find his Lebanese contact, he learned of a case in the village he had come to visit, Kornayel, some ten miles east of Beirut. It transpired that the father of the child concerned was a cousin of the man he had come to meet. On his first evening, Stevenson made complete written notes of his interview with this man, Mohammed Elawar, and his wife. On this occasion only an untrained interpreter was on hand: for a further four days, Stevenson used two other, trained, interpreters. Stevenson rechecked much of his material, and added new information, on a second visit five months later (with another interpreter).

On his first visit, Stevenson was told how Mohammed's son Imad had been born in December 1958. One might have suspected that something strange was going on when the first word he spoke was 'Jamileh', had one known that this was the name of the mistress of Ibrahim Bouhamzy, the man whose reincarnation Imad appears to have been. As soon as he could string sentences together, Imad was speaking of his past life. His father scolded him for telling lies, but Imad persisted. At the age of two years he had spontaneously recognised a neighbour of Bouhamzy's in the street. He had given many details of his (i.e. Bouhamzy's) house, his relatives, his own life. Nonetheless his family did not feel moved to do any checking. Mohammed, the father, had once attended a funeral in the town of Khriby, where Bouhamzy had lived, but had not met any member of the Bouhamzy family.

The two villages were separated by some 20 miles, but the people of

REINCARNATION : THE CASE OF IMAD ELAWAR

In all cases, there was at least one informant for each item and at least one corroborator.
In many cases, there were two or more informants and corroborators.
Evidence from Imad Elawar in advance of Stevenson's visit to Khriby.

Item	Comments
1. His name was Bouhamzy and he lived in Khriby.	1. The first name was never used (i.e., Ibrahim).
2. He had a woman called Jamileh.	2. Correct : Ibrahim's mistress.
3. She was beautiful.	3. Jamileh was famous in Khriby for her beauty.
4. She wore high heels.	4. Correct, and very unusual amongst Druse women.
5. He had a brother 'Amin'.	5. Amin was a close relative. Close relatives may be termed 'brother'.
6. Amin worked at Tripoli.	6. Correct.
7. Amin worked in a courthouse.	7. Amin was an official of the Lebanese Government. His office was in a courthouse.
8. There was someone called 'Mehibeh'.	8. Cousin of Ibrahim Bouhamzy.
9. He had brothers called Said and Toufic.	9. Ibrahim had cousins called Said and Toufic : see point 5.
10. He had a sister, Huda.	10. Correct.
11. A truck ran over a man, broke both his legs, and crushed his trunk.	11. All details correct for Said Bouhamzy (note 9).
12. He (Ibrahim) was a friend of Mr Kemal Jouhblatt.	12. Ibrahim was a friend of this Druse politician and philosopher.
13. He was very fond of hunting.	13. Ibrahim was passionately fond of hunting. Imad frequently asked his father to take him hunting.
14. He had a double-barrelled shotgun.	14. Correct.
15. He also had a rifle.	15. Correct.
16. He had hidden his gun.	16. Correct. Presumably refers to rifle, which is an illegal possession in Lebanon.
17. He had a brown dog and had once beaten another dog.	17. Ibrahim had a brown dog, which had once fought with another dog which Ibrahim had beaten.
18. His house was in Khriby : there was a slope before it.	18. Correct.
19. There were two wells at the house, one full and one empty.	19. Correct. These were not spring wells, but concrete concavities used for storing grape juice. During the rainy season one became filled with water, whilst the shallower one did not, since water evaporated from it. Hence one was full and one empty.
20. They were building a new garden when he died.	20. When Ibrahim died, the garden was being rebuilt.
21. There were apple and cherry trees in the garden.	21. Correct.
22. He had a small yellow car, and a minibus.	22. Both correct.
23. He also had a truck.	23. Correct.
24. He used the truck for hauling rocks.	24. Correct.
25. There were two garages at his house.	25. Almost correct. Ibrahim kept his vehicles in the open, outside two *sheds*.
26. The tools for the car were kept in the attic.	26. Correct.
27. He had a goat, and sheep.	27. Correct.
28. He had five children.	28. Quite wrong : he had none. Said (note 9) had five sons.

Lebanon in this region tended not to travel very much, and members of the Elawar and Bouhamzy families were adamant that they had not met. After collecting all the information he could about Imad, Stevenson set out for Khriby to collect as much information as possible from the Bouhamzy family itself.

Finally Imad and his father were taken to Khriby, where Imad was introduced to the Bouhamzy family. He recognised many of them spontaneously, addressing them in the correct manner. The Bouhamzies were astonished at the way Imad *behaved*, which is not the least important aspect of such cases. This five-year-old child behaved, the family said, just as Ibrahim had.

The sum total of correct statements made by Imad about his past life, involving intimate details, precise statements about his home and his relatives, is summarised overleaf. The sheer wealth of information seems to rule out coincidence completely as an explanation of the correspondences. Of 57 statements checked by Stevenson, no less than 51 were correct.

What possible explanation – apart from that of reincarnation – could we conceive of for this case? Since the families insisted that they had not met, there is no chance of a member of one family discussing Ibrahim with a member of Imad's family, and that second person getting confused and thinking that Imad had said it. It is perhaps possible that one or two incidental meetings had been made and forgotten, but is implausible in the extreme that so many of Imad's statements could have been correct as a result of a few casual comments long forgotten.

Some details the Bouhamzy family would surely have preferred to keep quiet: Ibrahim's mistress, for example. Fraud is really unlikely when one's claimed past life risks the embarrassment of social disapproval. One might simply consider that a conspiracy between 17 people with no conceivable motivation for undertaking it is much more implausible than reincarnation.

Stevenson has reported scores of cases of possible reincarnation. Errors of testimony, memory, and fraud – 'conventional' explanations – do not appear able to cope with the facts. Stevenson considers that some paranormal explanation is justified by the data. As we have seen consistently throughout this chapter, the 'survival' and 'Super-ESP' explanations are the two major rivals.

Stevenson accepts that Super-ESP could explain much of the correct *information* reported by the children in reincarnation cases. However, he points out that it is difficult to explain the fact that the children only appear to have ESP related to *one person*, the person whose reincarnation they appear to be. Above all, Stevenson says, it is the *personality* aspect which strongly suggests survival. In Imad's case, his natural manner of behaviour strongly resembled that of the dead Bouhamzy. In some cases families have spontaneously recognised similarities in the personality of the deceased person and that of the child in which the deceased is allegedly reincarnated. How can this possibly be just

Super-ESP? Alan Gauld has written that he has studied many of the older psychical researchers in great detail, and knows more about them that anyone could possibly expect to learn by ESP: but he is also sure that not for a moment could he accurately impersonate them in this way. Now, certainly, there are excellent mimics in show business; but could one of them convince the mother of a dead man that he was a reincarnation of that person? Surely not. So how can we reasonably entertain the idea that children of four or five, even using ESP-acquired information, could effect a convincing impersonation of a dead stranger?

We have made much of Stevenson's pioneering research, but a caveat must be added with which we are sure Stevenson himself would agree. A clear priority is for other dedicated researchers to replicate, in broad fashion, Stevenson's enquiries. Certainly some others have researched reincarnation cases, but no-one has conducted such an exhaustive and extensive enquiry over many years as Stevenson. It is understandable why this is so: the expense in terms of time and money is considerable. But it is a crucial next step in reincarnation research.

The question of survival

Some decades ago, J. B. Rhine nearly managed to exorcise the survival problem from the realm of parapsychology. For him, it was not a scientific question: the Super-ESP hypothesis would always provide a possible alternative, so the question was ultimately beyond scientific proof one way or the other.

This was an extraordinary attitude for Rhine to take, even given the times he lived in. For exactly the same attitude of mind is exemplified by those sceptics who believe that all parapsychology is fraud or bad experiment. It is in principle impossible to disprove that. It could indeed be the case that scores of scientists have conspired to defraud their colleagues (which would have to include both of the authors). We reject that 'explanation', as all intelligent people will, because while not impossible it is an absurdly unreasonable argument to offer. Similarly, some of the best evidence in survival research, especially the detailed behavioural evidence from Stevenson's reincarnation studies, is getting close to reducing the Super-ESP hypothesis to absurdity – even though it is not possible to rule it out completely. We cannot decide the issue scientifically: but we can decide it rationally, just as we decide rationally to reject the notion that ALL significant ESP results are the product of a gigantic conspiracy.

Rhine did live and work in an age in which death was a taboo topic. There is some truth in the notion that the twentieth century replaced sex with death as the topic not to be discussed in polite company. Recently attitudes have changed. The interest in euthanasia, the hospice movement, the experiments of Stanislav Grof with hallucinogens to ease the deaths of terminally ill people; all these things and more suggest that we are trying now to come to terms with death, and the growing interest in survival research amongst parapsychologists reflects this. Attitudes to survival, of course, vary enormously. Spiritualists anticipate their deaths with happy certainty of a blissful after-life, while the Cambridge philosopher C. D. Broad expressed a hope that there was no survival on the grounds that this world was bad enough without having to put up with another one. Other philosophers have established to their own personal satisfaction that survival after death is inconceivable, since a linguistic analysis shows that our concept of 'personality' is irretrievably bound up with the notion of a physical continuity. Only one thing remains certain: death is the one experience which all human beings can be sure that they will experience alone. None of us will 'know' for certain whether we survive physical death until a few minutes after our brains have finally stopped functioning. Some people have been so fascinated by this problem that they have actually committed suicide in order to find out. Whilst few of us have so keen an interest as that, it seems unlikely that human beings will not continue to direct their ingenuity to the problem which has obsessed people from time immemorial.

As we have seen already, a clear majority of scientists believe that ESP is either an established fact or a likely possibility, and that parapsychology is a bona fide scientific enterprise. We have also seen that a flat assertion that psi is incompatible with physics is ill-judged.

On the other hand, it is clear that most scientists do not feel that parapsychology has made much progress, and some remain hostile to it. Why is this? The consensus view of poor progress can only really be put down to ignorance. We have shown that modern research areas (like the 'altered state' experiments and the covert psi testing) are superior to older experiments on several counts. First, they are more repeatable. Second, the psi effects are generally more powerful. Third, there has been a development of clear theories and models underpinning the new research. Now, maybe some scientists would say 'The effects still aren't repeatable enough: the effects aren't strong enough: the theories are unconvincing.' Fine (although subjective and not our view): but the point is, *parapsychology has clearly made progress on all these counts*. That many scientists do not realise this can only be ascribed to ignorance: they don't read the journals, they don't seek out the facts.

Psi: the historical problem

In our experience many scientists become very uncomfortable when parapsychology is discussed. They know they know little about it; they realise that they ought to know more about it; yet they fight shy of it. Why is this?

One factor must be the dubious history of parapsychology. Mediumship has been riddled with fraud since time immemorial. Parapsychology has emerged from a shady background. Yet this is true for other areas of science too: hypnosis would be an obvious example. Further, modern experimental techniques for studying psi in the laboratory eliminate almost any possibility of subjects' cheating. This anxiety is surely misplaced.

Sceptics point with glee to the one established case of fraud by a *researcher* in parapsychology (in 1974: he had worked on psi in animals). However, this is certainly not unique to parapsychology. Is all I.Q. testing dubious because of the probable fraud of Sir Cyril Burt? Is cancer research to be viewed as suspicious because of the fraud of the Sloan–Kettering research institute (also in 1974)? Is genetics suspicious because of the faking of results by Mendel or his assistants? Hardly. When one finds that a particular experimental result has been replicated by ten different experimenters in five different countries (as is the case with the ESP/extraversion correlation), then fraud by the researchers is hardly a credible explanation of the findings as reported. One of us wrote a quarter of a century ago:

Unless there is a gigantic conspiracy involving some thirty University departments all over the world, and several hundred highly respected scientists in various fields, many of them originally sceptical to the claims of the psychical researchers, the only conclusion that the unbiased observer can come to must be that there does exist a small number of people who obtain knowledge existing either in other people's minds, or in the outer world, by means yet unknown to science.

The only revision necessary now would be that the number of people involved is larger than it was then!

To have a concern about fraud in science is reasonable. To try and 'explain' everything in terms of fraud is disreputable.

Another historical factor which concerns some scientists is that parapsychology reeks of magic, long declared an enemy of science. Some scientists fear that the very attempt to set psi on a scientific basis will somehow encourage a superstitious, irrational anti-scientific attitude. The perfect reply to this has been given by the astronomer Carl Sagan, attacking a repressive editorial in the (American) *Humanist* about astrology:

The fundamental point is not that the origins of astrology are shrouded in superstition. This is true as well for chemistry, medicine and astronomy, to mention only three.

The repeatability issue

Some sceptics also profess a concern about repeatability. They claim that, if an experiment is conducted on a particular theme, examining some hypothesis, then it should generally be counted upon to produce the same results. The nearest we get to this in parapsychology is probably the Ganzfeld/relaxation studies, where some 50–60 per cent of experiments do produce results well above chance: 10-12 times more than chance would predict. This is claimed by the sceptics to be too low; a higher percentage of success is required.

But just what *is* that higher percentage, and can it be justified? How high can we expect? How repeatable is repeatable? One cannot expect from human beings behaviour as predictable as that of chemicals in flasks or electrons in cloud chambers. Just what yardstick are we going to use for deciding whether the results of ESP experiments are repeatable enough to be deemed up to a scientifically acceptable standard?

In the complete absence of any sceptical writing on this topic we have to do some clear thinking here. We might, say, compare ESP experiments with other areas of research in psychology – perhaps on a weak sensory system, like the sense of smell. If we do that we find something very interesting: psychologists do not actually pay much attention to repeatability. T. X. Barber, a noted methodologist of psychology, has shown that only 10 per cent of introductory textbooks of psychology even include the word 'repeatability' in the index! Now, since repeatability is supposed to be a criterion of scientific acceptability for experimental research, which is the better group of scientists here? Who is paying more attention to the real issues? Obvious: Barber's comment is that parapsychology is easily the most sophisticated branch of experimental psychology.

We would not profess to *know* for sure whether the results of the best ESP experiments are adequately repeatable or not, for there are no objective rules to judge this by. What we do know is that progress is being made here, and that all the discussion of evidence and standards on this issue is being produced by parapsychologists, rather than their critics.

Answering the critics

Finally, scientists have queried the research methods and statistics of parapsychologists – in isolated skirmishes. This seems to be a symptom of their concern rather than part of it. The statistical issues were settled many years ago, and whilst some researchers occasionally make slips, parapsychologists generally are extremely careful and even over-conservative in their evaluations of experiments. Similar comments would apply to methods of experimenting: the average standard is better than it was, say, 30 years ago, and a pinnacle of achievement like Schmidt's work has produced many laudatory comments from para-psychologists and sceptics alike. Anyone trying to mount a comprehensive critical attack on parapsychology from a statistical viewpoint would be doomed to failure (no-one has tried for the last 30 years). An attack based solely on criticism of research methods could not survive without extensive appeal to fraud (which, as we've seen, is an unsci-entific and *corrupting* argument – like heroin, once you get the taste for it you can't stop).

This exhausts all the rational sceptical arguments which are brought to bear on parapsychology. However, it is clear that a purely rational perspective will not suffice to explain scientific attitudes. What makes John Taylor utter emotive (and amusing) phrases like 'ESP is dead'? What made one colleague of Sargent's say to him, after a discussion of his, and other researcher's, Ganzfeld-ESP work, 'The results you presented would convince me of anything else, but this: I just *cannot* believe it and I don't know why?' A story told to us by Dr Bernard Dixon, an ex-editor of *New Scientist* and someone broadly sceptical about parapsychology, which really brings this irrational component home is this. After a lecture at the Royal Institution on PK metal-bending, one physicist sitting close to Dixon leapt to his feet and shouted, 'It's all nonsense. Nonsense! Heard it all before! Nonsense!' Dixon stated that he was so purple that he, Dixon, worried for a moment about whether the man might have a coronary or not. What is it that drives normally sane enough people to such extremes of virtually speechless irrationality?

We are familiar enough with *irrational belief*. There are some people who will believe almost anything. But, on the other hand, there are people who will refuse to believe anything. A perfect example would be the great scientist Helmholtz: 'Neither the testimony of all the Fellows of the Royal Society, nor even the evidence of my own senses, would lead me to believe in the transmission of thought from one person to another independent of the recognised channels of sense.' Here we have *irrational disbelief*: just another Lavoisier. Helmholtz has put himself beyond the pale of science: not the testimony of every single Fellow of the Royal Society would persuade him to revise his irrational disbelief. In short, Helmholtz has stated: My mind is made up and no evidence is going to change it. Now, whatever rules science has (and these are constantly debated), this nonsense violates most of them.

So, why is irrational disbelief not seen for what it is? Why do newspapers detail excesses of gullibility but remain silent on this issue? Possibly because the irrational disbelievers have played a classic con-trick on us: they have pretended to be the 'real' scientists, defending the purity of science against the dangerous nonsense of parapsychology. But they may be seen, on closer inspection, to be nothing of the kind. *Indeed they are not sceptics at all!*

Consider what the irrational disbeliever is saying. First, there are certain Laws of nature (and the sceptic will frequently use the disreputable tactic of appealing to authority, in Inquisitional vein, here) – and psi contradicts them (which cannot be stated, as we've seen). Therefore psi cannot possibly occur, and one can dismiss any 'evidence' for it on any grounds which happen to be convenient – bad experiments, fraud, conspiracy, that kind of thing ('arguments' which contravene all rules of scientific discourse).

The parapsychologist is the true sceptic. He says, 'There is evidence of the existence of phenomena not generally accepted by science and not incorporated into scientific theories. I am not prepared to accept it on the word of some authority (or group thereof) that these things cannot possibly exist. *I question orthodoxy*, and if you define dissent as heresy, so much the worse for science. I'm going to look at the facts without preconceptions.

New knowledge is often acquired by people who refused to accept the so-called Laws of nature, and authoritarian pronouncements about what was possible and impossible. Parapsychologists are in this tradition. They have generated new knowledge.

The future of psi research

The parapsychologist has earned a place in the scientific research laboratories of the future. He will have to measure up to scientific standards – and he will make sure that other people do too! As an example, recently a journal of parapsychology has been initiated in which, to get a paper published, it is strongly advantageous to submit a design for an experiment and state exactly what results you expect *before you do the experiment* (they may ask you to change something, which stops you from doing the experiment and then sending in the proposal). This ensures that statistical malpractice, for example, is eradicated. The reactions of certain of our psychological colleagues to this can be easily summarised: (1) It's good that parapsychologists do this, and (2) I'm damn glad I don't have to. Certainly the parapsychologist's colleagues will keep him on his toes – and he'll keep them on theirs.

The parapsychological research laboratory of the future will have to contain researchers from many disciplines. Since human beings will be tested there, psychologists will be essential; physicists will be needed, as will physiologists, electronics workers, and so on. Such laboratories are just coming into existence, at Duke University in North Carolina and the McDonnell laboratory at Washington University in St Louis, Missouri. It is the work of researchers in laboratories like these which will explain the unexplained and reveal more and more about the mysterious human faculties we denote with a simple three-letter word: *psi*.

THE PSI FACTOR EXPERIMENT

This is your chance to take part in a mass ESP experiment and to find out if you possess ESP ability to a more than ordinary degree. In addition this experiment will help us to check our research findings against a large sample of the population.

All correctly filled-in replies will be scored, but since this takes a lot of time we will not be able to inform everyone of their score. Only people who score exceptionally well will be contacted, and asked if they would like to take part in further testing.

THE EXPERIMENTS

This experiment uses the five symbols conventionally used in ESP card-guessing experiments:

For convenience these are usually written as:

In each of the 50 guessing boxes below, write clearly ONE of the five symbols; that symbol will be your guess for that box. An *example* of how you *might* begin is shown.

1	✳
2	▢
3	✳
4	○
5	+

The targets for this experiment will be a sequence of 50 symbols generated randomly by computer. The computer will be asked to generate a random sequence for each complete set of guesses received. So everyone who takes part in this experiment will have an individual series of targets to guess at. This is therefore a *precognition* experiment: we are asking you to guess the order of 50 symbols generated by computer *after* you have made your guesses. This may seem off-putting, but remember that many experiments of this type have given firm evidence of ESP. There is no reason why this one should not do so as well. You might like to relax before you do the experiment – just sit in a comfortable chair, somewhere quiet.

Please write down a guess in *every one* of the 50 boxes. Unless you do this we cannot include your guesses in the experiment.

Good luck!

1		11		21		31		41	
2		12		22		32		42	
3		13		23		33		43	
4		14		24		34		44	
5		15		25		35		45	
6		16		26		36		46	
7		17		27		37		47	
8		18		28		38		48	
9		19		29		39		49	
10		20		30		40		50	

Questions about the ESP experiment

It would help us to know something about your state of mind while you were doing your guessing, so please answer the following questions.

1 When you were making your guesses, did you feel (tick off ONE)
Very relaxed
Quite relaxed
Neither relaxed nor tense
Quite tense
Very tense

2 When you were making your guesses, was your mood
Very good
Quite good
Neutral
Quite bad
Very bad

3 At what time of day did you make your guesses? Time
Now fill in your name and address. You may remain anonymous if you wish – your answers will still help us with our experiment, but we will not be able to contact you in the event that your ESP score is unusually high.

Name

Sex (male or female)

Address

Thank you very much for helping with this exploration of ESP. Please copy out or photocopy page 187, and mail it to: *Dr C. L. Sargent, The Psychological Laboratory, University of Cambridge, Cambridge CB2 3EB (United Kingdom).* Please do NOT mail them to Professor Eysenck or to the publishers of this book.

FURTHER READING

Chapter 1 and General

BELOFF J.* (Ed.). *New Directions in Parapsychology*. London: Paul Elek, 1974.
RANDALL J. L.* *Parapsychology and the Nature of Life*. London: Souvenir, 1974, (especially recommended).
RHINE L. E.* *ESP in Life and Lab*. NY: Macmillan, 1967.
THOULESS R. H.* *From Anecdote to Experiment in Psychical Research*. London: RKP, 1972.

Chapter 2

BURTON J.* *Heyday of a Wizard*.
Home D. D. Earl of Dunraven, 'Experiences in Spiritualism with D. D. Home'. *Proceedings of the Society for Psychical Research*, 1924, vol. 35, pp 1–285.
MEDHURST, R. G., GOLDNEY K. M. AND BARRINGTON M. R. (Eds). *Crooks and the Spirit World*.
NY: TAPLINGER. London: Souvenir, 1972.
Stepanek. PRATT J. G. 'A decade of research with a selected ESP subject: an overview and reappraisal of the work with Pavel Stepanek'. *Proceedings of the American Society for Psychical Research*, 1973, vol. 30, pp 1–78. Chapter by J. G. Pratt in J. Beloff (ibid)*.

Chapter 3

Helmut Schmidt. Only technical references exist for Schmidt's work. Details of his machine can be found in his manuscript 'Anomalous Prediction of Quantum Processes by some human subjects' Boeing Scientific Research Laboratories Document DI.82.0821, Plasma Physics Laboratory, (Feb) 1969. Articles by Schmidt can be found in the *Journal of Parapsychology* and the *Journal of the American Society for Psychical Research* from 1969 on.

Chapter 4

ANGOFF A. AND BARTH D. (Eds). *Parapsychology and Anthropology*. NY: Parapsychology Foundation, 1974.
PALMER J. Chapter in B. B. Wolman (Ed). *Handbook of Parapsychology*. NY: Van Nostrand Reinhold, 1977.
RAO K. R. Chapter in J. Beloff (ibid)*.
SARGENT C. 'Extraversion and Performance in "Extra-sensory Perception" Tasks'. *Personality and Individual Differences*, 1981, vol. 2, pp 137–143.

Chapter 5

HONORTON C. Chapter in B. B. Wolman (ibid).
HONORTON C. Chapter in B. Shapin and L. Coly (Eds). *Psi and States of Awareness*.
ULLMAN M., KRIPPNER S. AND VAUGHAN A. *Dream Telepathy*. London: Tumstone, 1973. (NY: Macmillan)*.
VAN DE CASTLE R. L. Chapter in B. B. Wolman (ibid).

Chapter 6

HONORTON C. Chapter in B. B. Wolman (ibid).
HONORTON C. AND KRIPPNER S. Hypnosis and ESP: a review of the experimental literature. *Journal of the American Society for Psychical Research*, 1969, vol. 63, pp 214–252.

Chapter 7

GAULD A. O AND CORNELL A. D. *Poltergeists*. London: RKP, 1979.
HASTED J. B. *The Metal Benders*. London: RKP, 1980.
RHINE L. E. *Mind over Matter*. NY: Macmillan, 1970*.
STANFORD R. G. Chapter (pp 324–381) in B. B. Wolman (ibid).

Chapter 8

STANFORD R. G. Chapter (pp 823–858) in B. B. Wolman (ibid).
STANFORD R. G. *Journal of the American Society for Psychical Research*, 1974, pp. 34–57 and 321–356.

Chapter 9

PUHARICH A. (Ed). *The Iceland Papers*. Essentia Associates, 1979. Chapters by Walker & Mattuck and de Beauregard.

Chapter 10

GAULD A. O. 'A series of drop-in communications'. *Proceedings of the Society for Psychical Research*, 1971, vol 55, pp 273–340.
GAULD A. O.Chapter in Wolman (ibid).
MOODY R. *Life After Life*. NY: Bantam Books, 1975*.
SCOTT ROGO D. (Ed.) *Mind Beyond the Body*. NY and Harmondsworth: Penguin, 1978*.
STEVENSON I. Chapter in Wolman (ibid).
STEVENSON I. *Twenty Cases Suggestive of Reincarnation*. Virginia: The University Press, 1974 (2nd revised edition).
WILSON I. *Mind Out of Time?* London: Gollancz, 1981.

Chapter 11

RANSOM C. 'Recent Criticisms of Parapsychology: A review'. *Journal of the American Society for Psychical Research*, 1971, vol. 65, pp 289–307.
RAWLINS D. 'sTarbaby'. *Fate*, October 1981. (An exposure of the so-called Committee for the Scientific Investigation of Claims of the Paranormal.).
ROCKWELL T. R. AND W. T. 'Irrational Rationalists: A critique of *The Humanist's* crusade against parapsychology'. *Journal of the American Society for Psychical Research*, 1978, vol. 72, pp 23–34.

* denotes least technical reference

INDEX